Reconstructing Shakespeare in the Nordic Countries

GLOBAL SHAKESPEARE INVERTED

Global Shakespeare Inverted challenges any tendency to view Global Shakespeare from the perspective of 'centre' versus 'periphery'. Although the series may locate its critical starting point geographically, it calls into question the geographical bias that lurks within the very notion of the 'global'. It provides a timely, constructive criticism of the present state of the field and establishes new and alternative methodologies that invert the relation of Shakespeare to the supposed 'other'.

Series editors
David Schalkwyk, Queen Mary, University of London, UK
Silvia Bigliazzi, University of Verona, Italy
Bi-qi Beatrice Lei, National Taiwan University, Taiwan

Advisory board
Douglas Lanier, University of New Hampshire, USA
Sonia Massai, King's College London, UK
Supriya Chaudhury, Jadavpur University, India
Ian Smith, Lafayette College, USA

Eating Shakespeare: Cultural Anthropophagy as Global Methodology, edited by Anne Sophie Refskou, Marcel Alvaro de Amorim and Vinicius Mariano de Carvalho

Shakespeare in the Global South: Stories of Oceans Crossed in Contemporary Adaptation, edited by Sandra Young

Migrating Shakespeare: First European Encounters, Routes and Networks, edited by Janet Clare and Dominique Goy-Blanquet

Shakespeare's Others in 21st-century European Performance: The Merchant of Venice *and* Othello, edited by Boika Sokolova and Janice Valls-Russell

Disseminating Shakespeare in the Nordic Countries: Shifting Centres and Peripheries in the Nineteenth Century, edited by Nely Keinänen and Per Sivefors

Forthcoming Titles
Recontextualizing Indian Shakespeare Cinema in the West: Familiar Strangers, edited by Varsha Panjwani and Koel Chatterjee

Global Shakespeare and Social Injustice: Towards a Transformative Encounter, edited by Chris Thurman and Sandra Young

Reconstructing Shakespeare in the Nordic Countries

National Revival and Interwar Politics, 1870–1940

Edited by
Nely Keinänen and Per Sivefors

THE ARDEN SHAKESPEARE
LONDON • NEW YORK • OXFORD • NEW DELHI • SYDNEY

THE ARDEN SHAKESPEARE
Bloomsbury Publishing Plc
50 Bedford Square, London, WC1B 3DP, UK
1385 Broadway, New York, NY 10018, USA
29 Earlsfort Terrace, Dublin 2, Ireland

BLOOMSBURY, THE ARDEN SHAKESPEARE and the Arden Shakespeare logo are trademarks of Bloomsbury Publishing Plc

First published in Great Britain 2023
This paperback edition published in 2025

Copyright © Nely Keinänen, Per Sivefors and contributors 2023

Varsha Panjwani and Koel Chatterjee have asserted their right under the Copyright, Designs and Patents Act, 1988, to be identified as copy editors of this work.

For legal purposes the Acknowledgements on p. xi constitute an extension of this copyright page.

Cover design by Maria Rajka
Cover image © Yrjö Ollila, imagined set design for *The Merchant of Venice* (1924), reproduced with the kind permission of the Theatre Museum Archive, Finland

All rights reserved. No part of this publication may be reproduced or transmitted in any form or by any means, electronic or mechanical, including photocopying, recording, or any information storage or retrieval system, without prior permission in writing from the publishers.

Bloomsbury Publishing Plc does not have any control over, or responsibility for, any third-party websites referred to or in this book. All internet addresses given in this book were correct at the time of going to press. The author and publisher regret any inconvenience caused if addresses have changed or sites have ceased to exist, but can accept no responsibility for any such changes.

A catalogue record for this book is available from the British Library.

A catalog record for this book is available from the Library of Congress.

ISBN: HB: 978-1-3502-5125-0
PB: 978-1-3502-5129-8
ePDF: 978-1-3502-5127-4
eBook: 978-1-3502-5126-7

Series: Global Shakespeare Inverted

Typeset by Deanta Global Publishing Services, Chennai, India

To find out more about our authors and books visit www.bloomsbury.com and sign up for our newsletters.

CONTENTS

List of figures vii
Notes on contributors viii
Acknowledgements xi

Introduction Nely Keinänen and Per Sivefors 1

1 Early Icelandic translations of Shakespeare: Settings, contexts, cultural transfer Ástráður Eysteinsson and Ingibjörg Þórisdóttir 35

2 Ida Aalberg and the first Finnish-language *Romeo and Juliet*, 1881 Nely Keinänen 69

3 Kaarlo Bergbom and the Finnish-language Shakespeare tradition: The Finnish national revival, German Romanticism, theatrical resources and personal wishes Pentti Paavolainen 99

4 Shakespeare and the Norwegian National Theatre, 1899–1914 Christina Sandhaug 143

5 Commemoration and conflict at Hamlet's Castle: The 1916 'Shakespeare *Mindefest*' in Elsinore Anne Sophie Refskou 179

6 Nynorsk and the Nordic spirit: Henrik Rytter's Shakespeare translations, 1932–1933 Svenn-Arve Myklebost 199

7 'A great interpreter of modern life': Eyvind
  Johnson and the changing perception of
  Shakespeare *Per Sivefors* 229

Afterword 251
Appendix 257
Index 267

FIGURES

0.1 Advertisement in the Finnish newspaper *Uusi Suometar*, 125, 1917   9
2.1 Axel Ahlberg (Romeo) and Ida Aalberg (Juliet) at the FNT, 1881   86
4.1 Johanne Dybwad as Rosalind in *As You Like It, eller Livet i Skogen*, 1912   161
4.2 *As You Like It, eller Livet i Skogen*, 1912   166

CONTRIBUTORS

Michael Dobson is Director of the Shakespeare Institute, Stratford-upon-Avon, and Professor of Shakespeare Studies, University of Birmingham, having previously taught at institutions including Oxford, Harvard, the University of Illinois at Chicago and the University of London. He has lectured on Shakespeare in over thirty five different countries and holds honorary doctorates from Lund and Craiova. He is an honorary governor of the Royal Shakespeare Company, a trustee of the Shakespeare Birthplace Trust and an honorary member of the Academy of Sciences of the Higher School of Ukraine. His publications include *The Making of the National Poet* (1992), *Shakespeare: A Playgoer's and Reader's Guide* (with Stanley Wells, 2021), and many chapters, essays, theatre reviews and programme notes.

Ástráður Eysteinsson is Professor of Comparative Literature at the University of Iceland. He has worked in the areas of literary and cultural theory, modernism and translation studies, and is a practising translator. His publications include co-translations of most of Franz Kafka's narrative works into Icelandic, numerous articles and the following books: *The Concept of Modernism* (1990), *Tvímæli* (1996), *Umbrot* (1999) and *Orðaskil* (2017). His edited books include *The Cultural Reconstruction of Places* (2006), *Translation – Theory and Practice: A Historical Reader* (with Daniel Weissbort, 2006) and *Modernism* (with Vivian Liska, two vols., 2007).

Nely Keinänen is Senior Lecturer in the Department of Languages at the University of Helsinki, Finland. She is the co-editor with Per Sivefors of the Arden Shakespeare volume *Disseminating Shakespeare in the Nordic Countries* (2022), editor of a special issue of *Synteesi* (*Journal of the Finnish Semiotics Society*) on

Shakespeare in Finland (2016), *Shakespeare Suomessa* [Shakespeare in Finland], a collection of essays by translators, directors and actors on Shakespeare (2010) and numerous essays connected to Shakespeare in Finland. Keinänen has also translated over thirty contemporary Finnish plays into English. She is on the board of the Nordic Shakespeare Society (NorSS).

Svenn-Arve Myklebost received his PhD from the University of Bergen in 2013 and subsequently worked for eight years at the University College of Volda in the *Nynorsk* heartlands of northwestern Norway. He is currently employed at the Inland Norway University of Applied Sciences in Hamar as an associate professor of English literature and culture. Aside from articles on adaptation theory, Shakespeare and esotericism and Laurence Sterne's *Tristram Shandy*, Myklebost has published extensively on Shakespeare comics, manga and graphic novels and is in the final stages of preparing a book manuscript on this topic.

Pentti Paavolainen is a docent at the University of Helsinki and from 1993 to 2007 held the chair of theatre research in the Theatre Academy (presently the University of Arts in Helsinki), where he developed the first doctoral programmes. His doctoral dissertation (1992) is a political analysis of changes in Finnish Theatre repertories in the 1960s, and he has published widely on theatre in Finland. His major academic work is his three-volume biography of Kaarlo Bergbom, a key figure in nineteenth-century theatre and opera in Finland, which came out in 2014, 2016 and 2018.

Anne Sophie Refskou is a research assistant at Aarhus University, Denmark, where she teaches comparative literature. Her publications include the Arden Shakespeare volume *Eating Shakespeare: Cultural Anthropophagy as Global Methodology*, co-edited with Vinicius Mariano de Carvalho and Marcel Alvaro de Amorim (2019). She is currently completing a monograph on Shakespeare and compassion in early modern culture.

Christina Sandhaug is Associate Professor of English Literature at Inland Norway University of Applied Sciences. Her main research interests are renaissance textuality, rhetoric and poetry; court masques, theatre and drama; and teaching and learning English.

She has published articles on printed court masques, Shakespeare and vocabulary learning, and co-written a book for English teacher trainees. She contributed to *Thomas More's 'Utopia' in Early Modern Europe: Paratexts and Contexts* (2008) and was text consultant for Edvard Hoem's Norwegian translation of *Hamlet* (2013). She is currently part of a collaborative research project called 'Literature, Teacher Education and Climate Change'.

Per Sivefors is Associate Professor of English Literature at Linnaeus University, Sweden. His latest books are *Representing Masculinity in Early Modern English Satire, 1590–1603: 'A Kingdom for a Man'* (2020) and the collections *Changing Satire: Transformations and Continuities in Europe, 1600–1830* (2022), edited with Cecilia Rosengren and Rikard Wingård, and *Disseminating Shakespeare in the Nordic Countries: Shifting Centres and Peripheries in the Nineteenth Century* (2022), edited with Nely Keinänen. He works extensively on the reception of Shakespeare in the Nordic countries and has recently contributed to the Arden Shakespeare volume *Migrating Shakespeare: First European Encounters, Routes and Networks*, ed. Janet Clare and Dominique Goy-Blanquet. He is chair of the Nordic Shakespeare Society.

Ingibjörg Þórisdóttir is a PhD student in translation studies at the University of Iceland. Her doctoral research focuses on the early translations of William Shakespeare's plays into Icelandic, especially the translation of the poet and pastor Matthías Jochumsson. The research also sheds light on their relevance for Icelandic literary and theatre history. Þórisdóttir´s main fields of academic interest are theatre and performance studies, and translation studies. She has taught courses at university level in cultural management and media, theatre history, Shakespeare, modern drama, theatre translation and theatre studies. For the past five years, she has been on the board of the Institute of Research in Literature and Visual Arts on behalf of PhD students at the Faculty of Icelandic and Comparative Cultural Studies.

ACKNOWLEDGEMENTS

As with our previous volume in the series Global Shakespeare Inverted, our work on this book has amply demonstrated the joys of collaboration and common discoveries. While we initially planned for a single volume, we – and the editors at Bloomsbury – soon realized that the material was rich enough for two books, the second of which we now present.

Many of our debts acknowledged in the previous volume remain the same. The editorial team at Bloomsbury, especially Mark Dudgeon, has been professional and eminently supportive of our work during the changing stages of a global pandemic. Repeated thanks are also due to David Schalkwyk, Silvia Bigliazzi and Bi-qi Beatrice Lei for generously putting their Global Shakespeare Inverted series at our disposal. Delilah Bermudez Brataas continues to serve as secretary of the Nordic Shakespeare Society and does much of the practical work with this international network of scholars.

For the present volume, Kent Hägglund has been an abundant source of information and support regarding the Swedish context, as have Pentti Paavolainen and Pirkko Koski for the Finnish. Anne Sophie Refskou supplied important notes on Shakespeare performances in Elsinore in the 1930s. Kimmo Absetz provided invaluable help with translations from the Finnish. We also wish to acknowledge our continuing debt to Richard Wilson, for his initiatives concerning the Nordic Shakespeare Society and for his own ongoing work on Shakespeare in the interwar period.

Nely wishes to thank the members of the Nordic Shakespeare Society, her colleagues at the Department of Languages, University of Helsinki, as well as Kimmo and Lea who bring such joy to her life.

Per would like to thank the members of the Nordic Shakespeare Society, the Early Modern Seminar at the University of Gothenburg and his colleagues at the Department of Languages, Linnaeus University, as well as Ellinor Broman, for being her incomparable self.

Introduction

Nely Keinänen and Per Sivefors

In one sense, this book continues where our previously edited volume, *Disseminating Shakespeare in the Nordic Countries: Shifting Centres and Peripheries in the Nineteenth Century*, left off. Our focus now moves the chronology forward to the late nineteenth and early twentieth centuries, with a broad perspective on Shakespeare reception in Northern Europe until approximately 1940. However, the initial emphasis is now squarely on the independence movements, the development of national literary and theatrical cultures and the way Shakespeare was incorporated into these. The period covered in this volume saw the creation of two new independent countries: Norway's personal union with Sweden was dissolved in 1905, and Finland, having been a Grand Duchy in the Russian Empire, declared its independence in 1917 (Iceland would follow in 1944). In this period, national theatres were created where Shakespeare was frequently performed. Historically and culturally, what followed was a period of shifting allegiances and political unrest, and of course the looming threat from Nazi Germany would follow in the 1930s, which means that the early 1940s constitute a suitable end date to the present volume since the cultural and political landscape of Northern Europe would change considerably in the wake of the Second World War. A significant theme of this volume is therefore the way in which Nordic authors, translators and performers related to new impulses – modernism, new media and new conceptions of theatre, to name a few – and what they meant for the reception of Shakespeare.

What characterizes the period under discussion is an extremely complex set of political affiliations, which inevitably coloured the cultural life of the countries, including their translations, productions and other work related to Shakespeare. The close linguistic ties between modern Norwegian, Danish and Swedish were of course a contributing factor as well, along with the continuing presence of the latter two languages in Iceland and Finland respectively. Taken together these factors amount to a set of micro-dependencies even in seemingly small details, such as the reliance of Shakespeare translators on similar work in other Nordic languages or the fairly frequent guest performances by Nordic actors in other countries. Even despite an often high-flown national rhetoric, especially in the first part of the period we examine here, there was also a tendency towards 'pan-Nordic' perspectives – which were moreover boosted in the later part of the period following the rise of fascism in Europe. Needless to say, therefore, translating and performing Shakespeare never amounted to mere straightforward 'influences' from the Anglophone world: it is no exaggeration to say that adapting Shakespeare reverberated at the level of intra-Nordic relations, but also in the larger political arena, particularly involving the more immediate neighbours of Northern Europe such as Germany and Russia (later the Soviet Union). Conversely, the representation of Shakespeare was affected at a more regional level, with new, publicly funded theatre institutions founded in various parts of the countries, often enough with Shakespeare on the repertoire. In short, this can be described as a 'rhizomatic' rather than linear movement, in line with contemporary scholarship on Shakespeare's dissemination then and now.

Significantly, it was also in this period that more important academic research on Shakespeare began to be carried out in the Nordic countries. Georg Brandes's three-volume work, for example, was translated into English and German,[1] and there were various other book-length studies by Nordic scholars, often intended for a general audience.[2] What is more, the history of Shakespeare in the Nordic countries was now considered substantial enough to merit scholarly attention: from this period there is a small but significant body of work tracing 'Shakespeare in Denmark', 'Shakespeare in Finland' and so forth.[3] Arguably, these works also feed into general narratives of national culture, implying the merits and values of each vernacular Shakespeare. While pioneering and vital, this body of work is in strong need of updating, and the present volume hopes to make a contribution towards that goal, emphasizing that Nordic Shakespeare was not simply and only 'national' Shakespeare even if

– as we shall see – national movements were pronounced, especially in the earlier part of the period we cover here. In other words, the 'reconstructing' in our title can be said to be reflected on two levels. One is obviously the way in which translation, performance and other aspects of Shakespeare reception were shaped by the shifting political and cultural climate of Europe and the rest of the world. Nordic Shakespeare was now an entity that, even from a local perspective, could be redefined in dialogue with broader international influences. The other, more oblique perspective involves the scholarly discussion on Nordic Shakespeare, which we hereby hope, in some limited way, to reconstruct in the sense of updating and rethinking it.

Translation projects in the period

In the cases of Finland, Norway and Iceland, it is certainly fair to say that national independence movements coloured the perceived need for a Shakespeare in the native language, although the practical outcome differed considerably between countries.

Paavo Cajander's translations in 1879–1912 were crucial not only in shaping a readerly Shakespeare in Finnish but also because many of them were performed soon after their completion owing to the translator's close collaboration with Kaarlo Bergbom (see later and Paavolainen's chapter). Cajander's translations held up well, and re-translations only began to be done in the 1930s and 1940s, when Yrjö Jylhä translated seven plays, mainly using Cajander as a base. And while such updating was considered necessary, reviewers cautioned that correcting Cajander needed to be done 'with a careful hand'.[4] A second complete works translation project into Finnish was not undertaken until 2002–2013, this time with a team of translators.[5]

Norway presents a special case in the period since comprehensive sets of translations appeared in both written forms of the language, in what was then known as Rigsmaal and in Nynorsk. In the former case, the most important effort by far was the twenty-one plays by a team of six translators that were collected in eight volumes during 1923–1942. As for Nynorsk, single plays began to appear around the turn of the century, although it was not until the early

1930s that Henrik Rytter's idiosyncratic translations of twenty-three plays were published. These translations embodied a vision that was at once nationalist and internationalist and, in Svenn-Arve Myklebost's words in the present volume, 'blend[ed] the familiar with the ancient'. While not widely read or performed today, these 'Modern Romantic' translations arguably mirror a Norway that was characterized by both an outward- and future-looking cosmopolitanism and an inward-looking concern with its Nordic past.

In Iceland, Shakespeare was a more divisive presence, and the cultural need to translate foreign classics was questioned (see Eysteinsson and Þórisdóttir's chapter). The first large-scale translation project had been Matthías Jochumsson's four tragedies (*Macbeth*, *Hamlet*, *Othello* and *Romeo and Juliet*) in 1874–1887; his adversary Eiríkur Magnússon, who condemned Jochumsson's translations for being too free, would publish his own version of *The Tempest* in 1885, a translation that prompted his critics in turn to object 'who wants to read Shakespeare now-a-days anyway?'.[6] It was, however, Indriði Einarsson's translations of twelve plays from 1922 onwards that would be the quantitatively most important effort in the period. Two of his translations were performed in Reykjavík in 1926 although apart from brief excerpts they all remained unpublished by his death in 1939. As a project, they reflect Einarsson's ambition 'to make the plays available to that National Theatre of the future which for years had been his favourite dream'.[7] That dream, however, only came true in 1950, well after Einarsson's death and a few years after Iceland's formal independence from Denmark.

As mentioned earlier, Denmark and Sweden had been independent countries for many centuries, and here the link between nationalist politics and national Shakespeare was obviously less pronounced. There was also a larger, and older, body of translations available from the late eighteenth century and onwards, and some of these translations exerted a continuing influence on the dissemination of Shakespeare. In Denmark, Edvard Lembcke's translation, published in 1861–1873, was the only 'complete' one for a century until Johannes Sløk's in the 1960s; however, beginning around the turn of the century Valdemar Østerberg (1865–1945) translated a good dozen plays that were reissued several times until the 1950s, and in his work as a teacher Østerberg also produced a school edition of

The Merchant of Venice (1915). While not performed on the national stage, his translations found their way to smaller venues and were also used in Norwegian theatre.[8] In addition to Østerberg's, there was also a volume of translations by Niels Møller in 1901, although critics at the time expressed some doubt as to whether these new versions would be capable of replacing Lembcke's earlier work.[9] The case of Sweden is somewhat similar: the translations by Carl August Hagberg, first published in 1847–1851, continued to be read, performed and reprinted well into the twentieth century, for example in 1925–1928 in a revised version by Nils Molin, whose research on Shakespeare in Sweden also resulted in a PhD dissertation in 1931.[10] Around the same time, in 1922–1931, the author and member of the Swedish Academy Per Hallström (1866–1960) published a new complete translation of his own. With prefaces by literary historian Henrik Schück, whose two-volume monograph *Shakspere och hans tid* [Shakespeare and His Time] had appeared in 1916,[11] Hallström's translations were considered – in the diplomatic words of a later Swedish encyclopaedia – 'particularly excellent in their lyrical parts',[12] yet failed in the end to replace Hagberg's as the standard version. Indeed, Hallström's translations, like Østerberg's, seem to have been more read than performed. It was instead Hagberg's Swedish versions that became exceptionally important in the Nordic context, as they were consulted by a number of Nordic translators into other languages, including Cajander in Finland and Jochumsson in Iceland. Icelandic and Norwegian translators also had recourse to Danish versions.

Shakespeare in Nordic theatre: Material, economic and aesthetic contexts

In terms of Shakespeare and national projects, by the late nineteenth century there were nationalist and independence movements underway in Finland, Norway and Iceland, in part influenced by German Romanticism which emphasized the importance of folk cultural traditions and national mythologies.[13] Theatre was 'one of the principal and most visible'[14] forces promoting a sense of nation, and national(ist) theatres were established in all three countries: in Finland in 1872 (independence 1917), in Norway in 1899 (independence 1905) and in Iceland in 1950 (independent state in a personal union with the Danish crown in 1918, full independence in 1944). As Bruce McConachie points out, key features of national theatres during the period 1850–1920 in Europe included 'strong bourgeois patronage, a theatrical repertoire that had as one of its main goals the celebration of the language, traditions, and culture of a people, and a National Theatre building prominently located in what was recognized as the national capital'.[15] In the Nordic countries, too, the shaping of theatre culture was crucially reflected at the material level, in the various buildings that were expressly designed to house 'national theatres'.

In Oslo, the new Nationaltheatret opened in September 1899 and is centrally located near the Royal Palace and Norwegian Parliament. Designed by Henrik Bull, it is a grand building very much in keeping with the idea of a 'national theatre':

> [I]t has a royal box that is still very much in use, grand foyers and lofty painted rococo ceilings, and paintings and sculptures by some of Norway's greatest artists. Its imposing *trompe l'oeil* fire curtain has a special place of affection in the hearts of actors and audiences alike. Part theatre, part art museum, the building gives off an air of dignity and solidity, not unlike a 'pillar of society'.[16]

The language of this theatre was Bokmål, closer to Danish, the language also used by Ibsen. The first steps towards a national theatre had in fact been taken in Bergen, Ole Bull's Norske Teater (founded 1850), later revived as Den Nationale Scene (The National Stage, 1876), but by the 1880s Norwegian efforts to secure a national theatre were centred in the capital.[17]

In Finland, too, at the turn of the century there were efforts to move the Finnish Theatre from the old wooden Arkadia Theatre to a more central location and larger building. Designed by Onni Törnquist-Tarjanne, the imposing granite structure in the National Romantic style is located next to the Central Railway Station. It was inaugurated on 9 April 1902, the hundredth anniversary of the birth of Elias Lönnrot who had collected the oral folk poetry making up the Finnish national epic *Kalevala*. The new theatre was described in the press as a 'stone castle built by the people's love',[18] and indeed collections for the building were taken up all over the country.¹⁹ Decorations were gradually added, for example an impressionist ceiling mural in the main theatre by Yrjö Ollila (1932), whose sketches for a set design for *Merchant of Venice* (1924) appear on this book's cover. Two of the likenesses depicted on the mural have a Shakespeare connection: Ida Aalberg is pictured as Ophelia (which she first played in 1884); and Elli Tompuri, the first Nordic woman to play the role of Hamlet, is also included as Thalia.²⁰ In keeping with nationalist ideals, the inaugural programme featured a Finnish play, Aleksis Kivi's *Lea*, though the farewell performance at the Arkadia Theatre had also included Act 4 of *Merchant of Venice* starring Benjamin Leino as Shylock.²¹ In conjunction with its move to the new building, the Finnish Theatre changed its name to the Finnish National Theatre (FNT). If the former had been largely constructed to highlight the distinction from the lingering Swedish heritage, the latter name hints at the accrued centrality of 'Finnish' to the construction of national culture.

Even in Sweden, which had been independent for centuries, the fashioning of architectural statements around a 'national theatre' now occupied the agenda. The Royal Theatre institution in Stockholm had been located in various places in the nineteenth century but was finally housed in the still standing Royal Dramatic Theatre.²² This was inaugurated in 1908 after a complicated planning process and resulted in a building and organization that in many ways failed to sever the links with past structures and modes of thinking.²³ By comparison, the Royal Danish Theatre, which had been located on the same address in Copenhagen since 1748, had an even less radical transformation, although here too a new building had been inaugurated in 1874.

Especially in Finland and Norway, the creation of a national theatre was complicated by struggles over competing languages,²⁴ in Norway between Bokmål and Nynorsk (see the chapters by Sandhaug and Myklebost in this volume). In Finland the struggle was less about language per se, as the Swedish-speaking intelligentsia sought to raise the status of Finnish. Many Swedish-speaking Finns even adopted Finnish names (e.g. the founder of the Finnish National Theatre went from Karl to Kaarlo Bergbom). But initially there was discussion of whether the government would support both Swedish- and Finnish-speaking companies, and the companies competed for audiences and over repertoire.²⁵

The role of Shakespeare in the development of national theatres varied between the countries. Finns seem to have been the most eager to seize Shakespeare as a means of enriching the language and culture. Translation and performance arguably went hand in hand in that enrichment. In an almost gloatingly positive review of the first play translated in the Finnish Literature Society's new complete works translation project (*Hamlet* 1879), B. F. Godenhjelm starts with the sentence: 'The translation of these brilliant works by Shakespeare is a project which we hope will bear the most delectable fruits for the furthering of our national culture and civilization, as his magnificent genius is everywhere, helping us to invigorate and uplift our national poetry.'[26] Reviews of the first Finnish-language performance (of *Romeo and Juliet* in 1881) also emphasized the cultural significance of performing Shakespeare (see Keinänen's chapter). As Christina Sandhaug discusses in this volume, there were 'great expectations' for the Norwegian National Theatre's first Shakespeare (*Twelfth Night*, 1899), but they were 'thoroughly disappointed', though later productions of *Dream* (1903) and *Merchant* (1907) were more successful. As for Iceland, Shakespeare performances in the period were limited to two comedies in 1926, but, as mentioned in the previous section, in the 1920s, when Indriði Einarsson began translating plays by Shakespeare he did so with an eye towards their eventually being performed in a national theatre.[27] And the two productions in 1926, both using Einarsson's translations, may have been the only Icelandic ones before Iceland's formal independence in 1944, but they were perceived 'as milestones in the history of Icelandic theatre, emphasizing the symbolic significance of staging Shakespeare for the cultural identity of the nation'.[28] Indeed, as the local theatre society, the *leikfélag*, became a professional national theatre institution, or a *leikhús*, Shakespeare was 'instrumental' in that transformation.[29]

Obviously, theatre as a commercial enterprise was not simply governed by national(ist) agendas. At the dawn of the twentieth century, it was clear that, even in the Nordic countries, 'Shakespeare' had become a brand with a global potential: indeed, at the time, Denmark's biggest bicycle factory was ingenuously named 'Hamlet Cycler' and exported their products as far as China, England and Russia (Figure 0.1).[30] Such an appeal arguably extends beyond simple uses of the name to seeing Shakespeare as a viable role model for playwrights; August Strindberg may certainly, as Gunnar Sorelius

FIGURE 0.1 Advertisement in the Finnish newspaper Uusi Suometar, 125 (1917). 'Just in, Hamlet bicycles from Hamlet, Denmark's largest and best-known bicycle factory. Hamlet bicycles for men and women, Hamlet competition bicycles, Hamlet two-speed bicycles'. The National Library of Finland, digital archives.

suggests, 'have looked upon himself as a Swedish Shakespeare', but that was arguably in part because Strindberg's own history plays such as *Gustav Vasa* (1899) were considerable box-office hits that established him as a national playwright in more than just his own imagination.[31]

In the long run, however, playwrights and producers would come to draw on new impulses from abroad (as indeed the example of Strindberg shows), and it is clear that in the early twentieth century, there was a reaction against the elaborate staging (and commercialism) of nineteenth-century theatre. Thus, in 1901, the Gothenburg newspaper *Göteborgs Handels- och Sjöfartstidning* featured a letter to the editor that mentions actor and impresario August Lindberg's then recent one-man version of *The Tempest* (the first Swedish performance of this play): 'Successful attempts at simplified staging are made in Copenhagen with Shakespeare, among us with Strindberg, and what are August Lindberg's recitations of "The Tempest" if not such an extreme simplification, where one single actor represents the entire cast and the stage exists only in the audience's imagination?'[32] The letter also reveals the broad outlook of theatrical culture at the time, with an eye on developments in the other Nordic countries as well as Europe. This is evident at the Finnish National Theatre too when, influenced by trips to the continent and England, Jalmari Finne brought in simpler and more practical sets (see Paavolainen's chapter). But there were exceptions to this as well, as, for example, the 1926 production of *The Winter's Tale* in Iceland which brought in a German set- and costume designer and was apparently rather glamourous.[33]

Acting styles were also moving away from the more declamatory style favoured by German Romanticism towards a simpler more naturalistic style. For example, at the turn of the century, the Finnish actor Kaarle Halme was praised for his 'clear, strong and simple performance' of Othello which nevertheless had 'sufficient dramatic power'.[34] As the century wore on, acting styles would move even further away from the perceived stiffness of classical declamation. Indeed, to Per Lindberg (son of the previously mentioned August L) in his noted modernist productions of Shakespeare in Gothenburg and Stockholm in the 1920s, 'the chief prerequisites' of the actor were 'physical freedom, elimination of strain, and vocal and muscular control'.[35] In short, the perceived need for a more 'modern' Shakespeare also entailed close attention to emerging theatrical practices elsewhere in Europe.

Tendencies like these obviously have international parallels. Cary DiPietro suggests that for all their dissimilarities, authors like G. B. Shaw and T. S. Eliot helped to disconnect Shakespeare from 'what they understood to be the bourgeois commercialism of an increasingly massified culture industry' and 'prepare him for the anti-commercial academic and national theatre cultures of the twentieth century'.[36] To an extent, this claim is valid also for the Nordic countries, and significantly it reverberates at the level of regional, rather than simply national, culture. In Sweden, the period saw a considerable expansion of the funding system of public theatre, with regional institutions established in various parts of the country, thus providing access to 'high' culture. Indeed, for the inauguration of the first Swedish city theatres with public funding and permanent ensembles, Shakespeare was a standard choice: Helsingborg's theatre (founded in 1921) performed *Twelfth Night* and that of Gothenburg (1934) *The Tempest*; the theatre of Malmö (1944) featured *A Midsummer Night's Dream* as its first production; and that of Norrköping and Linköping would stage *Romeo and Juliet* in 1947.[37] Thus, if the 'regional' had previously been somewhat of a counterforce against the cultural hegemony of the capital, regional theatres were now integrated in a national system of theatre institutions.[38] That is not to say that differences were necessarily flattened out: theatres in the capital and in the provinces could still draw on different foreign and local influences compared to the capital.[39]

In Finland as well, new theatre companies were being established in larger cities, often two, as there were separate theatres for the upper and working classes.[40] While these theatres were usually inaugurated with a domestic play, many sought to perform Shakespeare early on. For example, a travelling company based in Vyborg, Finland's second largest city at the time, performed several Shakespeare plays to varying success in its early years.[41] In the 1906–1907 season, *Merry Wives of Windsor* was performed in three cities to good reviews, while a production of *Othello* fell flat.[42] Both at the FNT and regional theatres, Shakespeare productions were often done on the initiative of an actor who wanted to play a specific role, such as Teuvo Puro (Shylock), Adolf Lindfors (Falstaff), Wilho Ilmari (Lear), Aarne Orjatsalo and Kosti Elo (Hamlet); these roles became part of an actor's portfolio and could be repeated if the actor moved from one theatre company to another.[43] And indeed, in Finland, the promise of playing a Shakespeare role seems to have been used to lure actors from one theatre company to another: in 1904, Kosti Elo was promised Hamlet and Sigismund in Calderón's *Life Is a Dream* if he would return to Vyborg and, angry that he was not able to get leading roles at the Finnish National Theatre, Kaarle Halme moved over to the Swedish Theatre to play Lear and Othello.[44] During the time Paavo Cajander was working on his complete works translations project (1879–1912), the FNT continued its goal of performing newly translated plays, but elsewhere the repertoire was more based on popularity: *Romeo and*

Juliet was a mainstay, and comedies such as *Twelfth Night* and *The Taming of the Shrew* were often done. Wilho Ilmari at the Turku Finnish Theatre had his favourites, including *Hamlet*, *King Lear* and *As You Like It*.[45]

The situation regarding regional theatres in Norway was especially complex, as in the first half of the twentieth century there were two theatrical centres, in Bergen and Oslo, as well as two competing language forms, as discussed earlier (and in more detail in Myklebost's chapter). The choice of language was a crucial and hotly contested political issue. Det Norske Teatret (The Norwegian Theatre) was founded in 1912 and entirely devoted to plays in Nynorsk and dialects. In Iceland, there were few theatre companies outside Reykjavík, and none seem to have performed Shakespeare. But it seems that Shakespeare was slowly spreading away from the capital region as well, as attested by a recently published translation of *Hamlet* by Ingivaldur Nikulásson, a local artist in Bíldudalur in the Westfjords, done in the 1930s or 1940s.[46] Records of staging, however, have not been found.

The story of Shakespeare performance around the turn of the century was in other words governed partly by the ambition in some circles to create a national Shakespeare, partly by a restructuring of the theatre into more organized regional theatre institutions, partly by recognizing what was commercially and technically viable in the first place. As for the latter, in what seems like a clear attempt at attracting crowds, Norway's new National Theatre would put on four Shakespearean comedies before its predictable first choice of tragedy, *Hamlet*, in 1907 (see Sandhaug's chapter). Over time, the case seems to have been similar in Denmark, where comedy generally dominated over tragedy.[47] Similarly, in Iceland, as already mentioned, the first two plays performed (in the 1920s) were comedies, *Twelfth Night* and *The Winter's Tale*. And Shakespeare's Nordic play continued to hold sway over its audiences: in Sweden, for example, it was the most frequently staged one in the canon, as it had been since the earliest performances of Shakespeare back in the eighteenth century.[48] Thus, in the period 1889–1947 there seem to have been twenty-six Swedish *Hamlet* productions, well ahead of the closest contender *Twelfth Night* at sixteen.[49] While there were fewer domestic ones in Denmark, the country saw several non-Danish guest performances of the play, which seems to have been deemed suitable fare by foreign touring companies.[50] In Finland during the same period, the division was more even, with *Hamlet* and *Taming of the Shrew* (twenty productions), followed closely by *Merchant of Venice* (nineteen) and *Romeo and Juliet* (seventeen). If the earlier part of the period covered here was characterized by navigating between national and commercial interests, it could be added that, increasingly, the reception of Nordic Shakespeare came with its own brand of modernity and social engineering. In the eyes of some critics, Shakespeare both represented a seemingly nostalgic ideal of pre-industrial beauty and a bygone, less standardized and – indeed – less hygienic age. This conflicting view is neatly captured in Brandes's widely read study, which describes Stratford as lying in 'a pleasant and undulating tract of country, rich in green meadows and trees and leafy hedges, the natural features of which Shakespeare seems to have had in his mind's eye when he wrote the descriptions of scenery in *A Midsummer Night's Dream, As You Like It*, and *A Winter's Tale*'. Yet, Brandes continues, 'Stratford-on-Avon was an insanitary place of residence. There was no sort of underground drainage, and street-sweepers and scavengers were unknown. The waste water from the houses flowed out into badly kept gutters; the streets were full of evil-smelling pools, in which pigs and geese freely disported themselves; and dunghills skirted the highway.'[51] Both the beauty and ugliness of Shakespeare's landscape seem by implication to be contrasted to Brandes's own, perhaps less beautiful but certainly better smelling present.[52]

For all this apprehension connected to the literary past, there was a sense in which Shakespeare could (even should) be made to speak to the modern world and modern audiences, and, as we have seen, that state-funded theatre institutions contributed to that dissemination.[53] Arguably, in some ways the egalitarian ideals of such a project were different from, for example, Eliot's version of Anglo-American high modernism even if, as we have seen, both insisted on warding off 'high' culture from pure commercialism.[54] Echoing continental and modernist ideas, directors and producers would state their explicit intention to create a more public and democratic theatre. In an article in *Dagens Nyheter* in 1926, the previously mentioned director Per Lindberg articulated the need to revitalize the theatre amid the competition from the film medium. Lindberg emphatically seeks his inspiration from abroad, from experimental theatres in Europe and in the proletarian theatres of the Soviet Union; in practical terms he also insists on reconfiguring the architecture of the theatres so that audiences and performers shared the same physical space instead of being separated by the proscenium arch.[55] This is an aesthetic choice that we also see implemented, if for apparently different reasons, in the famous British production of *Hamlet* at Elsinore in 1937 starring Laurence Olivier.[56] Adult educational associations similarly fostered an egalitarian idea of access to culture in all its forms, yet non-professionals could be actively discouraged from meddling with Shakespeare: in *Teaterhandbok för amatörer* (1931), a handbook for amateur theatres published by the Swedish workers' association ABF, the author advises against taking on Shakespeare due to the verse and the number of roles.[57] In other words, the advice is said to be based on practical rather than ideological considerations.

In Finland, by contrast, workers' theatres, which had been established in cities such as Helsinki, Tampere and Turku, embraced Shakespeare. For example, in 1919, Kosti Elo became the actor-manager of the Tampere Workers' Theatre (TTT), where in his first season he triumphed as Hamlet, a role he had been playing to growing acclaim since 1904. Panu Rajala suggests that in the turbulent years following independence (1917) and civil war (January–May 1918) in Finland, Shakespearean classics with their perceived timeless themes were indeed preferred to contemporary Finnish drama: *Romeo and Juliet*, which had been performed at the TTT the previous spring, and especially *Hamlet* played to full houses, as 'art depicted the evil of humanity but also how to free oneself from it'.[58] Elo reprieved his Hamlet in 1926 at the theatre's twenty-fifth anniversary (also celebrated with a performance of *Twelfth Night*) and again in 1929, the tenth anniversary of his coming to the theatre.[59] *The Merchant of Venice* also proved popular with workers' theatre companies: from 1931 to 1937, it was put on by five different companies in as many cities.[60] While theatre circles were small, and actors mainly moved freely between workers' and city theatres, Wilho Ilmari reveals that when in 1917 he was asked to play Lear at the Tampere Theatre, he 'secretly' worked on the role with Aarne Orjatsalo, then director of the Tampere Workers' Theatre, who would himself play Hamlet to great acclaim in November. When the Finnish civil war broke out not much later, Ilmari (a conservative 'white') found himself in a shouting match with Orjatsalo (a 'red').[61]

Part of the work of theatre in this period was seen as educating audiences to understand and appreciate classics like Shakespeare, and this was not always easy. Ilmari tells of a 1920 performance of *Othello* in Turku in which he played Othello to his wife Litja's Desdemona: in 'the moment of utter hopelessness' where he kisses Desdemona before strangling her, someone in the audience let out a loud smacking kiss, similar 'to how movie audiences react to love scenes'. He was so upset he refused to finish the performance, but when he found out later that many in the audience had been first-time theatregoers, he regretted his decision (and indeed went on to direct a total of twelve Shakespeare productions during his fourteen years as director of the theatre).[62] In rare cases, this could also include educating theatre critics, as seen in Aarne Orjatsalo's published response to criticism of his portrayal of Othello in 1910, where interestingly from a modern perspective he discusses at length Iago's racism and how this influences Othello.[63]

In addition to attempts at making theatre itself more publicly accessible, performed Shakespeare would also be supplied by the new media of radio and film. For example, from the mid-1920s, when regular radio broadcasts began and national radio services were established, to 1940, there were fifteen Shakespeare plays broadcast on Danish radio.[64] Sweden presents even more striking statistics: in the same period there were thirty-seven performances of Shakespeare on national radio, making his works the most performed ones by any non-Swedish playwright.[65] In Finland, scenes from Shakespeare were broadcast on the radio in the 1930s, including monologues by Elli Tompuri, who decades earlier had become the first Nordic female Hamlet (discussed later). The first radio performance in Iceland was in 1943, directed by Lárus Pálsson who had studied in Denmark. Of course, commercial film would also offer numerous remediations of Shakespeare especially after the advent of sound, and English-language productions such as the Douglas Fairbanks and Mary Pickford vehicle *The Taming of the Shrew*, George Cukor's *Romeo and Juliet*,[66] Max Reinhardt's *A Midsummer Night's Dream* and the British *As You Like It* starring Laurence Olivier all reached Nordic cinemas in the 1930s. Actual Nordic interpretations of Shakespeare on film were obviously fewer, although there is a strong Nordic element in the German *Hamlet* production of 1921 in the form of its female star, the Danish Asta Nielsen (discussed in the next section). There had also been a domestic Danish production based on *Hamlet* in 1911 by prolific silent film director August Blom.[67]

Nordic Shakespeare and international impulses

If this introduction began with an emphasis on the ambition in various countries to create 'national Shakespeares', it is also fair to say that not even the most fervent stages of Nordic nationalism were devoid of broad and significant international influences. As we have seen, there was a close attention to European trends, and this tendency was demonstrably sustained over time. A typical example is the previously mentioned Finnish actor (and later director) Wilho Ilmari, who in May of 1914 left for his first 'study trip' abroad, with stops in Copenhagen, Berlin, Dresden, Prague, Vienna and Munich. In his autobiography he recalls being so impressed by Shakespeare performances directed by Max Reinhardt in Berlin that he forgot everything else he saw that trip.[68] In the 1920s he studied in Germany with Ferdinand Gregori and Julius Bab, whom he credits with opening his eyes to the dramatic possibilities of Shakespeare, and Oscar Rasco, with whom he worked on voice techniques.[69] In 1933–1934, the Finnish actress Glory Leppänen, in part disappointed in the availability of roles for mature actresses, decided to study directing at the Max Reinhardt seminar.[70] And Indriði Waage, the first director of Shakespeare in Iceland, had spent time in Germany studying theatre.[71]

That said, the emergence of national theatres and new independent states may have resulted in a somewhat smaller degree of intra-Nordic collaboration compared to the nineteenth century. Even so, there were certainly exceptions. For example, in 1885, the Finnish actress Ida Aalberg performed Ophelia in Finnish to Ernesto Rossi's Italian Hamlet at the Royal Dramatic Theatre in Stockholm (the rest speaking Swedish), gleefully writing to a friend afterwards that the King had called her an 'amazing revelation' and signing the letter 'your little Ophelia'.[72] In 1922, the Norwegian actor Ingolf Schanche, who had been a very successful Hamlet at the National Theatre in Oslo, also performed the role in Stockholm.[73] Danish actors came to Iceland for short performances, reciting scenes from Shakespeare. And in Finland, with its significant number of Swedish speakers, Swedish-language culture continued to be a vital force. This was not just a matter of Swedish culture influencing Finnish: for example, in the 1880s, the Finnish academic and theatre director Wilhelm Bolin (1835–1924) was responsible for updating Hagberg's Swedish translation of Shakespeare's plays and publishing the revised version with Gleerups, who had also issued Hagberg's original translation.

Rossi's performance in Stockholm attests to the fact that the late 1800s had seen guest performances by foreign troupes and actors performing in the Nordic countries.[74] In the twentieth century, these impulses from abroad continued, for example in the various performances of Max Reinhardt's Shakespeare productions, in both Denmark and Sweden, in 1915–1920, and in the *Hamlet* that the Moscow Art Theatre staged in Stockholm and Copenhagen in 1922.[75] Moreover, in Denmark, the celebration of the Shakespeare *Mindefest* in 1916 at Elsinore, which Anne Sophie Refskou discusses in depth in this volume, meant that European and global politics also entered the Shakespearean arena, even though, as Refskou demonstrates, there was a clear ambition to keep current events on the outside. To an extent, the same is true of the guest performances of *Hamlet* at Elsinore, beginning with the already-mentioned British production in 1937, which inaugurated a tradition of foreign-language performances that lasts to this day.[76] The very next year saw a production from England's soon-to-be adversary Germany featuring the star actor and Nazi collaborator Gustaf Gründgens. As we emphasize in our previous collection *Disseminating Shakespeare*, Nordic Shakespeare was in other words about much more than influences between Nordic countries or from the Anglo-American world: indeed, French and German ones continued to be significant well into the twentieth century.

Growing feminist movements in Europe also affected Shakespeare on Nordic stages. Theatres and their audiences became more interested in the choice of repertoire, and certain plays, such as *The Taming of the Shrew*, were criticized for their outdated ideas about women. For example, while not exactly radical in its gender politics, a Danish review of a performance in Aarhus in 1921 described the

Shrew as 'a play that may seem particularly prehistorical in a time like ours, when women can be not only members of parliament and municipal commissioners, but police officers and infantry soldiers'.[77] The successful production of the play at the Norwegian National Theatre in 1900 had similarly been met with some consternation since its morals were thought to be 'incredibly odd' for 'present-day people' (see Sandhaug's chapter). And Bergbom's 1890 production of the play in Finland was not well received, for what seem like similar reasons (see Paavolainen's chapter).

Yet, at the same time, Shakespeare could be put to the service of the 'new woman'. At least in Finland, especially regional theatres were almost always short of money, and this sometimes resulted in women getting opportunities they might not have otherwise. Reviewers of the Vyborg production of *Merchant* (1902), for example, made snide comments about Hilda Martin playing Lorenzo in pink tights, and in the same production Rosa Pulkkinen also played a male role.[78] Elli Tompuri more famously took on a male role in her travelling production of *Hamlet* (1913). Following Sarah Bernhardt, she had long thought that any actor, male or female, should familiarize themselves with the role even if they never act it. After her son was born Tompuri felt she had to play it, even though she felt uncomfortable by the thought of appearing onstage in tights.[79] Tompuri toured *Hamlet* in part because despite being hailed as one of the leading actresses of her generation, she was thought by some to be difficult, and she never got a permanent contract at the Finnish National or one of the regional theatres.[80] Reviewers did not quite know how to react to the performance, calling it 'reckless', sometimes discussing at length their discomfort with seeing a woman in a man's part:

> Elli Tompuri's power rests on her passionate feminine sensuality, the way she uses her voice, her plasticity, everything points towards that. Watching her Hamlet is disconcerting, because there's something so strange in the performance, entertaining only for being so different.
>
> By saying this I don't mean to imply that Mrs. Tompuri wouldn't be Hamlet, or that she doesn't understand his soul. But all the externals, all her means of playing the role which would allow the viewer to understand how she understands the character, work

against her. . . . We don't understand why Mrs. Tompuri would subject herself to the temptation when she could be playing roles such as Hugo's Lucretia Borgia.'[81]

A potentially even more radical reinterpretation of *Hamlet* was perhaps that of Asta Nielsen in the previously mentioned German film production from 1921. This film, which took its premise from an essay by Edward P. Vining claiming that Hamlet was in fact a woman, allowed its star, in the words of Delilah Bermudez Brataas, 'to perform gender fluidity and to convey that fluidity as the means to achieve ambition and agency'.[82]

The development of regional theatres also created more opportunities for female directors, some of whom took on Shakespeare, such as Glory Leppänen who directed to great acclaim *Two Gentlemen* in Turku (1937) and *Shrew* in Vyborg (1938).[83] Thus, Nordic Shakespeare in one sense offers an index to the ideological and political rift lines of the interwar period.

By the 1930s, then, Shakespeare had become firmly established in the repertoire and was extensively represented in the Nordic vernaculars, often in several different translations that were used more or less interchangeably by performers. Arguably, this also meant that 'Shakespeare' had become something of a blank slate on which various ideologies and positions could be inscribed. In the late 1930s, as Per Sivefors's chapter discusses in this book, to an author like the Swedish Eyvind Johnson, Shakespeare could symbolize the weak defence offered by culture and learning in the face of the Nazi threat, yet also help to articulate that very dilemma. Similarly, as mentioned previously Henrik Rytter's vision of Shakespeare in his translations from the early 1930s was firmly grounded in an internationalist, anti-fascist political stance (see Myklebost's chapter). To be sure, Shakespeare could be mustered to more squarely represent defiance vis-à-vis totalitarian enemies. In the newspaper *Norsk Tidend*, published in London by the Norwegian exile government during the Second World War, poet and novelist Nordahl Grieg reports from a performance of *All's Well That Ends Well* at the height of the Blitz: 'The Clown ran on to the stage and said, "There's an air-raid alert, anyone who wants to can seek shelter. We're proceeding with the show". . . . No one left, and while the air still trembled from the sirens, the young heroine continued her line.'[84] And despite its theatre building having been destroyed in the war, in Finland the previously mentioned Vyborg Theatre continued to operate. For example, during the 1943/4 season, a trip to Sweden to procure costumes made possible a well-received production of *Much Ado*. Of course, during the war and in countries that were occupied (Denmark, Norway) or claimed to be neutral (Sweden), co-opting Shakespeare in the struggle against fascism was often less than easy,[85] and putting on Shakespeare, especially his comedies, could be an act of escapism rather than one of open defiance.[86] Indeed, Nordic wartime theatre was hardly anti-fascist in any consistent way – far from it.[87] However, at least in Sweden, explicitly anti-Nazi Shakespeare became more of an option as Germany was increasingly perceived to be on the losing side, as witnessed by Alf Sjöberg's well-received *Merchant* in Stockholm in 1944.[88]

The structure of the book

Although some of the chapters in this book have a wide chronological sweep, the organization of the volume is, in the main, chronological, beginning with the early representation of Shakespeare on national stages and gradually moving on to more 'modern' conceptions, as well as discussing how Shakespeare was politicized in the interwar period up until approximately 1940.

Ástraður Eysteinsson and Ingibjörg Þórisdóttir's chapter on early Icelandic translations and performances partly describes a familiar development, with the advent of Romanticism sparking an interest in Shakespeare, though chronologically later than most of Europe. Denmark and Germany were vital influences, but, for example, Carl August Hagberg's Swedish translations eventually became an important point of reference for translators like Matthías Jochumsson in the second half of the nineteenth century. It was only later, in the 1920s, that Shakespeare began to be performed in Icelandic and on the whole, 'Icelandic Shakespeare' turned out to be a contentious project: on the one hand, Shakespeare represented a desirable high European culture; on the other hand, there was a great deal of discussion on the general value of translating his work into Icelandic. Thus, perhaps more than in other Nordic countries, alongside often fervent celebration, there was a perception of Shakespeare as a foreign element that might impact negatively on the vernacular literary tradition.

Focusing more on performance, Nely Keinänen analyses the first professional Finnish-language performance of Shakespeare, *Romeo and Juliet* (1881), starring Ida Aalberg (1857–1915) as Juliet. Shakespeare was eagerly embraced by the nationalist cause, which saw translating and performing Shakespeare as a cultural test. Early in Aalberg's career, the theatre cultivated the image of her as a living embodiment of the nation-as-female, the Finnish Maid, a characterization which was then problematized through her portrayal of Juliet, and reviewers reacted to the 'innocent' versus 'erotic' parts of her portrayal. This study also illuminates tensions in the uses of Shakespeare as cultural capital: Aalberg can also be seen as part of a larger theatrical trend in the late nineteenth century, whereby theatrical divas, frustrated by the paucity of good female roles in Shakespeare, turned instead to modernist authors more interested in the pressing gender questions of the day, though Aalberg was not above trying to use Shakespeare to advance her career as well. Expanding from this focused exploration of the first Finnish-language Shakespeare, Pentti Paavolainen's chapter follows the long career of Kaarlo Bergbom (1843–1906), who staged no less than fourteen Finnish-language premieres of Shakespearean plays in the period 1881–1902. Working closely with the poet Paavo Cajander, who was responsible for the translations, Bergbom's Shakespeare was part of the Fennoman movement that sought to develop Finnish language and culture, but it also owed a substantial debt to German Romanticism especially in the earlier phases of Bergbom's career. Arguably, this conception of Shakespeare was therefore both backward-looking in some of its aesthetic preferences (indeed removing much of Shakespeare's perceived crudity) and innovative in its attempts at fashioning a distinctly Finnish Shakespeare.

Examining another emerging national culture and its relation to Shakespeare, Christina Sandhaug discusses productions of Shakespeare during a pivotal moment in Norwegian history in general and that of Norway's National Theatre in particular. The period 1899–1914 saw eight productions of Shakespeare, all of which testify to the complexity of Norway's own ideological transition from a provincial National Romanticism towards a more cosmopolitan notion of nationhood. Tracing that development, Sandhaug draws on a broad range of material on the reception of the productions, but also discusses the sway that 'Shakespeare' held in the popular imagination and in the press. While Shakespeare could not compete with national icons such as Ibsen and Bjørnson, the staging of his plays, and the reception of them, testifies to the transformation of Norwegian national sensibilities and the complex ways 'Shakespeare' resonated in the period.

Anne Sophie Refskou's chapter focuses on the tercentenary commemoration of Shakespeare's death at Elsinore in 1916. This international event, Refskou suggests, embodied a tension between lingering National Romantic conception of Shakespeare with little or no reference to the ongoing world war and a more outspoken and politically explicit agenda, as represented by, for example, the internationally renowned Danish Shakespeare scholar, Georg Brandes (whose book on Shakespeare we cited earlier as an example of a more 'modern' view of Shakespeare mixed with nostalgia). The latter, more outspoken position seems, however, to have been largely suppressed in the interest of avoiding contention, and in Refskou's analysis the 1916 *Mindefest* therefore represents both Nordic self-assertion and an attempt at occupying a politically 'neutral' position during the First World War.

Whereas many of the contributions to this volume focus squarely on performance, Svenn-Arve Myklebost's chapter engages with the translations of Shakespeare into Norwegian by Henrik Rytter, which appeared in the early 1930s. As reflected in especially his introductions to the plays, Rytter's own political position had changed from right-wing sympathies towards a more Romantic and peculiarly left-leaning view of national identity, framing his translations in an ideology that is both nationalist, vitalist and socialist. In that sense, Rytter's Shakespeare is markedly different from the elitist and conservative Shakespeare found in Eliot's brand of Anglo-American modernism. Rytter's actual translations, however, do not always reflect the ideological positions of his introductions, yet in their 'linguistic plurality' they have the power to make the plays seem 'new'. A similar distance towards high modernism characterizes Shakespeare's presence in the works of Swedish author Eyvind Johnson (1900–1976) as discussed in Per Sivefors's chapter: here, for example, the Hamlet figure – a common persona in Johnson's early work – becomes an emphatic representative of modernity. What is more, Johnson's numerous references to Shakespeare can be said to reflect the author's own changing political outlook. The early novels from the 1920s are densely populated by Hamlet-like characters that embody the lack of direction and initiative after the First World War, whereas Johnson's later work in the 1930s and early 1940s reflects on the possibility of overcoming this passivity by, for example, anti-fascist struggle and solidarity with the working classes. During the Second World War, the concluding lines from *The Winter's Tale* come to sum up Johnson's sense of hope in defeating Nazi powers in Europe.

Taken together, the essays reveal the complex interconnections between local, national, Nordic and European Shakespeares, and what 'Shakespeare' came to signify in changing political, social, literary and theatrical contexts. The risk perhaps in a collection like this is to overstate the significance of Shakespeare in larger developments, to forget that Shakespeare is one influence among many, that while translators and actors could make a name for themselves with Shakespeare, they also translated or performed other works/roles. Especially during an age when the average theatrical repertoire could encompass dozens of plays per season, Shakespeare was not the only playwright on offer. But having said this, one senses in the discourse around Shakespeare a particular pull, the sense that this translation, this performance, this literary allusion is more special because it is Shakespeare. Book and theatre reviewers pause to discuss the significance of Shakespeare, an actor or director writing a memoir devotes more pages to their Shakespearean productions. The sense is not what Shakespeare means to me but what he means to us, defined ever more broadly. The next significant developments in Nordic, and indeed global, Shakespeare will come in the 1960s, a topic we hope to return to in later publications.

Notes

1 Brandes's book, which originally appeared in 1895–1896, was published in English in 1905 by William Heinemann under the title *William Shakespeare: A Critical Study*. He moreover wrote introductions to a multivolume edition in English that appeared around the same time, also with Heinemann. For discussion of Brandes as a Shakespeare scholar, see, for example, Hansen, 'Observations'. Unless otherwise indicated, translations into English are our own.

2 Such popular studies include the Danish Goll, 'Forbrydertyper'; the Swedish Schück, *William Shakspere* and *Shakspere och hans tid*; and Brunius, *Shakespeare och scenen* and *Shakespeare*. For Brunius as a Shakespeare critic, see the recent Gedin, *August Brunius*, 276–81. See also the 'Timeline' appended to the present volume.

3 On Denmark, see Ruud, *Denmark*; on Finland, see Hirn, 'Shakespeare i Finland'; on Iceland, see Einarsson, 'Shakespeare in Iceland'; for Norway, see Ruud, *Norway*; and for Sweden, Molin, *Shakespeare och Sverige*. These studies all appeared between 1916 and 1940.

4 Tiitinen, 'Kaksi viimeistä Shakespeare', 458. For a careful comparison of Jylhä's translations to Cajander's, see Mustanoja. In a wide-ranging essay, Rissanen compares these two to later Finnish translators.

5 On the reception of this complete works project, see Keinänen, 'Canons'.

6 Einarsson, 'Shakespeare in Iceland', 281.

7 Einarsson, 'Shakespeare in Iceland', 283.

8 See the entry on 'Valdemar Østerberg' in *Dansk Biografisk Leksikon*. Østerberg's translations were also used for radio performances in 1931 and 1940 (Albrectsen, *Shakespeareopførelser*, 80, 94).

9 See the review by P. A. Rosenberg, 'Shakespeareoversættelser', in *Dannebrogen*, 14 January 1901. Similarly, writing in 1917, Martin Ruud felt that despite their merits, the new translations were characterized by 'a modernity which dissipates the atmosphere of Shakespeare's English' (Ruud, *Denmark*, 38). As it turned out, these misgivings were partly correct, since Lembcke's translations, and even older ones by Peter Foersom and Adam Oehlenschläger, continued to be used for performances in Denmark well beyond the period covered in this book.

10 Molin, *Shakespeare och Sverige*, which covers the period until the mid-nineteenth century.

11 Schück's book was his second on Shakespeare and has a strongly contextual approach, with nearly the entire first volume taken up by discussion of political and cultural history as well as theatre before Shakespeare.

12 'Per Hallström', entry in *Nordisk familjebok*.

13 Wilmer, 'German', 15–16.

14 Wilmer, 'German', 25.

15 McConachie, 'Towards a History', 51. On the links between theatre and national identity, see also Holdsworth, *Theatre Nation* and

Holdsworth, ed., *Theatre and National Identity*, and Mäkinen et al., eds, *Theatre*.
16 Shepherd-Barr, 'Development', 86.
17 Shepherd-Barr, 'Development', 90.
18 *Opiksi ja Huviksi*, 1 April 1902, no. 4–6, 66.
19 Pirkko Koski, however, argues that the theatre 'by no means represents the "whole" nation . . . [although it was able to sell itself] as representative of the nation and of the people both to the media and the public, and even to many generations of researchers' ('Justification', 100).
20 Pyrrö, 'Taidekierto', parts 2 and 3.
21 *Opiksi ja Huviksi*, 4–6, 1 April 1902, 66.
22 For the Royal Theatre in the eighteenth and nineteenth centuries, see Rosenqvist, ed., *Den svenska nationalscenen*, chs. 1–5.
23 As Claes Rosenqvist points out, 'the recurring demands' for an entirely new national theatre 'were obstructed already during the projecting and building phases by the influence of old traditions and institutions' ('En teaterbyggnad', 261).
24 Wilmer, *National Theatres*, 3; Koski, 'Justification', 100–5.
25 Wilmer, 'German', 27–30.
26 Godenhjelm, 'Kotimaan kirjallisuutta', 36. See also Keinänen, 'Role'.
27 Einarsson, 'Shakespeare in Iceland', 284.
28 Þorbergsson, 'Staging the Nation', 30. In Þorbergsson's view, the responses to these performances indicate that 'Shakespeare somehow represented a connection to theatrical tradition, an entrance ticket to the cultural heritage of Europe, or even the membership of an exclusive club of culturally independent countries' (30).
29 Þorbergsson, 'Staging the Nation', 30.
30 See Hundebøll, 'Kjøbenhavns Cyclefabrik'. The commercial appeal of Shakespeare's prince clearly had its disadvantages: an article in *Jyllandsposten* (22 January 1922) complains of all the 'Hamlet humbug' that had been accruing in Elsinore in recent years, including visits to 'Hamlet's grave' and 'Ophelia's well' organized by local innkeepers.
31 Sorelius, 'Introduction', 12. It is worth keeping in mind that Strindberg's income from theatre royalties and book sales of his plays *Gustaf Vasa* and *Erik XIV* (both 1899) amounted to well above 15,000 Swedish krona (Ollén, 'Kommentarer', 510). This was about

fifteen times the annual salary of a baker in the first decade of the 1900s (cf. *Kollektivaftal*, 23).
32 *Göteborgs Handels- och Sjöfartstidning*, 25 January 1901.
33 *Visir*, 27 December 1926, 2.
34 Veistäjä, *Viipurin*, 51.
35 Marker and Marker, *A History*, 232.
36 DiPietro, *Shakespeare and Modernism*, 43. For Shakespeare, modernism and mass culture, see also Halpern, *Shakespeare Among the Moderns*, ch. 2.
37 Previously, smaller theatres without permanent ensembles had also often opened with a play by Shakespeare: the theatres of Kristianstad (founded 1906) and Sandviken (1908) featured *A Midsummer Night's Dream* and *Hamlet* respectively.
38 For the role of provincial theatres in the earliest dissemination of Shakespeare in Sweden, and the reluctance in Stockholm towards Shakespeare, see Sivefors, 'Trade Routes'. For the history of and ideas behind the system of city theatres – a concept imported from Germany – see Heed, 'Stadsteatertanken'.
39 As Ann Fridén suggests on the early twentieth century, '[i]n comparison with much of Sweden, Stockholm was greatly influenced by German culture and ideas. Stockholm had also looked to France for inspiration for a very long time. Gothenburg, however, looked westwards and several of its leading families were of British descent' (*Macbeth*, 75).
40 Paavolainen, *Suomen teatterihistoria*, ch. 4 (also available in Swedish, see the Works Cited). For example, in the city of Tampere, a Workers' Theatre, with amateur actors but a professional director, was established in 1901, followed by the Tampere Theatre in 1904, all professionals.
41 Productions include *Mac* (1901/2), *MV* (1902/3, 1915/16), *Ham* (1904/5, 1905/6, 1908/9, 1929/30), *TS* (1904/5, 1938/9), *AC* (1905/6) and *MW* (1906/7). Later productions included *KL* (1912/13), *TN* (1908/9), *AYL* (1918/19), *Tem* (1911/12), *Oth* (1906/7, 1937/8), *MA* (1906/7, 1943/4, in Viipuri, seven times), *RJ* (1910/11, 1911/12, 1923/4, twenty-seven performances), *MND* (1930/1).
42 According to one review, 'that it somewhat succeeded can be considered a merit, especially since there had been so little time to rehearse. The performance was certainly unfinished, but we're so used to that that anything different would have felt unusual' (qtd. in

Veistäjä, *Viipurin*, 71). That season the company performed thirty different plays.

43 Paavolainen, *Suomen teatterihistoria*, ch. 4.3. Orjatsalo even performed his Hamlet at a Finnish workers' theatre in the United States in 1923 (Pennanen, *Orjatsalo*, 322–5).

44 Paavolainen, *Suomen teatterihistoria*, ch. 4.1.

45 Paavolainen, *Suomen teatterihistoria*, ch. 4.3; Ilmari, *Teatterimiehen Lokikirja*, 69.

46 Shakespeare translations by Ingivaldur Nikulásson, Komedíuleikhúsið, 2022.

47 See the list in Albrectsen, *Shakespeareopførelser*, 34–95.

48 For the earliest performances of *Hamlet* in Sweden, see Sivefors, 'Trade Routes'.

49 Kent Hägglund, personal communication to Per Sivefors, 12 October 2021. Although statistics are hard to establish with any exactitude, especially if counting performances by non-professionals, the other most commonly performed plays in Sweden seem to have been *MV*, *Oth*, *RJ* and *TS*, making for a fairly even distribution across comedies and tragedies.

50 Among them are the French guest performances in 1899 and 1902 (the latter starring Sarah Bernhardt); Swedish ones in 1914 and 1934; Austrian actor Alexander Moissi's performance with the ensemble of the Betty Nansen-Teatern in 1922; the Soviet troupe that visited Copenhagen, also in 1922; and of course the performances at Elsinore by English and German troupes in 1937, 1938 and 1939. For foreign guest performances more generally, see the next section.

51 Brandes, *William Shakespeare*, 5.

52 Even in more specific matters of contemporary public health, Shakespeare could serve as a point of reference. A Danish newspaper reflects in 1922 on the fact that Hamlet is often represented as thin and nervous, despite his mother's comment that 'he's fat and scant of breath' (*Ham*, 5.2.269). The somewhat surprising conclusion is that Hamlet is 'a Danish type, whom we know from numerous less than energetic countrymen, prone to reverie, aestheticization, mental disease, cancer and suicide' (*Nationaltidende*, 26 November 1922). A certain amount of body fat is healthy; fatness in the vein of Shakespeare's Danish prince clearly isn't.

53 As an example of such promotional work, although musical settings of Shakespeare are not at the focus of the present volume, it bears remarking that public theatre institutions actively embraced the use

of incidental music by contemporary composers. The most significant case in point is of course Sibelius's score for *The Tempest*, which premiered at the Royal Theatre in Copenhagen in 1926. In Sweden, other well-known composers such as Wilhelm Stenhammar, Kurt Atterberg and Lars-Erik Larsson all contributed music to Shakespeare performances at public theatres or on the national radio.

54 Though, to be fair, neither necessarily embraced a narrowly 'national' conception of Shakespeare: as Janet Clare points out, '[a]s an expatriate writing during the interwar years, Eliot's criticism is free from the religiose Englishness that then predominated' ('*Hamlet* and Modernism', 237).

55 For discussion of Lindberg's programme, see Lagerroth, 'Modernismens genombrott', 72; for Lindberg's 'egalitarian ideal of a flexible, classless "folk theatre"', see also Marker and Marker, *A History*, 242. As previously noted, Lindberg became noted for his modernist productions of Shakespeare at Gothenburg's Lorensbergsteatern and, later, at the Konserthusteatern in Stockholm.

56 For this production, see Gaines, 'The Single Performance', and Refskou, '"Whose Castle Is It Anyway?"'.

57 'For amateurs, Shakespeare's verse drama . . . requires among many other things a fine-tuned diction; additionally, plays of these dimensions, with all their parts, require large stages, which amateur companies generally do not have access to. Thus, it is only recommendable in exceptional cases that Shakespeare, and verse drama in general, be performed by our Swedish amateurs' (Bergman, *Teaterhandbok*, 42–3).

58 Rajala, *Titaanien Teatteri*, 39–40.

59 Rajala, *Titaanien Teatteri*, 128–31, 169. According to reviews, Elo only got better in the role with each passing year, as did Elli Tompuri, of whom more later, who as a guest artist played Juliet in 1929 when she was nearly fifty. One reviewer commented on how 'a mature actress can play Julia as much more alive and naturally in love than an actress who is closer to an age which is not even worth trying to attain' (Rajala, *Titaanien Teatteri*, 171).

60 Statistics from Ilona, the database of the Theatre Info Finland and the Theatre Museum.

61 Ilmari, *Teatterimiehen Lokikirja*, 54–5; Pennanen, *Orjatsalo*, 201–3.

62 Ilmari, *Teatterimiehen Lokikirja*, 71–2.

63 Pennanen, *Orjatsalo*, 145–54.

64 Albrectsen, *Shakespeareopførelser*, 76–94.

65 See the statistics in Fredén, *Handbok*, 126–8. For specific discussion of voice and delivery in these and other recorded performances of Swedish Shakespeare, see Martin, *Eloquence Is Action*.

66 In the 1930s, prose versions of this play/film were sold, with stills from the movie (Pentti Paavolainen, personal communication, 29 March 2022).

67 Albrectsen, *Shakespeareopførelser*, 57.

68 Ilmari, *Teatterimiehen Lokikirja*, 49–50.

69 Ilmari, *Teatterimiehen Lokikirja*, 67, 69. Ilmari reports Gregori was amazed that a young actor from Finland would want to study abroad, as few from Germany went to study acting elsewhere (70).

70 Leppänen, *Elämäni Teatteria*, 131–65. In her autobiography, she tells of her disappointment at being offered the Widow in *Shrew* when she had originally been promised Kate (129).

71 Jónsson, 'Fyrsti íslenski leikstjórinn', 24.

72 Räsänen, *Ida Aalberg*, 199.

73 Other examples include Swedish guest performances at Copenhagen of *Hamlet* in 1934 and *Romeo and Juliet* in 1936 (Albrectsen, *Shakespeareopførelser*, 83–4, 87).

74 See Keinänen and Sivefors, 'Timeline'; Sivefors, '"A Blot"'.

75 For Reinhardt's influence on Nordic theatre, including his Shakespeare productions, see Marker and Marker, *A History*, 227–30.

76 Other foreign-language performances in Denmark include French ones of *Hamlet* in 1899 and 1902. There was also a guest performance of *Macbeth* by an English troupe at the Casinotheatret in Copenhagen in 1936 (Albrectsen, *Shakespeareopførelser*, 87).

77 *Aarhus Stifts-Tidende*, 14 April 1921.

78 Veistäjä, *Viipurin*, 35.

79 Tompuri, *Minun Tieni*, 250–1. It can be added that Bernhardt's interpretation was certainly known in Northern Europe: as noted elsewhere in this introduction (n. 49), in 1902 she starred as Hamlet in a French guest performance at the Folketeatret in Copenhagen (Albrectsen, *Shakespeareopførelser*, 48).

80 Mäkinen, 'Kamppailua', 133.

81 *Aamulehti*, 18 October 1913.

82 Brataas, 'The Shadow's Shadow', 4.

83 Leppänen, *Elämäni Teatteria*, 196–7, 211–13. The *Shrew* production was done in celebration of the theatre's fortieth anniversary; Leppänen did finally get to play Kate (with no rehearsal) when the regular actress sprained her ankle just before a sold-out performance. The next season Leppänen was planning on directing *Much Ado* in Viipuri, but those plans were shelved in November 1939.

84 *Norsk Tidend*, 25 October 1940.

85 Generally, for anti-Nazi theatre in Sweden in the 1930s, see Lagerroth, 'Antinazistisk trettiotalsteater'; for the war years, see Ek, 'Krigsskugga'.

86 As Sverker Ek puts it, Alf Sjöberg's production of *Much Ado* in early 1940 'was perceived as a much-needed reminder that there was more to life than angst in the face of an imminent war' ('Krigsskugga', 164).

87 For example, the Dramatic Theatre in Stockholm even mounted a guest production of Strindberg's *Gustaf Vasa* in Berlin in 1941; see Ek, 'Krigsskugga', 169–70, and the Finnish National Theatre had plans to visit in 1942/3, though nothing came of this; see Korsberg, 'Politiikan', 79–90. In 1938, the Schiller Theatre (Berlin) had toured in the Nordic countries (Finland, Sweden, Norway and Denmark), playing Calderón's *The Mayor of Zalamea*, travelling with a company of approximately thirty people (*Teatteri-Maailma*, 3, 1938, 44).

88 Sorelius, 'Anti-Nazi *Merchant*'. For earlier Swedish productions of this play and their relation to anti-semitism, see also Feiler and Sauter, 'Shylock', esp. 41–4.

Works cited

Albrectsen, Stig, *Shakespeareopførelser i Danmark 1792–1987* (København, 1988).
Bergman, Gösta, ed., *Teaterhandbok för amatörer* (Stockholm, 1931).
Brandes, Georg, *William Shakespeare: A Critical Study* (London, 1905).
Brataas, Delilah Bermudez, 'The Shadow's Shadow, or Gendered Ambition in Asta Nielsen's 1921 Hamlet', *Cahiers Élisabéthains*, 98/1 (2019), 3–21.
Brunius, August, *Shakespeare och scenen: Tre studier till trehundraårsminnet den 23 april 1916* (Stockholm, 1916).
Brunius, August, *William Shakespeare: Liv, drama, teater* (Stockholm, 1924).

Clare, Janet, 'Hamlet and Modernism: T. S. Eliot and G. Wilson Knight', in Dirk Delabastita, Jozef De Vos and Paul Franssen, eds, *Shakespeare and European Politics* (Newark, 2008), 234-45.
DiPietro, Cary, *Shakespeare and Modernism* (Cambridge, 2006).
Einarsson, Stefán, 'Shakespeare in Iceland: A Historical Survey', *ELH*, 7/4 (1940), 272-85.
Ek, Sverker, 'Krigsskugga och budkavle', in Tomas Forser and Sven Åke Heed, eds, *Ny svensk teaterhistoria*, iii (Möklinta, 2007), 163-74.
Erich, Mikko, *William Shakespeare ja hänen runoutensa* (Helsinki, 1916).
Feiler, Yael, and Willmar Sauter, 'Shylock i rörelse: Gestaltning och mottagande – Nu och då', in Yael Feiler and Willmar Sauter, eds, *Shakespeares Shylock och antisemitismen* (2nd edn, Stockholm, 2010), 27-54.
Fredén, Gustaf, *William Shakespeare: Handbok till radioteatern* (Stockholm, 1960).
Fridén, Ann, *Macbeth in the Swedish Theatre* (Göteborg, 1986).
Gaines, Barry, 'The Single Performance of *Hamlet* that Changed Theatre History', in Paul Menzer, ed., *Inside Shakespeare: Essays on the Blackfriars Stage* (Selinsgrove, 2006), 206-15.
Gedin, Per I., *August Brunius, kritiker* (Stockholm, 2022).
Godenhjelm, B. F., 'Kotimaan kirjallisuutta', *Kirjallinen Kuukauslehti* February (1880), 36-40.
Goll, August, *Forbrydertyper hos Shakespeare* (Copenhagen, 1907).
Halpern, Richard, *Shakespeare Among the Moderns* (Ithaca, 1997).
Hansen, Niels B., 'Observations on Georg Brandes's Contribution to the Study of Shakespeare', in Gunnar Sorelius, ed., *Shakespeare and Scandinavia: A Collection of Nordic Studies* (Newark, 2002), 148-67.
Heed, Sven-Åke, 'Stadsteatertanken i svensk teater', in Tomas Forser and Sven Åke Heed, eds, *Ny svensk teaterhistoria*, iii (Möklinta, 2007), 195-235.
Hirn, Yrjö, 'Shakespeare i Finland', *Finsk Tidskrift*, 4 (1916), 245-70.
Holdsworth, Nadine, *Theatre & Nation* (London, 2010).
Holdsworth, Nadine, ed., *Theatre and National Identity: Re-Imagining Conceptions of Nation* (London, 2014).
Hundebøll, Sune, 'Kjøbenhavns Cyclefabrik – Hamlet Meinungsgade 10-14', in *Nørrebro lokalhistoriske forening og arkiv: Årsskrift 2014* (København, 2014), 16-19, https://noerrebrolokalhistorie.dk/aarsskrifter/aarsskrift2014.pdf, accessed 10 December 2021.
Ilmari, Wilho, *Teatterimiehen Lokikirja* (Helsinki, 1971).
Jónsson, Klemenz, 'Fyrsti íslenski leikstjórinn', *Lesbók Morgunblaðsins*, 11/1 (1997), 24.
Keinänen, Nely, 'Canons and Heroes: The Reception of the Complete Works Translations Project in Finland, 2002-13', *Multicultural*

Shakespeare: Translation, Appropriation and Performance, 16/31 (2017), 109–25.

Keinänen, Nely, 'The Role of Hamlet in Finnish Nation-Building, 1879–84', in Márta Minier and Lily Kahn, eds, *Hamlet Translations: Prisms of Cultural Encounters Across the Globe*, 16 (2021), 81–100.

Keinänen, Nely, and Per Sivefors, 'A Timeline of Significant Shakespeare-Related Events in the Nordic Countries Before 1900', in Nely Keinänen and Per Sivefors, eds, *Disseminating Shakespeare in the Nordic Countries: Shifting Centres and Peripheries in the Nineteenth Century* (Bloomsbury, 2022), 297–315.

Kollektivaftal i Sverige träffade under år 1909 (Stockholm, 1912), https://share.scb.se/OV9993/Data/Historisk%20statistik/%C3%96vrig%20statistik%20fr%C3%A5n%20andra%20myndigheter%201877-/Arbetsstatistik%20utg.%20av%20Kommerskollegium%201899-1913/Arbetsstatistik-F2-Kollektivavtal-Sverige-traffade-1909.pdf, accessed 8 February 2022.

Korsberg, Hanna, *Politiikan ja Valta-Taistelun Pyörteissä: Suomen Kansallisteatteri ja Epävarmuuden aika 1934–1950* (Helsinki, 2004).

Koski, Pirkko, 'Justification as National Throughout Changing Times: The National Theatre of Finland', in S. Wilmer, ed., *National Theatres in a Changing Europe* (Houndmills, 2008), 99–110.

Lagerroth, Ulla-Britta, 'Antinazistisk trettiotalsteater', in Tomas Forser and Sven Åke Heed, eds, *Ny svensk teaterhistoria*, iii (Möklinta, 2007), 117–24.

Lagerroth, Ulla-Britta, 'Modernismens genombrott i huvudstaden', in Tomas Forser and Sven Åke Heed, eds, *Ny svensk teaterhistoria*, iii (Möklinta, 2007), 69–82.

Leppänen, Glory, *Elämäni Teatteria* (Helsinki, 1971).

Mäkinen, Helka, 'Kamppailua hegemoniasta kulttuurin kentällä: Elli Tompuri vastaan Suomen Kansallisteatteri', in Pirkko Koski, ed., *Niin muuttuu mailma, Eskoni* (Helsinki, 2000), 125–56.

Mäkinen, Helka, S. E. Wilmer, and W. B. Worthen, eds, *Theatre, History, and National Identities* (Helsinki, 2001).

Marker, Frederick J., and Lise-Lone Marker, *A History of Scandinavian Theatre* (Cambridge, 1996).

Martin, Jacqueline, *Eloquence Is Action: A Study of Form and Text's Influence on the Vocal Delivery Style of Shakespeare in Sweden 1934–1985* (Stockholm, 1987).

McConachie, Bruce, 'Towards a History of National Theatres in Europe', in S. E. Wilmer, ed., *National Theatres in a Changing Europe* (Houndmills, 2008), 49–60.

Molin, Nils, *Shakespeare och Sverige intill 1800-talets mitt: En översikt av hans inflytande* (Göteborg, 1931).

Mustanoja, Tauno, 'Suomalainen Shakespeare', *Suomalainen Suomi* (1957), 206–12.

Ollén, Gunnar, 'Kommentarer', in August Strindberg, *Folkungasagan, Gustav Vasa, Erik XIV*, ed. Gunnar Ollén, *August Strindbergs samlade verk*, xli (Stockholm, 1992), 467–582.

Paavolainen, Pentti, *Finlands teaterhistoria*, Teaterhögskolans publikationsserie, 69, trans. Katariina Torvalds-Wiik, https://disco.teak.fi/teatteri/sv/.

Paavolainen, Pentti, *Suomen teatterihistoria*, Teatterikorkeakoulun julkaisusarja, 53, https://disco.teak.fi/teatteri/.

Pennanen, Jotaarkka, *Orjatsalo: Taiteilija politiikan kurimuksessa* (Tampere, 2017).

'Per Hallström', in *Nordisk Familjebok*, ix (Malmö, 1952–1955).

Pyrrö, Katariina, *Taidekierto. Kansallisteatteri*, https://kansallisteatteri.fi/esitys/taidekierto/, accessed 17 March 2022.

Rajala, Panu, *Titaanien Teatteri: Tampereen Työväen Teatteri 1918–1964* (Tampere, 1995).

Räsänen, Ilmari, *Ida Aalberg* (Porvoo, 1925).

Refskou, Anne-Sophie, '"Whose Castle Is It Anyway?": Local/Global Negotiations of a Shakespearean Location', *Multicultural Shakespeare: Translation, Appropriation and Performance*, 15/1 (2017), 121–32.

Rissanen, Matti, 'Hämäläisiä Shakespearen Suomentajia Paavo Cajanderista Jukka Virtaseen', in Jari Alenius, Lari Ahokas and Jarmo Kosekela, eds, *Kaikuja Hämeestä* (Helsinki, 2003), 133–56.

Rosenqvist, Claes, ed., *Den svenska nationalscenen: Traditioner och reformer på Dramaten under 200 år* (Stockholm, 1988).

Rosenqvist, Claes, 'En teaterbyggnad för sin tid: Det nya Dramatenhuset vid Nybroplan', in Claes Rosenqvist, ed., *Den svenska nationalscenen: Traditioner och reformer på Dramaten under 200 år* (Stockholm, 1988), 229–61.

Ruud, Martin, *An Essay Toward a History of Shakespeare in Norway* (Minneapolis, 1917).

Ruud, Martin, *An Essay Toward a History of Shakespeare in Denmark* (Minneapolis, 1920).

Schück, Henrik, *William Shakspere: Hans lif och värksamhet* (Stockholm, 1883).

Schück, Henrik, *Shakspere och hans tid*, 2 vols (Stockholm, 1916).

Shepherd-Barr, Kirsten, 'The Development of Norway's National Theatres', in S. Wilmer, ed., *National Theatres in a Changing Europe* (London, 2008), 85–98.

Sivefors, Per, 'Trade Routes, Politics and Culture: Shakespeare in Sweden', in Janet Clare and Dominique Goy-Blanquet, eds, *Migrating*

Shakespeare: First European Encounters, Routes and Networks (London, 2021), 189–208.

Sorelius, Gunnar, 'Introduction', in Gunnar Sorelius, ed., *Shakespeare and Scandinavia: A Collection of Nordic Studies* (Newark, 2002), 9–16.

Sorelius, Gunnar, 'The Stockholm 1944 Anti-Nazi *Merchant of Venice*: The Uncertainty of Response', in Gunnar Sorelius, ed., *Shakespeare and Scandinavia: A Collection of Nordic Studies* (Newark, 2002), 193–206.

Þorbergsson, Magnús Þor, 'Being European: Staging the Nation in 1920s Icelandic Theatre', *Nordic Theatre Studies*, 25/1 (2013), 22–33.

Tiitinen, Teuvo, 'Kaksi viimeistä Shakespeare'in Macbethin suomennosta', *Virittäjä* 40 (1936), 450–8.

Tompuri, Elli, *Minun Tieni*, 2nd edn (Porvoo, 1942).

'Valdemar Østerberg', in *Dansk Biografisk Leksikon*, https:// biografiskleksikon.lex.dk/V._ Østerberg, accessed 14 March 2022.

Veistäjä, Verneri, *Viipurin ja Muun Suomen Teatteri* (Helsinki, 1957).

Wilmer, S. E., 'German Romanticism and Its Influence on Finnish and Irish Theatre', in Helka Mäkinen, S. E. Wilmer and W. B. Worthen, eds, *Theatre, History and National Identities* (Helsinki, 2001), 15–69.

Wilmer, S. E., 'Introduction', in S. E. Wilmer, ed., *National Theatres in a Changing Europe* (Houndmills, 2008), 1–5.

1

Early Icelandic translations of Shakespeare

Settings, contexts, cultural transfer

*Ástráður Eysteinsson and
Ingibjörg Þórisdóttir*

In Iceland, as elsewhere in Europe, interest in William Shakespeare's dramas, along with the recognition of his canonical status in Western literary history, was reinforced with the advent of Romanticism, in a cultural context doubly marked by growing attention to individual identity and expression, and by critical changes in the historical understanding of nationhood. The public Icelandic reception of Shakespeare's works, however, not to mention translation of his plays, is considerably 'delayed' compared to the scene of literature and drama in, for instance, France, Germany, Denmark and Sweden. The first Icelandic translations of plays by Shakespeare were not published until the 1870s, and translations of his plays first appeared on stage in Iceland in the 1920s.

In this chapter, we analyse the complicated positions and reaction with regard to Shakespeare in Iceland in the late nineteenth and early twentieth centuries, and trace important moments in the translation and reception of his works in this period while also paying attention to key participants in the contexts that shaped the entry of Shakespeare into Icelandic literary culture. On the one hand, Shakespeare was seen as a representative of high European culture who might have something to offer to Iceland's national aspirations, fuelled by its literary legacies, but at the same time his presence proved divisive. Prominent translators discussed how Shakespeare's blank verse could best be incorporated into the language, while critics and commentators argued about the cultural significance of translation and about the 'use' of translating foreign classics into Icelandic.

Since the rendering and publication of the Bible in the sixteenth century, few canonical works from Western literary history had been published in Icelandic translation. It should be noted in this context that there was no secular printing press in Iceland until 1773. It wasn't until well into the nineteenth century that the Homeric epics were brought out in Sveinbjörn Egilsson's prose translation, the *Odyssey* from 1829 to 1840 and the *Iliad* in 1855. Somewhat earlier, Alexander Pope's philosophical poem *Essay on Man* and John Milton's epic poem *Paradise Lost* had appeared in Icelandic, both translated from Danish and German by Jón Þorláksson. Given the role of Shakespeare in German and Danish Romanticism, one might assume that a passage had been reasonably cleared for at least some of his plays onto the Icelandic literary scene around or shortly after the mid-nineteenth century.

But that route proved somewhat complicated, not only due to the lack of a professional theatre in Iceland but also because Icelanders, during much of the nineteenth century, were quite busy exploring and revaluating their own literary history, for instance the ways in which some of their medieval literature, especially the sagas ('Íslendingasögur') and the Eddas (both the variety of medieval Eddic poetry and the mythology as portrayed in Snorri Sturluson's *Edda*), might constitute key canonical elements in a cultural foundation of a nation that needed to come into its own again. A substantial portion of the energy of Icelandic Romanticism went into this enterprise, which can only be briefly touched on here, but there is little doubt that for an extended period, the Icelandic rediscovery and structuring of its own 'Western' (and Northern) tradition restrained the urge to import various significant elements of the European canon.[1]

In focusing on the Icelandic reception of Shakespeare, we begin with a brief overview of the historical context of Romanticism in Iceland, effected mainly through contact with Denmark and Germany, and this includes the celebration of Shakespeare, especially Shakespearean tragedy. In addition, we discuss how the fledgling state of theatre in the country also had a damping effect on the advent of Shakespeare, as other genres were seen as more significant, though individual playwrights looked to Shakespeare for models.

Greetings from overseas

Icelandic Romanticism was slow to develop. A long-time rural society, with only minimal urban municipalities, Iceland saw increasing vocational diversity and initiatives in the late eighteenth century. The village of Reykjavik was granted a town charter in 1786 and around this time the ties between the administrative centres on the colonial island and their rather distant capital, Copenhagen, became more active and reciprocal. An increasing number of Icelandic students went to Denmark to continue their education at the University of Copenhagen. Some subsequently pursued careers in Denmark, but others moved back to Iceland, like the lawyer Bjarni Thorarensen (1786–1841) who studied and worked in Copenhagen from 1802 to 1811 and was an early Icelandic reader of Shakespeare.[2] Back on home turf he had a prosperous career and advanced to the position of district governor of northern and eastern Iceland. As such he oversaw an outpost of the Danish 'empire', but as a poet and pioneer of Icelandic Romanticism, he composed patriotic lyrics about Iceland as a separate realm with its own history and natural world.

Other Icelanders pursued this vision as part of their lives and work in Copenhagen, for instance Baldvin Einarsson (1801–1833), an early proponent of Icelandic independence. He co-edited the journal *Ármann á Alþingi* (1829–1832), the first of a number of journals, written in Icelandic and published in Copenhagen (and distributed both there and in Iceland), that were instrumental in the struggle to resurrect the Icelandic parliament, 'Alþing' (which was to happen in 1845), and to reclaim the independence of the country (a process which would not be completed until 1944). Another such journal was *Fjölnir* (1835–1847), one of whose editors was the poet and natural scientist Jónas Hallgrímsson (1807–1845), a central figure of Icelandic Romanticism. The Icelandic diaspora in Copenhagen would continue to grow throughout the nineteenth century, and its bipartite space, a home away from home, played a highly significant role in forming the world of Icelandic ideas, politics, education and literature in the nineteenth century, impacting several people who were shaping forces for the future of Icelandic society and culture. These individuals were not limited to a Danish horizon, and many of them grasped the cosmopolitan options Copenhagen had to offer – its connections to the wider world that Iceland had a hard time forming on its own terms.

The journal *Fjölnir* was not only a forum marked by Enlightenment concerns and contemporary issues but also a Romantic-historical mission that involved both creative innovation and a stock-taking of historical legacies found helpful in building a new and sovereign society. Foremost among these, as borne out in the first issue of *Fjölnir*, in its opening editorial and especially in Hallgrímsson's lead poem 'Ísland', was Iceland's initial four centuries of independence, starting with the settlement of the island in the ninth century and in particular its rich literary heritage of prose, poetry and mythology, in part based on oral transmission but having developed into writing which was preserved in the voluminous Icelandic collection of manuscripts. The next step is of course to talk about the preservation of the language and to interlace both the language and the medieval literary legacy with the island country itself, its landscape and nature, its separate destiny, in terms of geography and history. All this is done in *Fjölnir*, and this conglomerate was to become a cornerstone in the ideological argument for Iceland's claim for independence from Denmark.[3] This is an indication of what, to use Homi Bhabha's phrase, the 'double time of the nation' was in the case of Iceland, for the notion of nationhood always rests somewhere on a shared past, preferably a 'golden age' of some sort – a cultural construct, to be sure, and its rhetorical figures have a lot to do with the 'fissures of the present'.[4]

Among the fissures of the present that were probed by *Fjölnir* was a certain crisis in finding modern successors to its medieval saga genres.

The novel had a hard time finding its way into Icelandic, whether in translation or as original output. The most popular narrative genre in early nineteenth-century Iceland was in fact a form of poetry with roots in the late Middle Ages: the *rímur*. They were long rhymed narratives, 'almost always', to quote Vésteinn Ólason, 'versified prose sagas, most frequently the Legendary Sagas or prose romances known as the Knight's Sagas (*riddarasögur*)'.[5] Jónas Hallgrímsson wrote very critically about *rímur* in a review in *Fjölnir*, in spite of their having formed a continuous mainstay in Icelandic literary history for five centuries.[6] It was time for change and in *Fjölnir* the Romantic lyric poem was the spearhead of renovation, whether it was composed by Hallgrímsson himself or by foreign poets translated by him, for instance Schiller, but more prominently Heinrich Heine. In *Fjölnir*, Hallgrímsson also published his tale 'Grasaferð', which is often referred to as the first Icelandic short story in the modern manner, and he co-translated the short story '*Der blonde Eckbert*' by Ludwig Tieck, about which an anonymous subscriber commented in the journal that such tales were 'of little use for *most* Icelanders', who had a hard time deciphering their meaning.[7]

At this point, theatre and the art of drama appear not to be within the parameters of serious attention in Icelandic literary culture. They may in fact seem to have been absent from the Icelandic literary system from the outset, although it has been argued that certain types of Eddic poetry, stemming from an oral tradition, can be seen as containing ritual, dialogic and performative features which may escape our attention in their strictly written version.[8] *Fjölnir* does not report on theatre life in Copenhagen or elsewhere in Europe and the name of William Shakespeare is not to be found within its covers. But among the innovative poems by Jónas Hallgrímsson published in the journal, two are arguably quite important for the future entry of Shakespeare into Icelandic literary culture, that is, 'Gunnarshólmi' (1838) and 'Ég bið að heilsa!' ('I Send Greetings!', 1844).[9] The latter is the first sonnet to be published in Icelandic, and both poems are groundbreaking in their use and masterful wielding of iambic pentameter in the language. In the sonnet, the poet sends, from his abode in Denmark, spring greetings to Iceland with the southern winds, the waves and the migratory birds – but in aesthetic terms the message is also: We can accommodate new modes of expression in this language. Here are the opening four lines:[10]

Nú andar suðrið sæla vindum þíðum,
á sjónum allar bárur smáar rísa
og flykkjast heim að fögru landi Ísa,
að fósturjarðar minnar strönd og hlíðum.

Now the sweet south exhales warm winds,
on the ocean all the ripples rise
and flock home to the beautiful land of Ice,
to the coasts and slopes of my native soil.

The lines are rhymed, so the form cannot properly be called 'blank verse', and it also contains the regular Icelandic alliteration connecting each pair of lines (*s*uðrið, *s*æla / *s*jónum and *fl*ykkjast, *f*ögru / *f*ósturjarðar), a feature that has survived since the very early days of Icelandic poetry (when it was a widespread feature of Germanic poetry) – and is still generally considered an essential part of Icelandic metric poetry. But in terms of metre, Hallgrímsson has here gone far in laying the groundwork for those who would later attempt to translate Shakespeare's plays. He has transferred the form, the metric line, into the language, where it could be used, adapted and adjusted by those who wanted to recreate Shakespeare's blank verse in Icelandic.

Convergences

Romanticism came to Iceland mainly through contacts with Denmark. The Icelandic poet and scholar Grímur Thomsen (1820–1896) lived in Copenhagen for thirty years, working for the Danish foreign service after he had completed his MA in literary studies with a thesis on Byron's poetry in 1845: *Om Lord Byron*, a book for which he was later also awarded a PhD at the University of Copenhagen. In it he makes a Hegelian argument about a long-term historical path towards Romanticism (where Byron stands centre stage), a trajectory in which Shakespeare plays a significant role.[11] It is tempting to argue that the reverse flow might also be the case when it came to bringing these two writers into Icelandic through the effort of poets who form what could be called the second generation of Icelandic Romanticism. In this second wave, Byron and Shakespeare emerge in some sense as paired in the Icelandic domain of poetry, but it should again be stressed that this happens in a crucible also shaped by other languages and cultural forces. At the time, educated Icelanders usually had Danish as their second language and through the Danish connection, German had for a long time been a significant language of culture and scholarship for Icelanders, and Latin was for many the fourth string in this linguistic fiddle. The importance of other foreign literatures, including works in English, was therefore very often conveyed to Icelanders through Danish and/or German – and they were sometimes intermediate languages for Icelandic translators.

Thus, the poet and scholar Steingrímur Thorsteinsson (1831–1912), while living in Copenhagen, translated the collected tales of *Arabian Nights* from German into Icelandic. He had studied English, so his 1866 versions of Byron's poems 'The Prisoner of Chillon' and 'The Dream' were presumably based on the originals. Another poet-scholar living in Copenhagen, Gísli Brynjúlfsson (1827–1888) was a great admirer and translator of Byron, but he was also the first person to publish, in 1852, an Icelandic translation of Shakespeare, namely the poem or song 'Fear no more the heat o' the sun' from *Cymbeline*.[12]

Steingrímur Thorsteinsson would later bring out his own version of that poem as well as some others by Shakespeare. He noted in a letter that he had been 'Shakespeare-crazed' ('Shakespeare-óður') as a young man.[13] He was eager but also hesitant to bring some of Shakespeare's plays into Icelandic. Even for an experienced translator of poetry and prose, the move to translating canonical works of drama into Icelandic was by no means self-evident.

In an article published in 1937 about Icelandic Shakespeare translations, Stefán Einarsson suggests that a chance meeting of three Icelanders in Copenhagen in the autumn of 1856 may have been decisive for the future of Icelandic Shakespeare activity.[14] Matthías Jochumsson (1835–1920) had recently arrived in the city, where he would spend the winter, when he ran into Steingrímur Thorsteinsson and his friend, the visual artist Sigurður Guðmundsson (1833–1874), a painter whose stay in Copenhagen from 1849 to 1858 awoke in him a deep interest in theatre, in fact a passion that was to put its mark on Icelandic culture in years to come – and theatre was more than likely one of the topics of conversation when these three men first met. Thorsteinsson undertook to mentor Jochumsson this winter and together they read the Poetic Edda,

German literature, Ossian and translations of the Greek classics.[15] Their connection turned into a long-term friendship, a relationship that was not always easy, as they went on to become leading poets of Iceland in the coming decades, enriching their native literature with their original poetry as well as their translations.

From Thorsteinsson and Jochumsson's correspondence, even though only Jochumsson's letters appear to have survived, one may gain a good deal of insight into how they see themselves and view one another as poets and translators, for instance in the late 1860s and early 1870s, when they are both translating Shakespeare, trying their hands at different plays, although they both focused on the tragedies. In pursuing these translations, they seem to have been just as ambitious as in their original compositions. But their personalities were strikingly different. Jochumsson was an outgoing and expansive person, effusive even, for instance in declaring his admiration for Shakespeare. Thorsteinsson was a more withdrawn and restrained, to the point of being reclusive at times. However, judging by Jochumsson's letters, they both seem to have been frank in evaluating one another as translators. Thorsteinsson felt that Jochumsson was too loose in his renderings of Shakespeare and lacked subtlety, whereas Jochumsson found Thorsteinsson too stiff and lacking in spirit, and indicated that he could sense his friend had been living away from his homeland, the place of his mother tongue, for too long (Thorsteinsson moved back to Iceland in 1872 after twenty-one years in Copenhagen).

Hannes Pétursson, in his book about Thorsteinsson's life and work, stresses how hard it is to compare these two poets, even though precisely that became a pastime of Icelandic poetry enthusiasts in the last quarter of the century, when the pair of them were in the process of achieving canonical status as 'national poets' ('þjóðskáld'). But they were 'opposites', Pétursson says, 'one an intellectual poet, the other an intuitive one'. This is reflected in a conversation the two poets had at a dinner in Reykjavík in 1880, when they, mildly inebriated, started discussing and comparing what they had accomplished. Jochumsson was overheard saying: 'Your poetry reaches deeper than mine, but you will never catch me in flight.' Thorsteinsson assented, and they embraced one another.[16]

It is perhaps also symptomatic of their differences that Thorsteinsson ended up completing only *King Lear* for publication. He may not have appreciated this 'joint effort' as much as his colleague and former protégé. He gave a draft of his first translated pages of *Hamlet* to Jochumsson, who apparently made some use of them.[17] Jochumsson finished *Hamlet*, *Macbeth*, *Othello* and *Romeo and Juliet*, and he gradually came to be seen as chief pioneer in these endeavours. Jochumsson's English, however, was not as proficient as Thorsteinsson's, and he did not rely solely on the original plays. In fact, he appears to have learned to appreciate Shakespeare in Carl August Hagberg's Swedish translations, and he had recourse to them when translating, but he may also have made use of Danish translations which had been revised by Edvard Lembcke, and he noted how useful he found Nikolaus Delius's edition of Shakespeare's plays (not least, presumably, Delius's German commentary).

Using intermediate translations is not necessarily a doomed path. One of the highlights of foreign literature in Icelandic from the turn of the nineteenth century is Jón Þorláksson's translation of Milton's *Paradise Lost* (published in its entirety in 1828), based in part on a Danish version but mostly on a German one.[18] But unlike Þorláksson, Jochumsson did have the original at hand, and while it is occasionally obvious how he makes verbal choices based on Hagberg's translation, it is more than likely that his command of English grew gradually stronger. During the period when he rendered four of Shakespeare's plays into Icelandic, he also translated Byron's dramatic poem, or 'metaphysical drama', *Manfred* (in Icelandic: *Manfreð*, published 1875) – confirming yet again the Icelandic Shakespeare-Byron linkage. It is a spirited translation – in fact Jochumsson himself felt that he had never wielded the Icelandic language with such spontaneity[19] – and yet it stays remarkably close to the English original.

Untimely tragedies?

In keeping with Romantic ideals, the first plays selected for translation were mainly tragedies. Thorsteinsson and Jochumsson's translations of five tragedies by Shakespeare were all completed by 1871, but it took a while to have them all published. The first appeared in 1874 and the last one in 1887. In the interim, a sixth Shakespeare play was translated and brought out in 1885. This was *The Tempest*, and the translator was Eiríkur Magnússon (1833–1913). So, these are the first six Shakespeare plays to appear in

Icelandic and the only ones that were published in the nineteenth century:

Macbeth, translated by Matthías Jochumsson (Reykjavík, 1874).
Lear konungur (*King Lear*), translated by Steingrímur Thorsteinsson (Reykjavík, 1878).
Hamlet, translated by Matthías Jochumsson (Reykjavík, 1878).
Óthelló eða Márinn frá Feneyjum, translated by Matthías Jochumsson (Reykjavík, 1882).
Stormurinn (*The Tempest*), translated by Eiríkur Magnússon (Reykjavík, 1885).
Rómeó og Júlía, translated by Matthías Jochumsson (Reykjavík, 1887).

Given the fact that at this time the Icelandic book market and the local production of books were still in a fledgling state, these six plays in a span of thirteen years might seem to constitute a significant breakthrough in the transfer of world literature into the Icelandic language. Add to that a volume of foreign poetry: *Svanhvít*, selected and translated by Thorsteinsson and Jochumsson and published in Reykjavík in 1877 – a book that gave Icelandic voices to several foreign poets that were important for these translators but also more broadly for the scene of poetry in Iceland at this time. The selection contains poems by Schiller, Goethe, Shelley, Burns, Carsten Hauch, Hölderlin, Longfellow, Byron, Grundtvig, Karl Gerok, Runeberg, Heine and a few other poets – including Shakespeare, for Thorsteinsson translated the song 'Hark, hark! the lark at heaven's gate sings' from *Cymbeline*, the sonnet 'So sweet a kiss the golden sun gives not' from *Love's Labour's Lost*, and two poems from *As You Like It*: 'Under the greenwood tree' and 'Blow, blow, thou winter wind' (the last two appear as a single poem in Icelandic).

Svanhvít was very well received. It is an important book in the extended Romantic period of Icelandic poetry, a collection in which the two poet-translators bring a whole array of different poems into their language, enlarging its cultural stage – and Shakespeare's poetry seems quite at home in this company.[20] The Icelandic reception of his tragedies, around the same time, turned out to be a more complicated affair. In November 1878, Jochumsson's translations of

Hamlet and *Macbeth* are discussed in *Skuld*, a weekly paper whose subtitle ('Íslenskt þjóðmenningarblað') stresses that its focus is on 'Icelandic national culture'. The anonymous critic acknowledges that Shakespeare is considered one of world's most prominent poets, even the greatest since the ancient classics – and at this most general level of the Shakespeare reception there are many similar comments to be found in Icelandic publications around this time. Furthermore, the commentary is rounded up with the statement that Jochumsson's virtuosity as translator is unquestioned. But the central critical observation in the article is this:

> However, we would have expected to see the works of many other poets translated into Icelandic ahead of those by Shakespeare . . . because we would have doubted, and we still doubt, that our nation has any use for his works, generally speaking. We find, to be honest, that it does not measure up to them. The Icelanders who will appreciate these translations are principally the educated few who are able to read the original texts anyway, or the best foreign translations.[21]

For those aware of Iceland's long-standing literary tradition and its variety of poetry, some of it quite challenging in its form, imagery and metaphor, this timorous disposition may seem surprising. But it was to be echoed in later responses and one could say it was predicted in a letter that Thorsteinsson wrote to a friend in 1878, the year his *King Lear* translation appeared:

> Such books have, and this is to be expected, a small readership in Iceland, but I think that with time Shakespeare is bound to become the favourite author of all those in this country who have any spirit, even though dramatic writing is on the whole inaccessible for those who do not know or have not seen dramatic performances on stage.[22]

This is a matter which could be observed from a number of angles. At one level, the novelty of Shakespeare's plays *as reading material* may have been an impediment in itself, especially since their dialogic structure is at times radically hybrid, shifting between prose and dramatic verse, along with the occasional poems and songs. More importantly, while an increasing number of periodicals and journals were now being published in Reykjavík and the larger villages in Iceland, the literary critical establishment was still in an embryonic state at this public level. The apparatus that could have helped create a context in which to receive literary novelties in an informed way – especially texts as rich and resonant as the plays that had been so ambitiously selected for translation – was not really in place yet. When the first two books of Milton's *Paradise Lost*, in Jón Þorláksson's translation, were published in an Icelandic journal in 1794 and 1796, the editor arranged for Joseph Addison's *Spectator* commentaries on each book to be translated and published with them. A critical and explanatory discourse was thus provided alongside the literary work.[23] By the last quarter of the nineteenth century, there were of course Icelandic scholars who could have written or translated commentaries about Shakespeare's tragedies. The first tragedy to appear in Icelandic, *Macbeth*, does in fact contain an interpretive afterword, but it does not tackle basic questions regarding the new literary genre which was now being introduced in Icelandic. Eiríkur Magnússon had therefore almost free play, so to speak, when he brought out his two-volume edition of *The Tempest*, containing both the original and his translation, along with voluminous explanatory material. But, as we shall touch on later, he had in fact previously made an aggressive entry into the Icelandic discourse about Shakespeare by criticizing the work of a fellow early translator, in a way that probably diverted attention from his own contribution and from the literary innovation implicit in this array of Shakespeare's plays in Icelandic.

Theatre in the making

But another context that was also sorely missing in Iceland was the physical forum: the stage and the auditorium, along with an audience and skilled actors to create the live circumstances for which Shakespeare wrote the original plays. Thorsteinsson is of course right when he says that having experienced dramatic performance is vital for the act of reading dramatic writing (which of course does not mean that one needs to have seen each play performed on stage in order to enjoy reading it). Acting had been a limited school and amateur activity in Iceland, first in the school of the bishopric of Skálholt in the eighteenth century and then in Reykjavík. During the nineteenth century the ties with Denmark sometimes appeared in the form of plays staged in Danish or in the visits of experienced Danish actors who entertained the Icelandic public with Danish plays or with a medley of sketches from various famous plays, including scenes from one or more plays by Shakespeare, whose drama was therefore first performed in Iceland in Danish translation. With a growing interest by the mid-nineteenth century, the often make-shift staging process was gradually taken more seriously. Soon after Sigurður Guðmundsson returned from his studies in Copenhagen in the late 1850s, he had become a driving force of this theatre activity in Reykjavík, not only its chief organizer but a creator of the stage scenery and the one who found and trained actors as well as potential authors of Icelandic plays and translators of foreign ones – and he insisted on Icelandic being the language of performance. With an ambition to modernize Icelandic cultural life but to do so with a view to its history, Guðmundsson was in many ways a collector of cultural memory. This included an interest in the local handicraft traditions as well as the folk tales and the oral legacy of recent times, just as the medieval Icelandic writers had drawn on oral narrative and poetry.

Encouraged by Guðmundsson, Matthías Jochumsson started writing plays, some of which were quite popular, especially one called *The Outlaws* (*Útilegumennirnir*, 1862, publ. 1864), later revised as *Skugga-Sveinn* (1898) – a drama that in its formal composition may in part draw on lessons learnt from Shakespeare, while its topic comes from the history and legends of Iceland. Guðmundsson also kindled the interest of a young man, Indriði Einarsson (1851–1939), who wrote his first play before the age of twenty and would later translate the first Shakespeare plays to be staged in Iceland. Sigurður Guðmundsson died in 1874, at the age of forty-one, but he set so many things in motion that not only the ongoing development in Reykjavík – which resulted in the establishment of the Reykjavík Theatre Company in 1897 – is in no small part attributed to him, but the movement he started would spread around the country, with several amateur theatre groups being formed in various villages and rural communities throughout

Iceland towards the end of the nineteenth century and in the beginning of the twentieth century.

Guðmundsson clearly felt that for this endeavour to be successful, the dramas put on stage would have to connect with the public at a 'folk' level. While encouraging his friends Thorsteinsson and Jochumsson in their efforts to bring Shakespeare into Icelandic, he initially felt that the plays they focused on were not the ones needed for the theatre he envisaged. In a letter to Thorsteinsson in 1861, he challenged him to translate Shakespeare's *The Taming of the Shrew*, saying that it was perhaps 'the only one of his pieces that can be staged here'.[24] Thorsteinsson did not comply. Guðmundsson clearly felt that *The Taming of the Shrew* would fit his project of producing plays for an Icelandic audience, a repertoire in which comedies were a substantial part, including translations of Molière. He was eager to establish a network for and arouse general interest in a cultural enterprise centred around a 'national stage', a truly *Icelandic theatre*. Its appeal would have to be broad and the element of public entertainment was inevitable. There was still no specially designed theatre space in the country, but Iceland's history and its folk heritage comprised an abundance of stories that he felt deserved to be performed as dramas.[25] In this regard, Guðmundsson looked to Shakespeare's history plays, although more as a kind of precedent rather than as works to be translated for his theatre in the making. However, eight years later, again in a letter to Thorsteinsson, he praises his *King Lear* translation, which he must have read in manuscript, and says that the two plays which are ready (the other one is almost certainly Jochumsson's *Macbeth* translation) now 'need to be printed, for it is crucial to show Icelanders this kind of literary art, since I think they have quite a natural bent for it'. But the problem, he adds, 'is that most of them have not seen anything or have always kept their eyes closed (which is one of the flaws of our countrymen when they travel abroad)'.[26]

Guðmundsson's use of the verbs 'show' and 'see' as regards the first Icelandic translations of Shakespeare's drama is at once interesting and oblique. There is hardly any doubt that Guðmundsson would have liked to be the first person to direct a Shakespeare play in Icelandic, and he had already staged several unpublished plays in Reykjavík. In this case he felt it was important that the translations be *published* in order to 'show' Icelanders this *literary art* – he uses the word 'skáldskapur', which in Icelandic can refer to any kind of literary creation, including drama (although when used about prose literature the word is often limited to fiction). But when he says that Icelanders have not 'seen' anything, he may be referring not only to the meagre theatre tradition in Iceland but also to a limited visual horizon in more general terms and thus implicitly to the importance of performing challenging plays like these, turning them into live audio-visual experiences. And it matters here that both Guðmundsson and Thorsteinsson had seen Shakespeare several times on stage in Copenhagen. But how can that experience be brought to bear on Icelandic circumstances? The cultural transfer must pass through a new text in a 'new' language.

This brings us to the classic question of whether a translator of a play brings it across primarily 'for the stage', that is, as a 'performance text', and how to distinguish between that and the 'dramatic text' we encounter in the play as reading material, which may certainly be originally written primarily with the stage in mind but which connects with the broader literary world once it is read.[27] And in the case of Shakespeare, his plays – if not his oeuvre then at least the best-known plays – enjoy the status of *world literature*, a concept highly dependent upon translation activity and the dissemination of such works *as reading matter*. This may be one more reason why Guðmundsson wanted to see the works of the two pioneer translators in print – hoping these plays would not only claim their space in their new literary environment but create new goals, a renewed ambition, for an emerging theatre.

Blank verse – The Icelandic way

The pioneers, Jochumsson and Thorsteinsson, decided to respect the tripartite textual nature of Shakespeare's drama. The prose sections pose no significant obstacles as such, nor do individual poems and songs, or chants, as in the opening scene of *Macbeth*, the first Icelandic translation to be published:

1 WITCH
>   When shall we three meet again?
>   In thunder, lightning, or in rain?

2 WITCH
>   When the hurly-burly's done,
>   When the battle's lost, and won.

3 WITCH
>   That will be ere the set of sun.

1 WITCH
>   Where the place?

2 WITCH
>   Upon the heath.

3 WITCH
>   There to meet with Macbeth.

1 WITCH
>   I come, Gray-Malkin.

2 WITCH
>   Paddock calls.

3 WITCH
>   Anon.

ALL
>   Fair is foul, and foul is fair:
>   Hover through the fog and filthy air.[28]

1. *norn.*
>   Nær er stundin stefnu til,
>   við storm og regn eða skruggubyl?

2. *norn.*
>   Þá úti er þessi orrahríð
>   og unnið og glatað þetta stríð.

3. *norn.*
>   Það verður senn, um sólarlagstíð.

1. *norn.*
>   Á hvaða stað?

2. *norn.*
>   Á heiði hér.

3. *norn.*
   Helzt þar Macbeth finnum vér.
1. *norn.*
   Eg skal koma, Ketta grá!
2. *norn.*
   Padda kallar.
3. *norn.*
   Skjótt, skjótt!

Allar.
   Ljótt er fagurt og fagurt ljótt,
   flögrum í sudda, þoku og nótt.[29]

Jochumsson's version follows the original in rhyming the couplets and the triplets (with the word 'skjótt' ('quick') Jochumsson in fact turns the original final couplet into a triplet). According to the Icelandic tradition of metric poetry, each couple of lines interconnect through alliteration, a sound system in which all stressed initial vowels can connect internally, but initial consonants (or consonant clusters in the case of *sk*, *sp* and *st*) connect only with their counterparts. The first two lines are linked with the *st*-sound (twice in the first line and in the first stressed syllable of the second line), the next two lines with the vowels *ú*, *o* and *u*, the fifth line is treated separately with its own double *s*-alliteration, the following two lines connect with *h*, and then it gets a little chaotic and irregular, along with what happens in the original. The *k* in 'kallar' is not in the initial stressed position where one would expect it; the double *sk* in 'Skjótt, skjótt' is in a line by itself, and the second to last line connects with the last one through the *f*-sound, but also contains a double *l*-sound. This overabundance seems quite at home in this scene and Jochumsson – very much in his element here – has turned the heath into a trembling and ominous sound cave.

The third kind of text type in Shakespeare's plays, the dramatic poetry genre of *blank verse*, is the one that most clearly distinguishes the playwright's articulation and is a touchstone when it comes to bringing the plays into another language. How do translators fare in recreating Shakespeare's acclaimed flexible mastery of this unrhymed iambic pentameter – the ways in which he conjoins the formality of metric verse with the facility of spoken diction? This conjunction may sometimes intermesh with instances where the quotidian meets the extraordinary in Shakespeare's figurative language, both in individual instances and in the broader reaches of his metaphoric formations. In March 1867, after finishing his draft of the first scene of *Macbeth*, Jochumsson wrote to Thorsteinsson about the challenge of 'seizing the tropical alive' from Shakespeare's language. He notes that he sometimes cannot find the equivalent vocabulary in Icelandic.[30]

But as far as the metre is concerned, neither translator appears to have any doubt about alliteration as an inevitable feature of metric poetry in Icelandic, but they must have realized what a strain it would cause if they were to pursue the traditional coupling of every pair of lines with three alliterative staves. Hence, they chose, as a general rule, to limit themselves to a double alliteration within each black verse line. Here are a few lines (16–23) from Scene 2 of Act 1, where a captain describes Macbeth's heroic conduct in battle (initial letters of stressed and alliterated sounds are italicized in this example of Icelandic translation and those that follow on the next few pages):

> For brave Macbeth (well he deserves that name),
> Disdaining Fortune, with his brandished steel,
> Which smoked with bloody execution,
> Like Valour's minion, carved out his passage,
> Till he faced the slave,
> Which ne'er shook hands, nor bade farewell to him,
> Till he unseamed him from the nave to th'chops,
> And fixed his head upon our battlements.[31]

> hinn *h*rausti Macbeth – *h*ann ber nafn með rentu –
> að *h*amingjunni glotti og *h*risti brandinn,
> sem frægðin rauk af, *d*rifnum manna*d*reyra;
> og eins og *s*annur *s*onur hugprýðinnar
> hjó kappinn *b*eina *b*raut unz hittir þrælinn,
> bauð hvorki *h*önd né *h*irti um langar kveðjur,
> en ristir sundur *k*við hans upp í *k*ok,
> og festir *h*ausinn *h*æst á *v*irkis*v*egginn.[32]

These masterful lines betray no lack of appropriate Icelandic vocabulary, even as each line contains its separate alliterative ground beat within the pentametric rhythm (for instance *h*rausti and *h*ann in the first line). But Jochumsson has also found space for, and allowed himself to perform, additional formal manoeuvres within this framework, for the h-staves form a kind of thread through these lines which introduce the future king. Apart from four alliterative h-pairs, the verb 'hittir' and the noun 'hugprýðinnar' ('valor') also have a stressed initial h-sound. But one could ask whether the translator is pushing his mastery too far by augmenting the beat of the alliterative supplement in this fashion. In fact, he even goes a step farther, for he gives the final line an extra thrust by adding a second alliterative pair ('*v*irkis*v*egginn') to the first one ('*h*ausinn *h*æst'). In his translations of the tragedies, Jochumsson frequently responds to moments of intensity in the original, in action or in figurative expression, by enhancing the formal articulation of his verse. This means not only that critical words may acquire an additional (but perhaps unnecessary) weight through the alliterative sound structure, but that the Icelandic text risks overemphasizing the poetry aspect of the blank verse lines at the cost of the contrapuntal spoken diction.

In the opening scene of *King Lear* (1.1.35–40), the text shifts to blank verse when the king announces his intention to unburden himself of his state and divide it in three. This is his declaration in Steingrímur Thorsteinsson's Icelandic version:

Meantime we shall express our darker purpose.
Give me the map there. Know that we have divided
In three our kingdom; and 'tis our fast intent
To shake all cares and business from our age,
Conferring them on younger strengths, while we
Unburdened crawl toward death.[33]

Vort hulda ráð skal *l*eiðt í *l*jós á meðan.
Fram svo með kortið! – Vitið það, að *v*ér
Nú höfum *þ*rídeilt *þ*essu voru ríki,
Og ráðið fast, að *v*elta af *v*orri elli
á *y*ngri herðar *á*hyggjum og starfi,
Svo vér án byrðar *g*etum skreiðzt til *g*rafar.[34]

Here we see a very balanced use of the line-by-line alliteration of introductory lines that are as ironic as the ones describing Macbeth's heroics in battle. Although the king talks here about crawling without a burden to his 'grave' (as opposed to 'death' in the original), this is an accurate rendering, preparing us for the brutal fact that there is no such crawling without a burden, and freeing oneself completely from responsibility can be deadly business. In Goneril's subsequent declaration of love for her father (1.1.55–61), however, one sees Thorsteinsson underscoring her hypocrisy by letting an extra portion of alliterative stresses form a beat to her verbal overkill, with an emphasis on the 'f' from the word 'faðir' ('father', replacing 'Sir' in the original). One line contains three vowel-staves, another one three f-staves and in the final line, four of the five stressed syllables connect through opening vowels:

> Sir, I do love you more than word can wield the matter;
> Dearer than eye-sight, space and liberty,
> Beyond what can be valued, rich or rare,
> No less than life, with grace, health, beauty, honour.
> As much as child e'er lov'd, or father found,
> A love that makes breath poor, and speech unable,
> Beyond all manner of so much I love you.[35]

> Minn faðir!
> Eg *e*lska *y*ður meir en *o*rð fá lýst,
> *F*ram yfir augans *l*jós, *l*ífsandann, *f*relsið,
> *F*ram yfir allt, sem *f*ágætt er og dýrmætt,
> Sem lífið sjálft, dygð, heilsu, *v*ænleik, *v*irðing;
> Sem barns ást *f*ramast *f*anst og *f*aðir reyndi,
> Svo heitt að *a*nda þrýtur, *o*rðin deyja,
> Langt *u*mfram þetta *a*llt ég *e*lska *y*ður.[36]

Jochumsson, in one of his letters to Thorsteinsson, criticizes his friend for formal stiffness in the *King Lear* translation draft and remarks how important it is that the iambs stay close to daily speech.[37] This may seem unwarranted criticism from someone who tends to take even bigger risks in his formal treatment of blank verse in Icelandic. Are they perhaps both translators who get stuck in internal poetic clusters when they should be attending to the 'speakability' of their lines? Not necessarily, for this of course depends on the actual verbal delivery of these lines, an active interpretation that may inflect the lines in ways that avoid the clashing of interconnected sounds as much as the humdrum of regular rhythm. A good actor – and a good reader who 'performs' the lines either silently or aloud – will be able to work creatively with the alliteration in Goneril's speech as well as (but then differently) with the previous heroic description of Macbeth in battle.

But there is no denying that both these key poets are at times intuitive as well as intellectual, dive deep and fly high, in their encounter with Shakespeare's dramatic poetry, turning it into powerful and memorable poetry in Icelandic, poetry that opens up new realms of Icelandic Romanticism. Juliet's soliloquy, 'Gallop apace, you fiery-footed steeds' (*Romeo and Juliet*, 3.2.1–31), with its threefold reference to speed in the name of love, is brilliantly recreated by Jochumsson, who typically adds a fourth, opening the first line with the word 'eldur' ('fire'); the first line could be literally back-translated as 'Fire-swift horses, hasten fleet-footed':

> Gallop apace, you fiery-footed steeds,
> Towards Phoebus' lodging. Such a waggoner
> As Phaeton would whip you to the west
> And bring in cloudy night immediately.
> Spread thy close curtain, love-performing night,
> That runaways' eyes may wink, and Romeo
> Leap to these arms, untalked of and unseen.
> Lovers can see to do their amorous rites[.][38]

> Eldsnöru hestar, skundið *f*ráum *f*ótum
> til *F*öbuss heim; hinn bráði *s*ólguðs *s*onur
> Nú skyldi halda´ á *k*eyri hans og *k*eyra
> svo *k*erra' og hestar steyptust nið'rí vestrið,
> og *k*oldimm nóttin *k*æmi' á augabragði. –
> Þú elskendanna *f*óstra, *f*ölva njóla,
> svæf *d*agsins brá og *d*rag nú tjald þitt fyrir;
> leið *u*nnustann í *á*starfaðmlag mitt,[39]

And the reserved Thorsteinsson pulls out all the stops in his version of the retired King Lear raving on the heath, egging on the violent powers of nature (3.2.1–9). In his book about Thorsteinsson, Hannes Pétursson finds that in these nine lines of translation the poet reaches his peak in terms of both density and verbal flight.[40] In Icelandic as in English these lines could be said to express ominously not just Lear's fate but much about the state of the world as we move farther into the twenty-first century:

> Blow winds and crack your cheeks! Rage, blow!
> You cataracts and hurricanoes, spout
> Till you have drenched our steeples, drowned the cocks!
> You sulphurous and thought-executing fires,
> Vaunt-couriers of oak-cleaving thunderbolts,
> Singe my white head! And thou, all-shaking thunder,
> Strike flat the thick rotundity o'the world,
> Crack nature's moulds, all germens spill at once
> That make ingrateful man![41]

> Blás, blás! ríf hvopt þinn, ofsabylur, æddu!
> þér felli-stormar, steypihvolfur, grenjið,
> Unz turnar sökkva, veðurvitar drekkjast!
> Brennisteins-elding, bjarta, hugar-snara,
> sem blossar undan eik-kljúfandi skruggu,
> Svíð hærukoll minn! Heimsins skelfir, þruma,
> Slá hnöttinn flatan; bramla og brjót í sundur
> Öll eðlis mót, og eyðilegg í skyndi
> Hvern vísir til hins vanþakkláta mannkyns.[42]

As these examples demonstrate, early Icelandic translators were technically gifted, and Icelandic could creatively accommodate Shakespearean verse. But these early translations were not all well received, as we shall promptly see.

A Tempest – In more than one sense

In retrospect, the publication of the first Shakespeare plays in Icelandic obviously constitutes an important moment in Icelandic literary history, whose early centuries are in no small part shaped by medieval translations from Latin and French, followed by periods of varying activity in translation of both poetry and prose but with drama as a largely neglected field – in both translation and original writing. One can only wonder if it is this weak position of drama that undermines the ability of the Icelandic literary system to find room for and establish a dialogue with a foreign writer who is a canonical figure in that genre. And even after the first translations appear, the response could perhaps be compared to shyness, if not a touch of inferiority complex. Amid this lacklustre reception of an important addition to literature in the Icelandic language, the contents of a lengthy, and in a certain sense meticulous, review to appear about one of these translations apparently sent shock waves through Icelandic cultural life. In December 1883, Eiríkur Magnússon, an Icelandic librarian at the University of Cambridge, well-known for co-translating Old Icelandic literary works into English with William Morris, published in the Reykjavík paper *Þjóðólfur* an article about Jochumsson's translation of *Othello* which had appeared in 1882.[43] Jochumsson and Magnússon had once been good friends, but their friendship had ended abruptly some years before and Magnússon's fierceness in this article has been explained as a kind of personal revenge.[44] In any case, Magnússon finds nothing but faults with the translation. He is a critic full of sound and fury, and while he focuses on *Othello*, his survey seems to sweep up *Macbeth* and *Hamlet* along the way (Jochumsson's *Romeo and Juliet* had not appeared yet), for he tells his readers that there is *one* usable and in fact excellent Icelandic Shakespeare play available, that is to say Thorsteinsson's *King Lear*, and that Jochumsson has much to learn from his colleague.

Magnússon has clearly gone error-hunting from one line to the next in the *Othello* translation, and he lists and discusses numerous cases of blunders that he has spotted, including a few obvious ones, such as when a line in the original has been overlooked, as well as a number of places where Jochumsson clearly relies on Hagberg's Swedish translation (which Magnússon has also checked), that is to say, when Hagberg's choices are questionable and have led the Icelandic translator astray. In some instances Magnússon's critique is debatable and his own alternative renderings of several lines by no means commendable. Translation criticism is important, and while Magnússon's review clearly shows that the *Othello* translation has not been through a proper editing process, his many strongly worded generalizations about the translation as a whole are not grounded in a careful critique based on a thematic, structural and aesthetic overview of the translated work and an attempt to understand the translator's general approach. In fact, he finds that Jochumsson is resolutely 'killing the spirit of Shakespeare' ('deyða anda Shakespeares') and he ends by rebuking the Icelandic Literary Society for publishing this 'ramshackle work' ('ónýtt verk').

One of the three members of the committee in charge of the book on behalf of the Literary Society, the poet Benedikt Gröndal later published a short (humorous and sarcastic) newspaper article, saying that there is nothing unnatural in trusting someone like Jochumsson to translate correctly, but also noting that a flawed line in Shakespeare is not a question of life and death, as well as declaring his opinion that 'people in this country have nothing to do with him [Shakespeare], for they do not understand heads or tails of him'.[45] A more serious sign of the collateral damage of this unconstructive discourse had already appeared in another article where the author, having referred to Magnússon's review of *Othello*, states that the publication of such translations should not be the concern of the Icelandic Literary Society; it should focus on works such as 'the original poetry' of Iceland's most prominent poets ('þjóðskáld', i.e. 'national poets'), for in these poems one can hear 'the spirit of the nation itself'.[46]

Eiríkur Magnússon clearly had an ambition to be more constructively involved in the entry of Shakespeare onto the Icelandic literary scene, for he now embarked on a translation of *The Tempest* which he brought out in Reykjavík in 1885 under the title *Stormurinn*. And the opening words of his introduction indicate that his approach to translation is very different from Jochumsson:

> The following translation of *The Tempest* is especially intended for those who want to obtain a full and clear understanding of the original language. Hence, I have been at pains to keep it accurate and literal enough to achieve this primary goal. At the same time, I have striven to make it accessible and supple so that eager readers would find it more or less approachable and entertaining. I have therefore stuck to the rule of following the original from word to word whenever possible.[47]

Fortunately, Magnússon does not literally follow his own description in the actual translation, although he does stick quite close to the lines as units of meaning (and he limits his alliteration throughout to two words in each line). This may decrease the risk of errors but is no guarantee against them, as when Prospero tells Ferdinand he may have Miranda as his wife, 'worthily purchas'd' (i.e. obtained; he has earned her), which Magnússon translates as 'feng / Við dýru verði keyptan' ('a catch / bought at a high price').[48] The translation has its interesting and curious moments, but the wording is at times obscure and the language cluttered; it lacks fluidity and lyrical nuances. The translator has a lot to say in his commentary about the play's most famous lines: 'We are such stuff / As dreams are made on, and our little life / Is rounded with a sleep',[49] but renders them rather lifelessly in Icelandic: 'Vér sjálfir erum sama efni og það / sem drauma myndar, og vort litla líf / Er svefni kringt'[50] ('We ourselves are the same stuff as that / which forms dreams, and our little life / is by sleep surrounded').

Unlike the other early translations of Shakespeare, Magnússon's version of *The Tempest* has never been republished and is rarely discussed. But his project as a whole is extensive and deserves more attention than it has received. It is comprised of two volumes. The first one contains an introduction followed by a survey of Shakespeare's life, before we get to the Icelandic translation itself, which is appended by five pages of notes and a nine-page afterword in which Magnússon presents a general interpretation of the play. Volume two opens with a preface which touches on the making of the play and its possible sources, but also contains various other observations and notes, before we are told that Magnússon's 'aim with this edition' is to bring out a book 'helpful for those eager to learn English, to assist them in getting beyond the most basic sentences', and he adds that he would like to see this work being used as a schoolbook.[51] We then get to the text of the play in the original, taken from a nine-volume Shakespeare publication, edited by G. W. Clark and W. Aldis-Wright, published in Cambridge in 1863. Magnússon then includes 101 pages of his notes about words and phrases in the original play. Since these notes are in Icelandic, they do in some sense constitute a second and different 'translation' of a substantial part of the play's English vocabulary.

Coping with silence

Magnússon's publication of *The Tempest* was reviewed in two newspapers, and the response was quite critical. The treatment he got was not as hostile and vehement as the one he had given

Jochumsson, but the irony in Grímur Thomsen's review (which carries the signature 'Ariel') is scathing, especially when he remarks that given the notes and a little knowledge of English one can make good use of the second volume, but 'who wants to translate the translator?' he asks, adding that he barely understands the actual Icelandic translation. This is of course a pointed overstatement but one that he supports with a whole array of examples and critical observations.[52]

The two authors of the other review find that the translation is generally semantically accurate, but still complain about inaccuracies and unclear references, as well as a cumbersome verse structure. But here, as we have seen elsewhere, the reaction to a single work broadens to a discussion of the cultural role of such translations. When a book is selected for translation, the authors note, two factors are decisive: 'usefulness and distinction', and if the nation at the receiving end is a small one, 'usefulness must have absolute priority'. They go on to say that there is a certain distinction inherent in 'having access to these masterpieces in our language', but that the lion's share of that distinction goes to the translators themselves. 'Experience has shown us that the general public is not fond of these works, nor is this to be expected, since most people do not understand them at all.' Furthermore, since these translations turn out to be of such little use, 'it is wrong to support them through public funding'.[53]

One cannot help wonder whether the narrow cultural perspective reflected in these and similar observations that crop up a number of time around the first Shakespeare translations explains why neither Jochumsson nor Thorsteinsson attempted to bring more of Shakespeare's plays into Icelandic and why none of their five translations appeared on stage in their lifetime – and also why no other translators, except for Magnússon, attempt to follow in their footsteps for a long time. The first public sign of renewed activity in this area was a translation by Guðmundur Björnsson (under his pen name 'Gestur') of Act 3, Scene 2, from *Julius Caesar*, which appeared in the journal *Skírnir* in 1918. In a preface to the translation, Björnsson claims, rather daringly, that previous translations manifest no recognition of Shakespeare's genius in metrical construction and cadence, because, so he claims, they focus primarily on verbal accuracy (he had clearly not taken a close look at Jochumsson's translations from this perspective). Björnsson thus seeks to clear an area where he does indeed make some prudent arguments about translating Shakespeare's blank verse with the variable cadence as a primary objective (taking precedence over alliteration, which is skipped in some of his lines). The translation is interesting, and it is to be regretted that Björnsson did not complete his translation of *Julius Caesar*.[54]

At this point in time, the Reykjavik Theatre Company, established in 1897, had been active for more than two decades. These had been eventful years in Iceland, for the country had acquired home rule and its own minister in 1904 and sovereignty in its internal affairs in 1918. There was little doubt that enough people felt that Icelandic theatre was 'useful', especially when it undertook to 'stage the nation', as Magnús Þór Þorbergsson puts it in a recent article – that is to say represent on stage the nation's identity as it emerges in history and cultural memory, including folklore and myths.[55] This activity was very much based on the heritage and legacy of Sigurður Guðmundsson's theatre activity during the 1860s until his death in 1874. Two plays that came out of his 'workshop', Jochumsson's *Outlaws* (later named *Skugga-Sveinn*) and Indriði Einarsson's *Nýársnóttin* (*New Year's Eve*), were restaged by the Reykjavik Theatre Company during its first years and remained the most popular Icelandic plays for decades to come.

But there was another thread of Guðmundsson's legacy which was also still alive, although at times less prominent: his emphasis on the importance of translating foreign plays into Icelandic and learning from the masters of the genre. The second play that Einarsson wrote under Guðmundsson's guidance, and which premiered 30 December 1873, was *Hellismenn* ('Cave Men'), a tragedy in five acts, written in blank verse. This turned out to be the last play that Guðmundsson oversaw. Einarsson had been reading Shakespeare and, through Guðmundsson, might also have accessed the Icelandic translations of *Macbeth* and *King Lear* in manuscript. From 1872 to 1878 Einarsson lived mostly abroad, studying economics in Copenhagen and Edinburgh. He later wrote that Guðmundsson had encouraged him to go abroad, get to know city life and to attend theatres. He saw several Shakespeare plays during his years abroad.[56]

After his return to Iceland, although he worked full-time as an economist, Einarsson was a driving force in theatre life in Reykjavík; he was among the founding members of the Reykjavik Theatre

Company, wrote five more original plays and was instrumental in paving the way for the Icelandic National Theatre and is often called its 'father', although he did not live to see its opening performance, his own first play, *Nýársnóttin*, in 1950.

Shakespeare's plays were important for Einarsson when he was taking his first steps as a playwright. He also translated a number of plays, but it was only after his retirement from official duties, at the age of seventy, that he sat down to translate Shakespeare. This turned into a lengthy 'collaboration', for Einarsson ended up bringing fourteen of the bard's plays into Icelandic: *Twelfth Night*, *As You Like It*, *Henry IV* (I and II), *The Merchant of Venice*, *A Midsummer's Night Dream*, *The Winter's Tale*, *Much Ado About Nothing*, *Julius Caesar*, *Richard III*, *King Henry VI* (I, II and III) and *Cymbeline*.[57] It is interesting that Einarsson decided to bypass the six plays that had already been translated and published in their entirety, although they had never been put on stage.

Einarsson remarks in an article about Matthías Jochumsson that when Shakespeare is staged 'in a good translation', its language is modern and more accessible than the original is to native speakers of English. He adds that his main complaint about 'our Shakespeare translations' (presumably referring to the six plays that had been published) is that 'it is often hard to speak them'.[58] He is in all likelihood referring to the dramatic verse parts of the plays, and when one reads scenes from his own translations, for instance his rendering of *The Winter's Tale*, the blank verse often appears to be quite close to spoken diction, even though it is metrically arranged and each line contains a pair of alliterated words.[59] This low-key composition is in itself an achievement, but at the same time it raises questions about the functional contrast of prose and verse in the plays, and about the formal, emotive and figurative aspects of Shakespeare's language, especially in his dramatic verse.

Two of Einarsson's translations were staged by the Reykjavík Theatre Company: *Twelfth Night*, which premiered 23 April 1926, and *The Winter's Tale* in December 1926; these were the first Shakespeare productions in Iceland, coming in quick succession, and it must have felt as if a major new presence was in the air. As Þorbergsson notes in his previously cited article, a 'unanimous press not only described these productions as important events for the Reykjavik Theatre Company, but as milestones in the history of Icelandic theatre', and judging by public reactions Shakespeare seemed to represent 'a connection to theatrical tradition, an entrance ticket to the cultural heritage of Europe'.[60] But had Icelandic theatre really set course in that direction? Not if performances and publications of Shakespeare are anything to go by. The public reaction to *The Winter's Tale* was in fact not as exuberant as the reception of *Twelfth Night*, which was restaged by the Theatre Company in 1933, but none of Einarsson's other translations made it to the stage. And, much as he was praised for his translation effort, not a single one of his translations has been published.

Stefán Einarsson, in his overview article about Icelandic Shakespeare translations, calls attention to 'the long silence about Shakespeare' after Jochumsson brought out his version of Romeo and Juliet in 1887 until Björnsson's *Julius Caesar* fragment appeared in 1918.[61] But this was a silence after book publications – the stage silence had been there all along and would continue till 1926 and, after it had been briefly broken by *Twelfth Night* and *The Winter's Tale*, it was to resume and last for several more years. As far as publication of complete plays by Shakespeare in Icelandic is concerned, the silence beginning in 1887 would be unbroken until 1945, when Sigurður Grímsson's translation of *The Merchant of Venice* (*Kaupmaðurinn í Feneyjum*) was produced by the Reykjavik Theatre Company and published as a book by Helgafell publishers.

Since the majority of Icelandic newspapers and magazines from this whole period is now accessible through a very useful database (https://timarit.is) one can see that Shakespeare, especially from around 1890 on, is frequently mentioned, cited and praised to the skies in Icelandic publications. But in contrast to some of the other Nordic countries, which tended to celebrate Shakespeare and put him to political and/or theatrical use, in Iceland Shakespeare was also a disturbing factor, a precarious foreign element. Some found his plays to be of little 'use' to a nation that despite its small population possessed a strong vernacular literary tradition going back centuries. In addition, Iceland had but a limited theatre practice, which initially favoured its own folk-based Icelandic dramas along with foreign revues and comedies, while the first Shakespeare translators focused on tragedy. In this sense, the reception of Shakespeare in Iceland differs from that in the other Nordic countries during the late nineteenth and early twentieth centuries, as explored in the remaining essays in this volume. Still, the Icelandic pioneers did blaze a trail of cultural and aesthetic transfer. In 1982, when Helgi Hálfdanarson (1911– 2009) wrote the foreword to his translations of the complete plays of Shakespeare, he paid homage to Matthías Jochumsson and Steingrímur Thorsteinsson, emphasizing how fortunate it was 'that the first ones to render Shakespeare's plays into Icelandic were such champions of language and letters'.[62]

Notes

1. See the discussion and analysis of the Icelandic literary polysystem in Eysteinsson, *Tvímæli*, 223–57.
2. See S. Einarsson, 'Shakespeare á Íslandi', pt. 1, 27. A shorter version of his survey is available in English: see S. Einarsson, 'Shakespeare in Iceland'.
3. *Fjölnir. Árrit handa Íslendingum*, 1 (1835).
4. Bhabha, 'DissemiNation', 294. Cf. Eysteinsson, 'Icelandic Resettlements', 156–7.
5. Ólason, 'Old Icelandic Poetry', 56.
6. Hallgrímsson, 'Um rímur af Tistrani og Indíönu'.
7. 'Úr bréfi af Austfjörðum', 40 (emphasis in the original).
8. See Gunnell, *The Origins of Drama in Scandinavia*; and the same author's 'Eddic Performance and Eddic Audiences'.
9. Cf. Hálfdanarson, 'Fáein orð um Shakespeare', 23, and his 'Flutningur bundins máls', 71.
10. Hallgrímsson, 'Jeg bið að heilsa!', *Fjölnir. Árrit handa Íslendingum*, 105 ('Jeg' is spelled 'Ég' in contemporary Icelandic); translation by the authors. A translation by Dick Ringler, which reproduces the rhyme and metre, is available at: https://digicoll.library.wisc.edu/Jonas/Heilsa/Heilsa.html.
11. Cf. Thorgrímsson Thomsen, *Om Lord Byron*, 19–25.
12. Shakespeare, 'Greftrunarljóð'.
13. Pétursson, *Steingrímur Thorsteinsson*, 195.
14. S. Einarsson, 'Shakespeare á Íslandi', pt. 1, 30.
15. Jochumsson, *Sögukaflar af sjálfum mér*, 112.
16. Pétursson, *Steingrímur Thorsteinsson*, 206–7.

17 Thorsteinsson notes in a letter that quite a bit of this translation fragment was used by Jochumsson in his *Hamlet* ('up to page 8'). See Pétursson, *Steingrímur Thorsteinsson*, 195.

18 See Eysteinsson, 'Iceland's Milton'.

19 Jochumsson, *Sögukaflar af sjálfum mér*, 196.

20 Thorsteinsson and Jochumsson, eds and trans, *Svanhvít*. The book, which was reissued in 1913 and again in 1946, has, for a volume of translation, an unusually strong place in Icelandic literary history.

21 'Bókmenntir', *Skuld. Íslenskt þjóðmenningarblað*, 25 November 1878.

22 Cited in Pétursson, *Steingrímur Thorsteinsson*, 195.

23 Eysteinsson, 'Iceland's Milton', 223.

24 Cf. Sigurbjörnsson, 'Shakespeare og Íslendingar', 14.

25 Guðmundsson's legacy has lately received renewed interest, as reflected in an important collection of articles (Aspelund and Gunnell, eds, *Málarinn og menningarsköpun*).

26 Letter to Steingrímur Thorsteinsson, in Guðmundsson, *Sigurður Guðmundsson málari og menningarsköpun*.

27 The concepts 'performance text' and 'dramatic text' come from Elam, *The Semiotics of Theatre and Drama*, 3 and *passim*. Cf. Eysteinsson, 'Skapandi tryggð', 114.

28 Shakespeare, *Macbeth*, eds Clark and Mason, 1.1.1–9.

29 Shakespeare, *Leikrit*, 9 (this volume contains the second edition of the four tragedies that Jochumsson translated).

30 Jochumsson, *Bréf*, 42.

31 Shakespeare, *Macbeth*, eds Clark and Mason, 16–23.

32 Shakespeare, *Leikrit*, 10.

33 Shakespeare, *King Lear*, ed. Foakes, 35–40.

34 Shakespeare, *Lear konungur*, 2–3.

35 Shakespeare, *King Lear*, ed. Foakes, 1.1.55–61.

36 Shakespeare, *Lear konungur*, 3.

37 Jochumsson, *Bréf*, 72.

38 Shakespeare, *Romeo and Juliet*, ed. Weis, 3.2.1–8.

39 Shakespeare, *Leikrit*, 455.

40 Pétursson, *Steingrímur Thorsteinsson*, 196. Interestingly, both these examples show that when especially eager to recreate the 'flight' in the original texts, the translators are tempted to add the third

alliterative stave and thus build an acoustic bridge between lines, in accordance with the Icelandic metric tradition (cf. lines 1–2 and 3–4 in Jochumsson's text, lines 4–5 and 6–7 in Thorsteinsson).
41 Shakespeare, *King Lear*, ed. Foakes, 3.2.1–9.
42 Shakespeare, *Lear konungur*, 66.
43 Magnússon, 'Othello Mattíasar'.
44 Cf. S. Einarsson, 'Shakespeare á Íslandi', pt. 1, 33.
45 Gröndal, 'Út af "Othello"'.
46 H.Þ., 'Hvert er mark og mið'.
47 Magnússon, 'Formáli', in Shakespeare, *Stormurinn*, I, iv.
48 Shakespeare, *Stormurinn*, I, 67.
49 Shakespeare, *The Tempest*, ed. Vaughan and Mason Vaughan, 4.1.156–8.
50 Shakespeare, *Stormurinn*, I, 74.
51 Shakespeare, *Stormurinn*, II, xiii–xiv.
52 Aríel [Grímur Thomsen], 'Stormurinn eftir Shakespeare'.
53 Stefánsson and Guðmundsson, 'Stormurinn'.
54 Shakespeare, 'Bálför Sesars', trans. Gestur [Guðmundur Björnsson]; includes Act 3.2 from *Julius Caesar*. Gestur published his translation of Act 3.1 from the same play in his poetry book *Undir ljúfum lögum* (Reykjavík, 1918).
55 Þorbergsson, 'Being European'.
56 I. Einarsson, *Séð og lifað*, 120–4.
57 S. Einarsson, 'Shakespeare á Íslandi', pt. 2, 51.
58 I. Einarsson, 'Matthías Jochumsson', 30–1.
59 The authors of the present chapter were able to access the translation in manuscript.
60 Þorbergsson, 'Being European', 30.
61 S. Einarsson, 'Shakespeare á Íslandi', pt. 2, 48.
62 Hálfdanarson, 'Fáein orð um Shakespeare', in Shakespeare, *Leikrit*, i, 20.

Works cited

Anon., 'Úr bréfi af Austfjörðum', *Fjölnir*, 2 (1836), 40.
Aríel [Grímur Thomsen], 'Stormurinn eftir Shakespeare', *Fróði*, 6 September 1886.

Aspelund, Karl, and Terry Gunnell, eds, *Málarinn og menningarsköpun: Sigurður Guðmundsson og Kvöldfélagið 1858–1874* (Reykjavík, 2017).
Bhabha, Homi, 'DissemiNation: Time, Narrative and the Margins of the Modern Nation', in Homi Bhabha, ed., *Nation and Narration* (New York, 1990), 291–322.
Einarsson, Indriði, *Séð og lifað: Endurminningar* (Reykjavík, 1936), 120–4.
Einarsson, Indriði, 'Matthías Jochumsson eins og hann kom mér fyrir sjónir', in Einarsson, *Greinar um menn og listir* (Reykjavík, 1959), 22–35.
Einarsson, Stefán, 'Shakespeare á Íslandi', *Tímarit Þjóðræknisfélags Íslendinga*, 19 (1937), 25–36 (pt. 1); 20 (1938), 37–54 (pt. 2).
Einarsson, Stefán, 'Shakespeare in Iceland: A Historical Survey', *ELH*, 7/4 (1940), 272–85.
Elam, Keir, *The Semiotics of Theatre and Drama* (London and New York, 1980).
Eysteinsson, Ástráður, *Tvímæli: Þýðingar og bókmenntir* (Reykjavík, 1996).
Eysteinsson, Ástráður, 'Icelandic Resettlements', *symplokē*, 5/1–2 (1997), 153–66.
Eysteinsson, Ástráður, 'Iceland's Milton: On Jón Þorláksson´s Translation of *Paradise Lost*', in Angelica Duran, Islam Issa and Jonathan R. Olson, eds, *Milton in Translation* (Oxford, 2017), 215–30.
Eysteinsson, Ástráður, 'Skapandi tryggð: Shakespeare og Hamlet á íslensku', in Eysteinsson, *Orðaskil: Í heimi þýðinga* (Reykjavík, 2017), 109–38.
Gröndal, Benedikt, 'Út af "Othello"', *Norðanfari*, 14 March 1885.
Gunnell, Terry, *The Origins of Drama in Scandinavia* (Cambridge, 1995).
Gunnell, Terry, 'Eddic Performance and Eddic Audiences', in Carolyne Larrington, Judy Quinn and Brittany Schorn, eds, *A Handbook to Eddic Poetry, Myths and Legends in Early Scandinavia* (Cambridge, 2016), 92–113.
Guðmundsson, Sigurður, *Sigurður Guðmundsson málari og menningarsköpun á Íslandi 1857–1874*, https://sigurdurmalari.hi.is/wiki/index.php?title=Br%C3%A9f_(SG02–225), accessed 1 August 2022.
H.Þ, 'Hvert er mark og mið bókmenntafjelagsins?', *Fjallkonan*, 18 July 1884.
Hálfdanarson, Helgi, 'Fáein orð um Shakespeare og samtíð hans', in William Shakespeare, *Leikrit*, I, trans. Helgi Hálfdanarson (Reykjavík, 1982), 7–26.

Hálfdanarson, Helgi, 'Flutningur bundins máls', in Helgi Hálfdanarson, *Molduxi: Rabb um kveðskap og fleira* (Reykjavík, 1998), 67–83.
Hallgrímsson, Jónas, 'Um rímur af Tistrani og Indíönu', *Fjölnir*, 3 (1837), 18–29.
Hallgrímsson, Jónas, 'Jeg bið að heilsa!', *Fjölnir*, 7 (1844), 105–6.
Hallgrímsson, Jónas, *Selected Poetry and Prose*, ed. and trans. Dick Ringler, https://digicoll.library.wisc.edu/Jonas/.
Jochumsson, Matthías, *Bréf Matthíasar Jochumssonar*, ed. Steingrímur Matthíasson (Akureyri, 1935).
Jochumsson, Matthías, *Sögukaflar af sjálfum mér* (Reykjavík, 1959).
Magnússon, Eiríkur, 'Othello Mattíasar', *Þjóðólfur*, 15 and 22 December 1883.
Magnússon, Eiríkur, 'Formáli', in William Shakespeare, *Stormurinn*, I, trans. Eiríkur Magnússon (Reykjavík, 1885).
Ólason, Vésteinn, 'Old Icelandic Poetry', in Daisy Neijmann, ed., *A History of Icelandic Literature* (Lincoln and London, 2006), 1–64.
Pétursson, Hannes, *Steingrímur Thorsteinsson: Líf hans og list* (Reykjavík, 1964).
Shakespeare, William, 'Greftrunarljóð', trans. G[ísli] B[rynjúlfsson], *Ný félagsrit*, 12 (1852), 177.
Shakespeare, William, *Lear konungur*, trans. Steingrímur Thorsteinsson (Reykjavík, 1878).
Shakespeare, William, 'Bálför Sesars', trans. Gestur [Guðmundur Björnsson], *Skírnir: Tímarit Hins íslenzka bókmenntafélags*, 92 (1918), 89–108.
Shakespeare, William, *Leikrit: Macbeth, Hamlet, Óthelló, Rómeó og Júlía*, trans. Matthías Jochumsson, 2nd edn (Reykjavík, 1939).
Shakespeare, William, *King Lear*, ed. R. A. Foakes (London, 1997).
Shakespeare, William, *The Tempest*, eds Virginia Mason Vaughan and Alden T. Vaughan, rev. edn (London, 2011).
Shakespeare, William, *Romeo and Juliet*, ed. René Weis (London, 2012).
Shakespeare, William, *Macbeth*, eds Sandra Clarke and Pamela Mason (London, 2015).
Sigurbjörnsson, Lárus, 'Shakespeare og Íslendingar', *Félagsbréf*, 9/34 (1964), 7–15.
Stefánsson, Jón, and Valtýr Guðmundsson, 'Stormurinn', *Þjóðólfur*, 14 and 21 May 1886.
Þorbergsson, Magnús Þór, 'Being European: Staging the Nation in 1920s Icelandic Theatre', *Nordic Theatre Studies*, 25/1 (2013), 22–33.
Thorgrímsson Thomsen, Grímur, *Om Lord Byron* (Copenhagen, 1845).
Thorsteinsson, Steingrímur, and Matthías Jochumsson, eds and trans., *Svanhvít: Nokkur útlend skáldmæli* (Reykjavík, 1877).

2

Ida Aalberg and the first Finnish-language *Romeo and Juliet*, 1881

Nely Keinänen

In this chapter, I analyse the first Finnish-language production of a Shakespeare play, *Romeo and Juliet*, produced in 1881 at the Finnish Theatre (FT), focusing on how Shakespeare as cultural capital was harnessed for the Finnish nationalist project and how this collided with evolving attitudes about the role of women.[1] On the one hand, the theatre company had been formed in 1872 to elevate the status of Finnish language and culture, and aimed to nurture both new drama in the vernacular and the translation and performance of classic plays. As such, this first Finnish-language performance of a complete Shakespeare play generated wide public interest in Finland, as Shakespeare was seen as a central figure in the European culture to which Finland aspired.[2] The performance was widely cheered as a cultural victory.

By contrast, this first Finnish *Romeo and Juliet* also provides a fascinating case study into the intersections of nation building and gender in late nineteenth-century Finland.[3] The FT built this production around its star actress, Ida Aalberg (1857–1915), who the theatre saw as an early champion of both theatrical art *and* nationalist ideals, a 'warrior' with the 'honour of fighting in the front lines' in the cultural battle ahead.[4] To this end, early in her career Aalberg was constructed both inside and outside of the theatre as a living embodiment of the nation-as-female, the Finnish Maid, *Suomi-neito*, representing youth, innocence and vulnerability, the purity of rural Finland, images celebrated by the Fennomans pushing the nationalist cause.[5] But by the early 1880s, Aalberg was moving beyond the ingénue roles which called up images of the Finnish Maid towards more complex ones, Nora in Ibsen's *A Doll's House*, which she played to great acclaim in 1880, and then Juliet. These roles both overlapped with and challenged nineteenth-century gendered expectations of women, and specifically clashed with the virgin figure in the national imagery of the Finnish Maid. Juliet, as written by Shakespeare and performed by Aalberg, is both 'innocent' and 'erotic', according to reviewers. So while on the whole, reviews of this first *Romeo and Juliet* are very positive, one can sense an underlying worry about whether Juliet's character is appropriate for modern audiences, even as translating and performing Shakespeare is a worthy goal which will help the nation reach its full potential.

The late nineteenth century saw the rise of the New Woman, as well as the rise of the diva on theatrical stages. The example of Ida Aalberg adds to our knowledge of how the 'Shakespeare rhizome', to borrow a term from Douglas Lanier,[6] was adapted but also rejected by actresses at the time. Shakespeare's cultural authority was always going to be problematic for the female actors who managed to rise to the top of the theatrical profession, becoming magnets drawing patrons to the theatre. Especially in an age which valorized the great tragedies, the paucity of roles for women put them in an untenable position vis-à-vis Shakespeare. In 1899, Sarah Bernhardt, perhaps the most famous of these divas, would play Hamlet, since 'no female character has opened up a field so large for the exploration of sensations and human sorrows as that of Hamlet' (and since Ophelia, which she played in 1886, 'brought nothing new to me in the study of character').[7] Both Bernhardt and her rival Eleonora Duse were attracted to roles like Magda in Hermann Sudermann's *Heimat* [Home], a role Aalberg would play in 1897. Aalberg also favoured modernist plays by Henrik Ibsen and the Finnish author Minna Canth which spoke more directly to women's issues and the feminist cause. If, as Lanier argues, the Shakespeare rhizome is an 'aggregated field in a perpetual state of becoming, ever being reconfigured as new adaptations intersect with and grow from it',[8] we can analyse Aalberg's Juliet as an early effort to reconfigure Shakespeare to better fit the Finnish context, incorporating aspects of both the Finnish Maiden and Nora, as it were, part of a wider effort among female theatre professionals to claim roles worthy of their skills, as well as treatment within their companies equal to their status. In the early 1880s, Shakespearean cultural capital still had strategic value; it could be used to forward national, theatrical, linguistic – and perhaps also feminist – ideals in pre-independence Finland.[9] Aalberg's Juliet continued to resonate in the Finnish consciousness even decades later.

The early reception of Shakespeare in pre-independence Finland

Ida Aalberg was not the first woman to play Shakespeare in Finnish, and indeed female actors were crucial in the creation of a Finnish-language Shakespeare tradition. An important transitional figure in the shift from Swedish- to Finnish-language Shakespeare was Charlotte Raa, the first professional actor to perform Shakespeare in Finnish. Charlotte Raa and her husband Frithiof acted together in Swedish in several productions, including Desdemona and Iago (1868) and Beatrice and Benedict (1869).[10] In the late 1860s, she was recruited to the Fennoman cause, even though at the time the Swedish actress did not speak a word of Finnish. In 1873, her Finnish improved, Raa played Lady Macbeth's sleepwalking scene and Ofelia's mad scenes while on tour with the fledgling FT in the provincial city of Hämeenlinna.[11] *Macbeth* had been translated in 1864 by Kaarlo A. Slöör (Finnicized pen name: Santala) (1833–1905) for the tercentenary celebration of Shakespeare's birth. Raa's performance was excitedly praised, especially in the Fennoman press.[12] A reviewer in *Morgonbladet* commented on how difficult it is to perform an excerpt from a play, but that Raa proved herself more than equal to the task:

> As soon as . . . the wretched Lady Macbeth came onstage, the play's deeply tragic atmosphere became apparent, and in the next moments the audience could easily imagine the full desolateness

of the tragedy. The viewer could see the whole, not just an isolated scene.[13]

Another press report is equally laudatory about Raa's performance, and especially the comparative comment at the end shows how these Shakespeare performances were significant in building national self-esteem:

> Fear and dread were the feelings in the audience evoked by Lady Macbeth, as she walked in her sleep, troubled by her conscience, speaking of the murder of the king which hung so heavily on her mind. The viewer could see the whole of the desolate tragic world Shakespeare depicts. The two scenes from *Hamlet*, where the mad Ophelia comes to court and in her delirium speaks words of wisdom, evoke for us the oppressive atmosphere in which the noble Hamlet moves, daydreaming but incapable of action. We doubt whether these scenes of Lady Macbeth and Ophelia could be performed any better than how Mrs. Raa performed them.[14]

That these early efforts to perform Shakespeare were considered significant can be seen in Raa's being asked to perform the same Shakespeare excerpts in Helsinki during the 1875–6 theatre season.[15]

The significance of Raa's groundbreaking Finnish-language performances, and their importance in the nationalist project, is also evident in the ways they were often recalled in conjunction with later celebrations connected to Shakespeare. For example, in 1913 she is mentioned in an article celebrating the completion of the Finnish Literature Society's (SKS) complete works translation project: 'Shakespeare's poetry was presented for the first time on a Finnish stage on 19 September 1873. . . . [by] Mrs. Raa, who will always be remembered as a key figure in the history of Finnish theatre.'[16] Playing Shakespeare was only a small part of Raa's contribution to the early development of Finnish-language theatre, but her landmark Shakespeare performances clearly earned a place in the national imagination, paving the way for Ida Aalberg's later triumphs.

Charlotte Raa was a close associate and friend of Emilie and Kaarlo Bergbom, who founded the Finnish Theatre company in 1872. The Bergboms had ambitious goals for the theatre, to perform domestic plays (by such writers as Aleksis Kivi and Minna Canth), along with significant contemporary foreign plays (e.g. Henrik Ibsen) and classics like Shakespeare.[17] Although creating a vibrant domestic tradition was the main goal, translation of foreign works was nevertheless seen as significant. The reasoning was that foreign authors had much to offer the developing nation, a point often repeated in the Fennoman press:

> A national literature only fulfils its task if it can open for its readers a road to the highest peaks of human thought, to the loveliest imaginative fields, and to that end, it needs also to own the best products created by foreign literatures.[18]

Translating Shakespeare and others was thus seen as a way of enriching the Finnish language, as B. F. Godenhjelm writes in 1880 in his review of the first Finnish translation of *Hamlet*:

> The translation of these ever-brilliant works by Shakespeare is a project which we hope will bear the most delectable fruits for the furthering of our national culture and civilization, as wherever his magnificent genius has managed to take root, it has invigorated and uplifted the national poetry.[19]

Finnish translations were undertaken by Paavo Cajander (1846–1913), a poet and lecturer in Finnish at the Imperial Alexander University in Finland (later University of Helsinki) who, working closely with the Bergboms at the Finnish Theatre, began translating Shakespeare's plays into Finnish in 1879 as part of the previously mentioned complete works translation project supported by the SKS. Starting with *Hamlet*, Cajander continued at the rate of one or two plays a year until 1912, when he had finished translating thirty-six of Shakespeare's plays. When he died, he was working on a translation of Shakespeare's sonnets. In a review of Cajander's translation of *Romeo and Juliet*, the second in the series, B. F. Godenhjelm concludes: 'I cannot help but express my joy that this wonderful love tragedy has appeared in such charming Finnish dress, and I dearly hope that Mr. Cajander's brilliant skills will continue to enrich our national literature with many more Shakespearean works.'[20]

Gender, nation, theatre

Alongside its concern with developing literary and dramatic Finnish, now seen as possible through the early successes of Cajander, the FT also participated in the construction of a particularly gendered idea of nation, and Aalberg's Juliet of 1881 must be read in this context. As Laura-Elina Aho has explored, this gendered idea of the nation was embodied by the 'Finnish Maiden', emphasizing youth, innocence and vulnerability.[21] One manifestation of this was the plethora of plays presented in the FT's first years (1872–1876) depicting female orphans. In these stories (many adapted from continental sources), a pure and lovely young (motherless) woman from the countryside, representing an idealized view of Finnish folk culture, is found by a cultured and intelligent male character representing the urban elite, who takes it upon himself to educate the woman. According to Aho, this is the 'core narrative of Finnish-language nationalism: the orphan embodying the "true heart of Finnishness" located in the peasantry, to be found, loved and cultivated by the intelligentsia'.[22] As a young and upcoming female star in an age where leading ladies drew patrons to the theatre, Ida Aalberg was consciously shaped both inside and outside of the theatre as a female personification of Finnishness in support of the Fennoman cause.[23] In this view, a woman's primary significance was in the home, ensuring the well-being of her family as well as upholding social, sexual and cultural mores.[24]

Aalberg joined the theatre in 1874 at the age of seventeen, playing a series of ingénue roles, the young, good and innocent girl on the verge of womanhood as described in connection with the orphan plays earlier. Reviews of these early performances focused on qualities similar to those of the characters: Aalberg was described as 'young and graceful', 'playful and sensitive', 'gentle and pleasant', all qualities associated with women in late nineteenth-century nationalist movements across Europe.[25] Aalberg's rural roots, along with her being a native speaker of Finnish, were also celebrated as the epitome of 'pure' Finnishness; she was hailed as the 'daughter of the nation'.[26] There were contradictions in these views of femininity as well, particularly concerning education. Much was made of Aalberg's travels to continental Europe for training, even as the feminine ideal was to stay at home and care for the family.[27] Aalberg's characters longed for education, often provided by a higher-class, educated male from the city, and Aalberg was surrounded in real life by male admirers who fancied themselves her supporters and teachers, reinforcing existing gender and class stereotypes.[28] As Aalberg gained in popularity, the FT began to construct its repertoire around her, and her success became a symbol of the theatre's – and the nation's – success. As some of the characters she was playing, Aalberg was expected to sacrifice her own ambitions (in her case to become a theatrical diva playing on European stages) for the Fennoman cause.[29] This was the situation until about 1880, when Aalberg began to play more complex female roles (e.g. Nora) and also to assert herself more assuredly within the theatre, causing Kaarlo Bergbom no end of headaches in constructing his repertoire.[30] A year later she would play Juliet.

Romeo and Juliet at the Finnish Theatre

There had been much discussion about which Shakespeare play the young FT would take up first, and indeed how soon something so difficult as Shakespeare could be attempted; these concerns can be traced to the cultural imperative to perform Shakespeare in a respectable fashion. Raa's short scenes in 1873 were an encouraging first step. Cajander had finished the first play in his complete works project, *Hamlet*, in 1879, but it was felt there wasn't an actor who could handle the lead role. A prominent Finnish-speaking actor, Oskari Wilho, wanted to play Shylock, but his health was failing.[31] Emilie Bergbom, writing to her brother Kaarlo in the summer of 1879, mentioned that one of the Fennoman journals, *Uusi Suometar*, had hoped that more 'valuable' plays would be presented, and she herself would be very happy if one of them would be Shakespeare. In addition, she thought 'it would be nice to try Aalberg as Juliet'. Ever the businesswoman, she also pointed out that *Romeo and Juliet* 'will be cheaper for us, and bring in more money', adding that Aalberg's recent success in *Jane Eyre* proved she was a good box-office draw.[32] Emilie got her way, and Cajander was asked to translate *Romeo and Juliet* after *Hamlet*, instead of *The Merchant of Venice*. Interestingly, not long before the scheduled opening night almost two years later, Emilie, writing to her good friend Betty Elfving, worried that audiences would not be as interested in *Romeo and Juliet* as they were in a farce also in the FT repertoire that season: 'It's perhaps likely that *Romeo and Juliet* won't entertain audiences as much as [Gustav von Moser's] *War in Peace Time*, but it will bring great joy to *real* friends of the theatre, to be able to present a Shakespeare play in Finnish. It's helping me to forget many bitter experiences.'[33] *Romeo and Juliet* was planned for the spring of the 1880/1 season, only the ninth of the new theatre.

Emilie's reference to 'real' friends of the theatre hints at the complex economic issues the fledgling theatre had to overcome while training audiences to appreciate a classic author like Shakespeare, whose cultural capital might not automatically translate into money in the till. Audiences had to wait for their first Finnish Shakespeare, for work was apparently slow on the translation. Bergbom wrote to Cajander at the beginning of February 1880, asking about it.[34] By November 1880, there were excited reports in the press of a forthcoming new Shakespeare translation by Cajander of *Romeo and Juliet*, due in December.[35] The translation was approved by the SKS in January 1881, with B. F. Godenhjelm, on behalf of the Poetry Committee, writing that the translation has been done 'with great artistic merit and poetic sense'.[36] The translation was published on 16 March 1881, the fiftieth anniversary of the SKS, again pointing to the significance of Shakespeare in the national consciousness. It was widely advertised all over Finland in both Swedish- and Finnish-language publications through the spring and summer, with further advertisements in the fall including both the first and second plays in the SKS *Shakespeare Drama* series.[37] Godenhjelm also published a substantive and very positive review of the translation in *Valvoja*, a Finnish literary magazine, in April 1881, a month before the theatrical premiere.[38] Like many of the theatre reviews discussed later, it begins by commenting on the cultural significance of Cajander's translation, which shows 'how much our literature has developed in the last half century, for the assimilation of this great poetic work into a national literature is a significant stage in the cultural development of all nations'.[39]

The importance of the first Shakespeare production for the FT can be seen in the careful preparations made for it. Ida Aalberg and her co-star, Axel Ahlberg (1855–1927) as Romeo, were cast when both were twenty-four years old.[40] Aalberg was sent to continental Europe to hone her skills as an actress. In May 1880, she travelled to Dresden, to the acting school of Marie Seebach, where among other roles she was to work on Juliet. Seebach instructed her students in the German grand style, static and declamatory.[41] In late June, Aalberg travelled on to Munich, where she was able to observe performances of plays by Schiller, Goethe, Lessing and Shakespeare, performed by leading German and Austrian actors. During her time in Munich, she was introduced to Henrik Ibsen.[42] Aalberg by no means simply absorbed these lessons, but also filtered them through her own aesthetic judgement and experiences. For example, she had seen Josephine Wessely (1860–1887) play Juliet in Vienna and thought she was too 'sentimental' in the opening scenes.[43] A few years earlier, Emilie Bergbom had warned Aalberg about getting too interested in tragedy, which might lead to too much 'sentimentality', by which she seems to have meant the more declamatory style of a trained actor. This Emilie Bergbom opposed to the 'energetic and naïve colours' preferred by Finnish audiences, where 'naïve' means natural and spontaneous expression, a step on the road towards more realistic acting at which Aalberg excelled according to Emilie.[44]

More evidence of the cultural significance of Shakespeare to the FT was the rehearsal period, which began in February 1881. Bergbom declared this a 'teaching play' and required all FT actors to attend rehearsals, regardless of whether they were in the show.[45] Bergbom included extra time for rehearsals, for he thought that performing Shakespeare was such an important test that he did not want to rush it.[46] Within the FT, all eyes were on Axel Ahlberg, the young actor cast as Romeo: he had only been with the theatre for three years, and the others were wondering whether he would be able to manage the part.[47] In a letter to Betty Elfving (22 February 1881), Emilie Bergbom wondered why Axel Ahlberg had even been cast as in her opinion Bruno Böök would have been more suitable, as he looked the part.[48] Ida apparently helped the inexperienced Ahlberg a great deal ('*Romeo and Juliet* would have come to nothing if Ida hadn't advised me, a real beginner, as Romeo'), but also had fun at his expense. Once when Bergbom was away, she started directing him to stand in a place where he felt nobody in the audience could see him. She replied: 'Who is going to bother looking at you while I'm onstage!' 'Half the audience', Ahlberg replied, and both burst into laughter.[49] Due to the significance of the production, Bergbom apparently worked the actors very hard and had them repeating scenes over and over, sometimes cruelly cutting them off.[50] One story circulated later that Bergbom was so enraged by Aalberg's rehearsal of the sleeping potion scene that he jumped onstage and performed the scene as he thought it ought to be performed. Katri Rautio, who witnessed the event, said, 'We forgot the theatre, the play, ourselves, and even Bergbom, all we had before us was a desperate person who had to somehow empty that vial, for she had no other hope. It was inexplicable how he was able to get so deeply into such a brief scene.'[51] Ida eventually caught a cold but had to keep rehearsing during the days and perform Gustav von Moser's farce *War in Peace Time* in the evenings as previously mentioned.[52]

The FT's first foray into Shakespeare turned out not to be easy. Opening night had been scheduled for 16 March, significantly the fiftieth anniversary of the SKS, but around 7:30 pm on the night of 13 March, they received word that Czar Alexander II had been assassinated in St Petersburg. Alexander II was popular in Finland, and Bergbom's voice was shaking when he interrupted the performance of another play and informed the audience, who trooped out in shock.[53] A seven-week period of mourning followed, disrupting all the planned celebrations and indeed putting the theatre at financial risk as they would be without an income for so many weeks. The theatre decided to take additional loans and pay the actors half their wages.[54] Still sick, Ida was given off time to recover, quite welcome given the rigours of the season.[55]

Opening night finally arrived on 3 May 1881. There were more patrons than seats. All eyes were on Aalberg (Juliet) and Ahlberg (Romeo), in that order. Puff pieces before the premiere spoke of the national importance of this first Finnish-language Shakespeare production:

> Today is a significant day in Finnish theatrical history. Tonight for the first time there will be a performance of one of the greatest tragedies of the world-renowned poet Shakespeare, *Romeo and Juliet*, that wonderful and charming depiction of young love

which collapses under the weight of parental hate. We are sure the Finnish Theatre will perform the play with distinction.[56]

A few days later, the same paper gleefully proclaimed the performance a success:

> [The packed audience] was curious to see how well our young theatre company would perform its first Shakespeare tragedy. That it was a success, even better than the many devoted friends of the theatre dared to imagine, was confirmed by everyone.[57]

Nearly all the reviews refer in one way or another to the cultural significance of the first Finnish-language Shakespeare production. It was called a 'triumph', succeeding 'beyond expectations'.[58] It represented 'a step forward'.[59] A review in the Fennoman *Uusi Suomatar* comments that the day should be celebrated, for it was the first complete production of a work of one of the 'world's leading dramatists' done by the still relatively young theatre:

> When we remember that the Finnish Theatre is only nine years old, we have to admit that it has worked very hard and has come a long way in an incredibly short period of time. Or are there many examples in the world of a people's theatre being established from absolutely nothing, which in only nine years advances to performing Shakespeare?[60]

A similar point is made a few months later in *Valvoja*: discussing the good performances of the supporting cast, as well as the exquisite costumes and set, the reviewer declares that 'one can say that our theatre's first Shakespeare succeeded so well that even theatres much older than ours would be proud to mount such a production'.[61] The same reviewer wishes the theatre luck in continuing its work, 'whose importance for the history of our nation's cultural development can no longer be questioned'.[62] *Romeo and Juliet* was not as great a success as Ibsen's *A Doll's House*,[63] also starring Aalberg, but nevertheless many felt that some invisible barrier had been broken. At a party following a performance on 6 May organized by the man who would later become Aalberg's husband, there were lofty speeches and much singing of nationalistic songs, and Ida received her first laurel wreath.[64] A newspaper in the former capital city of

Turku printed a message 'signed by 11' sent to the FT in Helsinki, wishing them luck with the production which was 'advancing arts in the nation'.[65] But even as the production was seen as advancing the arts, there were worries about what images of woman it was embracing, what implications Ida as Juliet had for this female symbol of the Finnish nation.

Juliet/Ida as Finnish Maid and erotic lover

Before discussing Aalberg's Juliet, it is worth pausing to reflect briefly on tensions between innocence and eroticism in Cajander's translation, and how these might have affected the performance and its reception. On the one hand, some changes seem conservative, as, for example, in 1.3 Cajander gives to Lady Capulet the line given to Juliet by Shakespeare, asking the Nurse to cease talking after she has repeated the 'fall backward' joke twice: 'And stint thou too, I pray thee, Nurse, say I' (1.3.60), thus emphasizing the mother's power over the daughter and Juliet's role as chaste, silent and obedient.[66] In 1.5, Rome's calling Juliet a 'Lady' is translated with *impi*, which means a virgin. But just before that, in the telling of the joke itself, Cajander speaks literally of Juliet falling 'on her back', thus not shying away from the line's sexual connotations. Similarly, in 1.5 when Romeo kisses Juliet a second time after their shared sonnet, in English Juliet says, 'You kiss by the book', whereas in Finnish Juliet's response seems warmer and indeed more erotic: 'Yes you know how!' During the balcony scene, she asks not whether she should have been more 'strange' but more 'cold', language with perhaps more direct sexual innuendo (1.5.143). Cajander also very effectively uses internal rhyme and interjection to highlight erotic moments for Juliet, as in his translation of 'Sweet, so would I' with its resonating dipthong on /*oi*/ sounds: '*Armas, oi, jos oisit!*' This is a translation which gives the actress opportunity to emphasize Juliet's sexual desires should she wish to do so.

Not surprising given Aalberg's star status, reviews often focus on her performance. Of special interest here are the ways reviewers evoke tropes connected to the Finnish Maid or worry that the character/performance stray too far from gendered expectations.

For example, Aalberg is praised for her 'fine artistic instincts' as well as her youthful 'glowing enthusiasm'.⁶⁷ One reviewer was disturbed by Aalberg's failure to play the young ingénue as she had done in earlier roles, with part of the problem stemming from the way Shakespeare has written Juliet's character. The reviewer is then relieved that Aalberg finally gets back into the proper character. Gendered expectations are also clearly visible in the approving comment that the translator has assigned one of Juliet's lines to her mother to be more in keeping with nineteenth-century gender expectations:

> Aalberg's Juliet is full of both enthusiasm and power, love and despair ... but we want nevertheless to say that in our opinion in the first scene she did not display the innocence, naivete that we know that Miss A is very capable of expressing. Juliet did not to our mind look like a person for whom marriage would be 'an honour that I dream not of', for she is paying far too much attention to the Nurse's prattling. In our opinion, Juliet's words: 'And stint thou too, I pray thee, nurse, say I' are better spoken by Lady Capulet, as they are in Cajander's translation. ... But ... already by the balcony scene, Miss A is the perfect Juliet, innocent, childlike, a virtuous maiden enraptured by her first love.⁶⁸

A later review in *Valvoja* responds differently to the first scene, accepting that Juliet is perhaps more fiery and passionate than the Fennomanian idealized woman. He asks whether a well brought-up girl 'in our day' would even be able to utter lines that Juliet utters to her Nurse, such as 'Ancient damnation! O most wicked fiend!' (3.5.237), and explains his reasoning thus:

> We see already at the beginning of the play that Juliet is not and has not been raised to be well-behaved. Her father is bad-tempered, her mother insignificant, and the Nurse's witticisms not the most refined. It's natural that Juliet seems unstable at the beginning, that she looks at life through a child's wondering and inquisitive but at the same time nonresistant eyes.⁶⁹

Although female innocence and virginity were key tropes of the orphan and ingénue roles Aalberg was celebrated for performing earlier, Shakespeare's Juliet is cut from a different cloth, depicting the transition from child to wife and uttering the kind of passionate words not typically expected from a late nineteenth-century woman, as the same reviewer notes:

> Through her powerful performance, we learn to perfectly understand this incomparable love, a love that does not even fear death; and all those emphatic words by Juliet, which when we read this drama may easily seem exaggerated to us, when enunciated by Miss A assume their proper colour: they describe to us a fiery soul, the likes of which can scarcely be found in our weak-nerved times.[70]

Significantly, 'weak-nerved' (a literal translation from the Finnish) seems connected not to progressive notions of femininity but rather to masculinity, as seen in comments about Axel Ahlberg's performance as Romeo. The *Valvoja* critic had this to say about the emasculating influence of love on Romeo and even more on Finnish men in real life:

> Romeo, of course, cannot possibly please us as much as Juliet, because love, which increases the naturally weak power of women, by contrast diminishes Romeo's masculinity: at the beginning all he can do is sigh after Rosaline and upon his banishment he throws himself on the ground and wishes to end his life. On the other hand, Shakespeare has so powerfully described Romeo's hopelessness that when well-acted, as it was here, it forces us to acknowledge that a person like Romeo is much more whole and complete than our contemporary men who stroll up and down the Esplanade or serenade [their lovers] with song.[71]

One of the more provocative descriptions of Aalberg's performance can be found in a letter to her by one of her patrons, J. J. F. Perander (1838–1885), a classics scholar and philosopher, evoking both Juliet/Ida as Finnish Maiden *and* erotic lover:

Thank you from the bottom of my heart for your Juliet! Your interpretation, down to the smallest details, is masterful. From your first entrance, everything is soulful, true Shakespeare! A rose, smelling ever so sweet. Nobody should be allowed to touch it, and yet it's so wonderfully captivating and warm, that it simply cannot be left outside the battle of life and love.

How striking, how almost shocking and prophetic is the surprised look on your face when Juliet sees Romeo for the first time!

A few small gestures and looks intrigue the audience, giving us a taste of what's to come.

And the first kiss, how feminine, how soulful it was!

And yet Juliet's womanly reserve, her virginal innocence and purity, are so closely linked to her great happiness and at the same time her deep suffering, encompassing the heart of the play, the tragedy of love![72]

Perander was especially taken with the scene where Julia takes the sleeping potion from Friar Lawrence, his description conflating Aalberg with her role, with Aalberg expressing 'her' feelings:

And Romeo and Juliet's first night of love! You interpreted it with such admirable mastery: pure innocence and suffering joined together. And the unbelievable artistry, the dignified simplicity with which you show your feelings in the scene where Friar Lawrence gives you the sleeping potion. In that scene it was clear that Juliet had decided she would never belong to another man. That scene should always be performed exactly like you did it. In that scene Juliet cannot seem unwomanly, or like she has fallen in love with Romeo too suddenly.

Juliet does everything with her whole soul, her entire being.

Oh that a sculpturer could capture your face in that moment and immortalize it in marble or bronze![73]

As Suutela points out, another interesting feature here is the way that Perander sees that Juliet's love must be absolute, even sacrificial, which Aho also associates with the Finnish Maid motif.[74] Almost paradoxically, to be 'unwomanly' is to be erotic.

The full force of these gendered expectations about sexuality and the erotic for Aalberg and her character can be seen in a letter describing the production to Charlotte Raa, written by her friend Alma Wikström.[75] It is worth quoting at length for the behind-the-scenes view it gives of the FT, as well as the author's opinion of Aalberg's technique, at times accused of being too static and declamatory and elsewhere overly passionate:

> I wasn't completely satisfied with anyone, except Friar Lawrence (Leino) and Mercutio (Böök), they were really good. Leino was fantastic, but Romeo (Ahlberg) was weak, as was Capulet (=Wilho), Paris (Kivinen), Montague (Tervo) and the Prince of Verona (Kallio) – the latter was terrible, as you might guess, as you well know that Kallio can't play anybody but Eenokki in *Kihlaus*[76] – Aurora was miserable as the Nurse (a real 'simpleton'), so all that leaves is Ida. What can I say about her? Well – By far the best was the first act and the balcony scene. But in Friar Lawrence's cell she was too much a sculpted picture rather than a suffering Juliet, and the night scene at Juliet's I should have mentioned first. There she was, in my opinion, disgusting. When the curtain came up she was lying on the bed (really lying) and Romeo had his arms around her. – I don't know, it just didn't seem pure, but instead lewd. Or at least that's what I saw. In the poison scene she was in such a rage she looked like she was completely mad, I guess it has to be done like that, I can't really say, as I don't understand it – in the final scene she was good, but maybe a bit lame. I'm sure it was because she was so exhausted, she'd just run out of energy – The End. The night I saw *Romeo* Ida got a huge laurel wreath from [a university student group.][77]

As Paavolainen points out, it is revealing the way that a female actress lying on a bed onstage is experienced as 'dirty' or 'lewd'[78] and what were the limits of female expression in late nineteenth-century Finland. Aalberg's breakthrough role in 1877 had been as Boriska in *Kylän heittiö*, a Hungarian folk play, where famously Aalberg's character has a dramatic monologue at the beginning of the third act, waking up dishevelled and discovering she has been raped. It was risky for an actress to take on such an erotic role, and, for example, care had to be taken to arrange the actress' clothing as she half-lay on the ground before the curtain rose. According to Suutela, at the time simply assuming a reclining pose onstage opened up the actress to accusations of immorality.[79] Interestingly, a series of photographs by

Daniel Nyblin of the *Romeo and Juliet* production include somewhat risqué images along these lines, including the one reproduced here where Juliet is reclining on her divan, her hand touching Romeo's hair, looking him straight in the eye. Romeo is holding Juliet's braid in his right hand, but it almost looks as though he is touching her breast. On the divan is a crumpled sheet alluding to sexual activity. Suutela points out that in the nineteenth century only prostitutes were thought to look strange men in the eye, but she thinks these photographs show that perhaps that convention was fading.[80] Negotiating erotic scenes continued to be a delicate operation for Aalberg later in her career, as seen in her Cleopatra (1896): in the FT at the time, only an actress with Aalberg's rural and working-class background could be called on to play such a seductive woman but given Fennoman feminine ideals only within certain limits; one reviewer thought she played the role as a dutiful wife (Figure 2.1).[81]

Considering that the eroticized elements of Aalberg's performance were so much discussed, almost nothing is said about the actual language of the 'Come, night' speech, where Juliet explicitly expresses sexual desire. In his review of the translation, Godenhjelm somewhat cryptically comments on the exuberant 'euphemisms' of Shakespeare's original, saying that compared to *Hamlet* the translator has many more 'challenges' to be 'overcome', but the examples given do not seem to point towards erotic content.[82] In the period it is perhaps one thing to approvingly or disapprovingly call a character 'fiery' but another to discuss the nature of that fire in more detail. *Romeo and Juliet* also reverses what we saw earlier in Aho's analysis as the 'core narrative of Finnish-language nationalism', where an uneducated rural female orphan is found and educated by an urban educated male – in Shakespeare's play, Juliet, if anyone, is the teacher. One has to wonder whether there were underlying fears that Aalberg was emasculating men, and, for example, her refusal to accept a permanent contract at the FT (giving her the higher fees and flexibility that came with being a freelance actor) was not looked upon kindly.[83]

The afterlife of Aalberg's Juliet

The cultural significance of Ida Aalberg's Juliet continued to be recognized in later pre-independence Finland, most significantly in a publication connected to the tercentenary of Shakespeare's death

FIGURE 2.1 *Axel Ahlberg (Romeo) and Ida Aalberg (Juliet) at the FNT, 1881. Photo: Daniel Nyblin/Picture Collections of the Finnish Heritage Agency.*

in 1916. Nearly thirty-five years after witnessing Aalberg's *Romeo and Juliet*, the Finnish writer Juhani Aho wrote about it in *A Book of Homage to Shakespeare* (1916), which was published in England by Oxford University Press on the three-hundredth anniversary of Shakespeare's death. Aho describes Aalberg's physical beauty, her temperament; his rhapsodic descriptions include familiar tropes from the idealized Finnish Maid: Aalberg is 'slender, tall, vigorous and flexible'.[84] Aho seems to have been mesmerized by her performance and recalls some of it in astonishing detail. For example, he quotes a few lines then explains how she delivered them:

> My bounty is as boundless as the sea,
> My love as deep. The more I give to thee,
> The more I have, for both are infinite. (2.2)

> [Aalberg's] technical performance of the final outburst, and its artistic effects, were based on how well she managed to make the many vowels in the Finnish verse sing, punctuated by the rare use of consonants. Has the Finnish language ever sounded so beautiful as in those verses? The final effect especially depended on how she enunciated the word *ääretön* [infinite]. Into those long vowels, coming deep from within her chest, punctuated and supported by the rolled r-sound, she managed to include not just the sea, but also the heavens and the earth, almost making visible the breadth, depth and height of her love.[85]

Aho sees in the performance elements of progressive feminism which he describes as 'Scandinavian' and considers a product of the time rather than Shakespeare. Unspoken here but perhaps understood is that Aalberg was already moving away from German Romantic acting traditions, towards a more realistic 'Nordic' style which Aho sees as aligned with Nordic feminism:

> She especially emphasized a woman's right to love, based on the Scandinavian woman's battle for her individual right to her own feelings – maybe a characteristic wholly alien to the original work, an addition to the bard's Juliet, but nevertheless one that did not disrupt the theatrical illusion as the actress's interpretation was in other respects Nordic as well.[86]

In his tribute, Aho also reiterates the significance to Finland and the Finnish language of this first performance:

> Every [Shakespeare] performance has in some way furthered our young culture, deepened and broadened it. In this sense, that first Shakespeare premiere 35 years ago was not only an artistic victory, but also a national cultural victory.
>
> It helped us to prove to ourselves that our culture and our language were part of European culture and language. The Finnish language was no longer just the language of our ancient epic *Kalevala*, not just the language of lyrical national poetry and domestic drama, but a language capable of depicting the greatest dramatic feeling, the finest new poetry for a new age. Among other things, this is why Shakespeare in his Finnish garb becomes for us a kind of national poet. I am happy that I have been given the opportunity to express these belated thanks to his countrymen.[87]

One of the more interesting, but also unanswerable, questions connected to Aalberg is the extent to which she was able to manipulate nineteenth-century images of femininity to her advantage, both early in her career when she was mainly playing ingénue roles and later as a mature actress. Juhani Aho notes that young women imitated Aalberg's facial and vocal expressions, her 'sweet smile'[88] and as a student of acting Aalberg would have no doubt practised mannerisms likely to garner her roles and acclaim. While Aalberg's biographers have tended to read her as a genuine personification of the Finnish Maid, 'discovered' in the countryside and brought by well-meaning and more knowledgable men to the capital city to act, Laura-Elina Aho points out that Aalberg actively sought an acting career, further training and – mainly successfully – to control the trajectory of her career.[89] And far from being a mere passive symbol of the nationalist project, in 1914 (just a year before she died), Aalberg affirms her own nationalistic reasons for joining the FT:

> I believe it was the spirit of Finnishness that awakened me, even if I didn't realize it at the time, which had taken me, led me, awakened me and put in me the enthusiasm that I could almost see before me the goal even though I knew virtually nothing about the dramatic arts. And that inner enthusiasm that the spirit of Finnish nationalism had probably put in me led me through

everything, gave me the strength to do what I needed to do, even though I was a child, everything which my parents thought was evil, but which I believed was the highest of all. The spirit of true nationalism led me to Doctor Bergbom.[90]

As Suutela points out, in this speech Aalberg can be seen as constructing her own myth about her combined calling to the dramatic arts and the nationalist cause, a cause which continuously and in myriad ways brushes up against the cultural capital of 'Shakespeare'.[91]

Aalberg's career more broadly shows the significance of the actress as embodied symbol of the nation and the significant role of theatre in perpetuating this image. The discourse surrounding Juliet highlights the limitations of the image of the Finnish Maid, with its focus on virginity, the woman as a bride of the nation, someone to be protected, with no room for married women's sexuality.[92] This discourse, along with Aalberg's fears of what her parents would think of their daughter's career in the theatre, also reveals some of the pressures women faced in nineteenth-century Finland: how to be a working woman in a society which thought women were best married and at home; and how (not) to appear onstage as a woman.[93] Ultimately, playing Shakespeare was only a small part of Aalberg's career, though after Juliet she would go on to play Ophelia and Cleopatra to high acclaim. I think it is important to emphasize this point: for all his cultural value for the nation, Shakespeare was of limited use for female actors. Especially during the late nineteenth and early twentieth centuries, when female divas were filling theatres (see Chapter 4 for a discussion of the Norwegian actress Johanne Dybwad), they sought to portray the powerful and emotional women they hoped to be in real life, too, parts written by modern authors like Ibsen, Sudermann and Canth. Shakespeare was perhaps for Aalberg at least partially a means to this other end, her Juliet contains aspects of the Finnish Maid and Nora, just as performing Shakespeare at the FT was a means to raise the prestige of Finnish-language theatre enough to be able to perform lesser-known Finnish authors. At the same time, Aalberg helped to create a theatrical market for Shakespeare which later benefited other actresses, such as Elli Tompuri who in 1913 toured Finland playing Hamlet, ironically after being sidelined by the FT for being too much of a New Woman. With time, the ambivalence of leading actresses over Shakespeare would lead to changes in theatrical practices, including gender-blind casting. For all the talk in the late nineteenth century about women being the 'weaker sex', in terms of the transmission of Shakespeare to Finland, women played a significant role, as seen in the work of Emilie Bergbom behind the scenes, Charlotte Raa and especially Ida Aalberg.

Notes

1 The theatre was known as the *Suomalainen Teatteri* (literally: Finnish Theatre) until 1902, when it changed its name to *Suomen Kansallisteatteri* (Finnish National Theatre). For ease of reference, I use the abbreviation FT throughout. Unless otherwise noted, translations from Finnish are my own.
2 On the nationalist goals of the FT, see Suutela, 'Instrument'.
3 On nationalism and gender in the nineteenth century, see Blom et al., eds, *Gendered Nations*.
4 Letter to Aalberg from Emilie Bergbom, qtd. in Suutela, *Impyet*, 12.
5 Aho, 'Motherless', 183.
6 Lanier, 'Shakespearean', 27.
7 Qtd. in Howard, *Women as Hamlet*, 99.
8 Lanier, 'Shakespearean', 30.
9 As discussed by Bourdieu, cultural capital can exist in three forms, two of which are relevant here: the 'objectified' state in the form of cultural goods (e.g. a Shakespeare translation or production), as well as an 'embodied' state, whereby an individual through their own effort acquires knowledge of some cultural authority, such as Shakespeare. When Shakespeare is adopted as an instrument of national politics as in Finland, these processes take on a collective nature. Cultural capital can in one sense be seen as located in a centre outside of Finland, whereby German, French, Nordic and English Shakespeares become a model, but as this chapter demonstrates in the very act of appropriation, the dynamic is challenged. Local traditions are established and are themselves subverted, and tensions between various agents (e.g. between the idealized Fennomanian concept of Shakespeare versus the uses of Shakespeare for furthering Ida Aalberg's career) reveal cleavages in the cultural capital of Shakespeare itself. See also Lanier, 'Recent'.
10 Paavolainen, 'Bergbom', 42, n. 9.

11 Pentti Paavolainen (personal communication, 9 March 2022) thinks these madwoman scenes were chosen because they allowed the actress to display emotional acrobatics and other virtuoso and shock effects, as indeed seen in the newspaper reports about them. Perhaps this choice can also be attributed to the popularity of Charlotte Brontë's *Jane Eyre* with its madwoman in the attic and its many theatrical adaptations. In 1879, Ida Aalberg would play Jane in a production of Birch-Pfeiffer's stage adaptation.

12 Pentti Paavolainen (personal communication, 5 June 2019). For example, *Uusi Suometar*, 109, 17 September 1873, 4, has a detailed notice about Raa's upcoming performance. Newspaper materials have been accessed through the National Library of Finland's digital archives.

13 Qtd. in Aspelin-Haapkylä, *Suomalaisen Teatterin Historia*, ii, 68.

14 *Uusi Suometar*, 111, 22 September 1873, 2. Ismael Kallio, who played Claudius, did not fare so well. His performance was described as 'hopeless' and even Kaarlo Bergbom was indirectly criticized for not rehearsing the scene well enough.

15 Aspelin-Haapkylä, *Suomalaisen Teatterin Historia*, ii, 224.

16 *Suomen Nainen*, 15 January 1913, 15.

17 During the period of the Bergboms at the theatre (1872–1905), there were 462 plays presented, of which 300 were translated. The languages translated include German (80 plays), French (83), Swedish (41), Norwegian (27) and English (22). Of the foreign playwrights, the most popular was Henrik Ibsen (15 plays) followed by William Shakespeare (14). Other favourites were Schiller, Molière, Goethe and Gogol (Aspelin-Haapkylä, *Suomalaisen Teatterin Historia*, ii, iii and iv).

18 Godenhjelm, 'Kotimaan Kirjallisuutta', 135.

19 Godenhjelm, 'Kotimaan Kirjallisuutta', 36–40, esp. 36.

20 Godenhjelm, 'Kotimaan Kirjallisuutta', 197.

21 Aho, 'Motherless', 183. Aho's work develops Suutela's in 'Orleans' and *Impyet*.

22 Aho, 'Motherless', 193.

23 Aho, 'Ihanteiden', 1, 3.

24 Aho, 'Ihanteiden', 3.

25 Aho, 'Ihanteiden', 7–8. See also Lindskog Whiteley, 'Cold Maids', on Swedish translations of Ophelia in the early nineteenth century, which explores similar links between gendered ideas of nation and virginal female heroines.

26 Aho, 'Ihanteiden', 8–9.
27 Aho, 'Ihanteiden', 11.
28 Iho, 'Ihanteiden', 12–14.
29 Iho, 'Ihanteiden', 15–17.
30 See Paavolainen's chapter in this volume for how Aalberg's efforts to act on foreign stages affected the FT's Shakespeare repertoire.
31 Paavolainen, *Arkadian Arki*, 296.
32 Letter quoted in Aspelin-Haapkylä, *Suomalaisen Teatterin Historia*, iii, 11. See also Niemi, *Paavo Cajander*, 80. In 1879, Aalberg studied the role of Jane in Germany (Paavolainen, *Arkadian Arki*, 261).
33 Qtd. in Aspelin-Haapkylä, *Suomalaisen Teatterin Historia*, iii, 80 (letter dated 22 February 1881).
34 Niemi, *Paavo Cajander*, 80.
35 *Uusi Suometar*, 10 November 1880, *Ilmarinen*, 13 November 1880, *Sanomia Turusta*, 13 November 1880 and *Vaasan Sanomat*, 15 November 1880.
36 *Suomi* no.14 (1881): 485–6.
37 *Uusi Suometar*, 64, 18 March 1881, 4, had the following announcement: 'Now available, the second volume in the Shakespeare drama series, *Romeo and Juliet*, published and sold by SKS, translated by Paavo Cajander'. Similar announcements appeared in *Finlands Allmänna Tidning*, 65, 19 March 1881, 2; *Helsingfors Dagblad*, 76, 19 March 1881; *Uusi Suometar*, 65, 19 March 1881; *Morgonbladet*, 66, 21 March 1881; *Uusi Suometar*, 66, 21 March 1881; *Waasan Lehti*, 22, 21 March 1881; *Suomalainen Wirallinen Lehti*, 34, 22 March 1881; *Päijänne*, 12, 23 March 1881, 3 (Jyväskylä); *Tampereen Sanomat*, 23, 23 March 1881, 3; *Suomalainen Wirallinen Lehti*, 35, 24 March 1881, 7; *Karjalatar*, 12, 25 March 1881, 3 (Joensuu); *Vaasan Sanomat*, 13, 28 March 1881; *Tampereen Sanomat*, 25, 30 March 1881, 3; *Uusi Suometar*, 93, 25 April 1881, 4; *Tampereen Sanomat*, 27, 6 April 1881, 3; *Karjalatar*, 14, 8 April 1881, 4; *Uusi Suometar*, 96, 28 April 1881, 4; *Uusi Suometar*, 100, 3 May 1881, 4; *Valvoja* no 9, 10 May 1881; *Valvoja*, 13–14, 1 July 1881 (both *Hamlet* and *R&J*); *Valvoja*, 15–16, 1 August 1881 (both *Hamlet* and *R&J*); *Valvoja*, 17, 1 September 1881.
38 *Valvoja*, 8, 15 April 1881, 193–7.
39 *Valvoja*, 8, 15 April 1881, 193.
40 Paavolainen, *Arkadian Arki*, 377. Aurora Aspegren (1844–1911) played the Nurse, Bruno Böök (1852–1883) was Mercutio and

Benjamin Leino (1853–1908) was Friar Lawrence. Set and costume design were by Severin Falkman, a noted historical painter.
41 Suutela, *Impyet*, 68.
42 Aspelin-Haapkylä, *Suomalaisen Teatterin Historia*, iii, 53–9.
43 Räsänen, *Ida Aalberg*, 131.
44 Suutela, *Impyet*, 68–9.
45 Heikkilä, *Ida Aalberg*, 128.
46 Aspelin-Haapkylä, *Suomalaisen Teatterin Historia*, III, 74.
47 Heikkilä, *Ida Aalberg*, 128.
48 Aspelin-Haapkylä, *Suomalaisen Teatterin Historia*, iii, 80. There were rumours that Böök and Aalberg had had an affair, and this was the reason he had not been cast as Romeo (Paavolainen, *Arkadian Arki*, 369).
49 Räsänen, *Ida Aalberg*, 123.
50 Heikkilä, *Ida Aalberg*, 130.
51 Koskimies, *Suomen Kansallisteatteri*, 32.
52 Heikkilä, *Ida Aalberg*, 129.
53 Heikkilä, *Ida Aalberg*, 130.
54 Heikkilä, *Ida Aalberg*, 130.
55 FT was a repertoire theatre, travelling all over the country to do performances. In the 1880/1 season, there were ninety-seven performances, with a total of forty-two plays in repertoire. Of these eleven were Finnish plays, and twelve were new to the theatre. The most a single play was performed was nine times, *Romeo and Juliet* had five performances that season (Aspelin-Haapkylä, *Suomalaisen Teatterin Historia*, iii, 90).
56 *Suomalainen Wirallinen Lehti*, 52, 3 May 1881.
57 *Suomalainen Wirallinen Lehti*, 53, 5 May 1881.
58 *Helsingfors Dagblad*, 4 May 1881.
59 *Finsk Tidskrift*, 1 June 1881, 489–90.
60 *Uusi Suometar*, 4 May 1881, 2.
61 *Valvoja*, 11, 12 June 1881, 258–9.
62 *Valvoja*, 11, 12 June 1881, 260.
63 Heikkilä, *Ida Aalberg*, 134.
64 Heikkilä, *Ida Aalberg*, 134; Aspelin-Haapkylä, *Suomalaisen Teatterin Historia*, iii, 85.

65 *Sanomia Turusta*, 52, 5 May 1881, 2.
66 Interestingly, in an extended review of the Wilhelm Bolin's (a Swedish-speaking Finn) reworking of Hagberg's Shakespeare translations (published a month after the *RJ* premiere in June 1881), C. G. Estlander comments that while it is appropriate that these lines be included 'if she is to remain Shakespeare's world famous Nurse', they cannot be translated 'verbatim'. Estlander thinks it would be inappropriate to perform these lines in the theatre unless altered, but that 'none is better than that of Bolin' (215). Translation of the Swedish by Bo Pettersson.
67 *Suomalainen Wirallinen Lehtik*, 53, 5 May 1881.
68 *Uusi Suometar*, 107, 11 May 1881.
69 *Valvoja*, 11, 12 June 1881, 259.
70 *Valvoja*, 11, 12 June 1881, 259.
71 *Valvoja*, 11, 12 June 1881, 260.
72 Qtd. in Heikkilä, *Ida Ahlberg*, 133.
73 Qtd. in Heikkilä, *Ida Ahlberg*, 133. See also Suutela, *Impyet*, 96–7.
74 Suutela, *Impyet*, 97.
75 This description perhaps needs to be taken with a grain of salt, as Aalberg had taken over as leading lady from Raa, and it's possible that both she and Wikström were jealous of her success.
76 A one-act comedy by Aleksis Kivi first performed in 1869 (Paavolainen, *Nuori Bergbom*, 388).
77 Qtd. in Paavolainen, *Arkadian Arki*, 377. These laurel wreaths, of which Aalberg received many during her career, sometimes contained envelopes of money or jewels from her admirers and could be a significant source of income (Suutela, *Impyet*, 85–6).
78 Paavolainen, *Arkadian Arki*, 377.
79 Suutela, *Impyet*, 83.
80 Suutela, *Impyet*, 94–9. Suutela notes that the actor eye contact and physical closeness are different in these photographs than in earlier ones taken for the opera, and she wonders whether this might indicate a turn towards ensemble acting (96).
81 See Paavolainen's chapter in this volume. Also, as a newly married Baroness, Aalberg needed to negotiate any future acting roles with her husband.
82 *Valvoja*, 8, 15 April 1881, 193.
83 For Aalberg's refusal of the contract, see Paavolainen's chapter in this volume.

84 Aho, 'Ensimmäinen suomalainen Shakespearen', 539.
85 Aho, 'Ensimmäinen suomalainen Shakespearen', 540–1.
86 Aho, 'Ensimmäinen suomalainen Shakespearen', 541.
87 Aho, 'Ensimmäinen suomalainen Shakespearen', 542.
88 Qtd. in Suutela, *Impyet*, 63.
89 Aho, 'Ihanteiden'.
90 Suutela, 'Orleans', 185, n. 23. A shorter version of this speech is quoted in Wilmer, 'German', 33, from which I adapt part of this translation.
91 Suutela, 'Orleans', 177.
92 See Valenius, *Undressing the Maid*, for an excellent analysis of constructions of the Finnish Maid.
93 Wilkinson discusses similar issues in the work of the Swedish author Anne Charlotte Leffler; see Wilkinson, 'Anne Charlotte Leffler's Shakespeare'.

Works cited

Aaltonen, Sirkku, 'Shakespeare suomalaisessa kulttuurissa', in Pirkko Lilius and Henna Makkonen-Craig, eds, *Nerontuotteita maailmankirjallisuudesta – Välähdyksiä suomennosten historiaan.* Helsingin yliopiston käännöstieteellisiä julkaisuja 4 (Helsinki, 2003), 99–125.

Aho, Juhani, 'Ensimmäinen suomalainen Shakespearen ensi-ilta Suomessa', in Israel Gollancz, ed., *A Book of Homage to Shakespeare* (Oxford, 1916), 538–42.

Aho, Laura-Elina, 'Ihanteiden ilmiloihtija – Nuori Ida Aalberg suomalaisuuden personifikaationa', unpublished MS.

Aho, Laura-Elina, 'Motherless Girls and the Orphan Myth in the Making of Nation: The Gendered Representation of a Nation in the Repertoire of the Finnish Theatre Company, 1872–76', *Nineteenth Century Theatre and Film*, 47/2 (2020), 179–208.

Aspelin-Haapkylä, Eliel, *Suomalaisen Teatterin Historia*, ii, iii and iv (Helsinki, 1907, 1909, 1910).

Blom, Ida, Karen Hagemann, and Catherine Hall, eds, *Gendered Nations: Nationalism and Gender Order in the Long Nineteenth Century* (Oxford, 2000).

Bourdieu, Pierre, 'The Forms of Capital', in J. Richardson, ed., *Handbook of Theory and Research for the Sociology of Education* (New York, 1986), 241–58.

Cajander, Paavo, trans. *Romeo ja Julia, William Shakespearen Draamat*, 3rd edn (Porvoo, 1919).
Digital archives, National Library of Finland, https://digi.kansalliskirjasto.fi/
Estlander, C. J., 'Shakespeare och hans bearbetare', *Finsk Tidskrift* 3 (1 September 1880): 206–19.
Heikkilä, Ritva, *Ida Aalberg: Näyttelijä jumalan armosta* (Helsinki, 1998).
Howard, Tony, *Women as Hamlet: Performance and Interpretation in Theatre, Film and Fiction* (Cambridge, 2007).
Keinänen, Nely, 'The Role of *Hamlet* in Finnish Nation-Building, 1879–84', in Márta Minier and Lily Kahn, eds, *Hamlet Translations: Prisms of Cultural Encounters Across the Globe*, vol. 16 (Cambridge, 2022), 81–100.
Keinänen, Nely, and Per Sivefors, 'Introduction', in Nely Keinänen and Per Sivefors, eds, *Disseminating Shakespeare in the Nordic Countries* (London, 2022), 1–30.
Koskimies, Rafael, *Suomen Kansallisteatteri 1902/1917* (Helsinki, 1953).
Lanier, Douglas, 'Recent Shakespeare Adaptation and the Mutations of Cultural Capital', *Shakespeare Studies*, 38 (2010), 104–113.
Lanier, Douglas, 'Shakespearean Rhizomatics: Adaptation, Ethics, Value' in Alexa Huang and Elizabeth Rivlin, eds, *Shakespeare and the Ethics of Appropriation* (New York, 2014), 21–40.
Lindskog Whiteley, Cecilia, 'Cold Maids and Dead Men: Gender in Translation and Transition in *Hamlet*', in Nely Keinänen and Per Sivefors, eds, *Disseminating Shakespeare in the Nordic Countries* (London, 2022), 89–115.
Niemi, Juhani, *Paavo Cajander: Suomentajan ja Runoilijan Muotokuva* (Helsinki, 2007).
Paavolainen, Pentti, *Nuori Bergbom: Kaarlo Bergbomin elämä ja työ*, i: *1843–1872* (Helsinki, 2014).
Paavolainen, Pentti, *Arkadian Arki: Kaarlo Bergbomin elämä ja työ*, ii: *1872–1887* (Helsinki, 2016).
Paavolainen, Pentti, 'Bergbom and Shakespeare – Erään Kaanonin Synty', *Synteesi*, 1–2 (2016), 22–46.
Paavolainen, Pentti, *Kriisit ja Kaipuu: Kaarlo Bergbomin elämä ja työ*, iii: *1888–1906* (Helsinki, 2018).
Räsänen, Ilmari, *Ida Aalberg* (Porvoo, 1925).
Suutela, Hanna, 'Orleansin neitsyt – Kansallinen protagonisti', in Helka Mäkinen, ed., *Lihasta Sanaksi: Tutkimuksia Suomalaisesta Teatterista* (Helsinki, 1997), 169–89.
Suutela, Hanna, 'An Instrument for Changing Nationalist Strategies: The Finnish Theatre Company, 1872–1883', in Helka Mäkinen, S.

E. Wilmer and W. B. Worthen, eds, *Theatre, History, and National Identities* (Helsinki, 2001), 71–93.

Suutela, Hanna, *Impyet: Näyttelijättäret Suomalaisen Teatterin Palveluksessa* (Helsinki, 2005).

Valenius, Johanna, *Undressing the Maid: Gender, Sexuality and the Body in the Construction of the Finnish Nation* (Helsinki, 2004).

Wilkinson, Lynn R. 'Anne Charlotte Leffler's Shakespeare: The Perils of Stardom and Everyday Life', in Nely Keinänen and Per Sivefors, eds, *Disseminating Shakespeare in the Nordic Countries* (London, 2022), 247–67.

Wilmer, S. E., 'German Romanticism and Its Influence on Finnish and Irish Theatre', in Helka Mäkinen, S. E. Wilmer and W. B. Worthen, eds, *Theatre, History, and National Identities* (Helsinki, 2001), 15–69.

3

Kaarlo Bergbom and the Finnish-language Shakespeare tradition

The Finnish national revival, German Romanticism, theatrical resources and personal wishes

Pentti Paavolainen

This chapter is based on a conference presentation given at the Shakespeare and Scandinavia conference (Kingston-upon-Thames, 8–11 October 2015). An earlier version of this chapter was published in Finnish as 'Bergbom ja Shakespeare – Erään Kaanonin Synty', *Synteesi* [Journal of the Finnish Semiotic Society], 1–2 (2016): 22–46. Grateful acknowledgement is made to Eero Tarasti and the journal for permission to make this revised version available in an English translation by Kimmo Absetz and Nely Keinänen. The author has published in Finnish a three-part extensive biography of Bergbom (Part I *Nuori Bergbom*, Part II *Arkadian arki* and Part III *Kriisit ja kaipuu*), and most of the general remarks on Bergbom are based on that work. See also Keinänen, ed., *Shakespeare Suomessa*.

Theatre director Kaarlo Bergbom (1843–1906) staged the first Finnish-language premieres of fourteen of William Shakespeare's plays over a little more than two decades (1881–1902) at the *Suomalainen Teatteri*, Finnish Theatre (FT).[1] He worked closely with the Finnish poet Paavo Cajander (1846–1913), who translated the plays in an order mutually agreed upon with the theatre. This chapter will analyse the complex and shifting forces shaping the emergence of Finnish-language Shakespeare: political struggles against the Russian Empire; cultural and linguistic struggles vis-à-vis Swedish; the clear, if waning, influence of German Romanticism; the limits placed by the theatre itself, in terms of resources and personnel; and towards the end of the period in question, the personal wishes of its director.

The geographical area known today as Finland was an autonomous Grand Duchy of the Russian Empire from 1809 to 1917, but in terms of legislation, academic and family ties still a kind of 'Eastern Sweden' due to its long history of Swedish rule. German nationalistic ideals came via the university, which since 1830 had been located in Helsinki, and there was further contact with German culture via the Baltic region and the cities of St Petersburg and Vyborg. The national awakening came not from below but from above, as the Fennoman movement was spearheaded by the Swedish-speaking educated class of which Bergbom was a member. In the 1880s, the Fennomans were still loyal to the tsar, as in 1863, Tsar Alexander II decreed that Finnish could be used in administrative business. Encouraging the educated classes to favour Finnish was in the tsar's interest as this would allow the Grand Duchy to better align culturally with the capital city of St Petersburg, which was geographically closer, and also to distance itself from Sweden. Beginning in the 1890s, however, the tsar's efforts to unify and strengthen the Russian Empire led to the 'Russification period' in Finland, which turned opinion against him and towards independence, at which point the strong ties with Sweden were very helpful.

The emergence of the Shakespeare tradition in Finland is in some ways similar to that in Norway, particularly in the wish to acquire cultural prestige for the vernacular language.[2] In the 1870s Bergbom and Cajander adhered to the programme that Finnish-language literature and arts could best be promoted by making the European tradition available in Finnish. The alternative would have been to make do with original Finnish literature only, written by less-educated people lower down the social order. The hope was that esteem for Finnish-language literature and drama would increase if it could be shown that key works of world literature (German, French, Spanish, English) could be translated into the vernacular. In addition to other classic plays, Shakespeare was added to the programme given his prominence for the Romantics.

Theatre became a powerful organizing force for the national movement. The cultural elite wished to establish a permanent domestic theatre, first in Swedish and later in Finnish (for centuries prior the administrative and cultural language had been Swedish, despite Finnish being the main language of the population).[3] Three of the largest Finnish towns (Turku/Åbo, Helsinki/Helsingfors, Viipuri/Viborg/Vyborg) had built suitable theatre buildings in the 1830s–1860s, which were available for rent. Beginning in the 1830s, efforts to develop Finnish language and literature were rooted in German Romanticism, which meant that Berlin emerged as the capital of ideas, soon in opposition to Stockholm, the latter important for producing professional actors for the Swedish-speaking stage and later realistic plays. Bergbom's ambition was gradually to provide the actors of the FT with challenges and opportunities which at the same time would help realize the long-term Fennoman agenda of raising the cultural and educational standards of the Finnish-speaking common people. That Bergbom largely succeeded in this goal can be seen in how quickly after his death the plays of Shakespeare and Schiller spread to the new theatres that were being founded in different towns in Finland.

In this chapter, I provide an extended case study of the complex processes through which Finnish-language Shakespeare emerged during the last decades of the nineteenth century. As Douglas Lanier has argued, 'we cannot take full analytic account of a work or its politics without being attentive to the particular historical "Shakespeare" of the time'.[4] In order to better analyse the 'proliferating network of relations' that constituted 'Shakespeare' for Bergbom, I first examine the Shakespeare traditions that Bergbom learned as a young man, especially those of German Romanticism, and then those he himself created and left behind. As elsewhere in the Nordic countries, many of the first Shakespeare plays to be translated and performed were the tragic plays providing star vehicles for actors. To the extent possible, I map the political uses of Shakespeare for the Fennoman movement. Once the cultural imperative to perform Shakespeare's most important plays (i.e. the major tragedies) in Finnish had been accomplished, towards the end of his career Bergbom turned to plays that held the deepest personal significance for him.

In addition to political and cultural influences, Bergbom also needed to consider the ambitions of his leading actors as well as the box office, allowing us to analyse Shakespeare as a capitalist product in late nineteenth-century Finland. While in general Shakespeare was held in high esteem, nevertheless a taste for his plays needed to be developed in the audience, which was expanding from the cultural elite to the middle and lower classes flowing into the capital city. Bergbom's theatre also had to compete with the Swedish Theatre of Helsinki (founded in 1860) and its Shakespeare offerings (though here I limit myself to only a few comments about this rivalry as space allows).[5] In a relatively short time, Bergbom was able to develop surprisingly robust Shakespeare traditions, and I conclude by discussing the persistence of this first canonization of 'Bergbom's Shakespeare' in Finland.

Shakespeare and the young Bergbom

Bergbom's knowledge of Shakespeare came through Swedish and German sources. Karl Johan (later Kaarlo) Bergbom grew up in a cultured family of a high civil servant whose pastimes included literature, theatre and music. His mother tongue was Swedish, and he first learned German and then French. It is known that he attended his first opera performance at the age of six, and undoubtedly was no older when he saw his first theatre performances.[6] He was exceptionally well-read, and in the 1850s became familiar with Shakespeare's works by reading Swedish translations by C. A. Hagberg. German translations by the Schlegel brothers and Ludwig Tieck formed another textual base for Bergbom's knowledge of Shakespeare.

Bergbom's political ideals were likely shaped by events of his youth. His mother died of cancer when he was ten, and the same year English navy cannons pounded Finland's coastal towns and the fortress of Viapori (Sveaborg) in Helsinki. During the Crimean War (1854–1855), the newly orphaned sons were sent to the countryside for safety. We do not know what sentiments towards England these experiences left on Bergbom and his generation. Nevertheless, in the 1860s the English parliamentarian system of government served as an ideal among all the liberal-minded university students of countries under authoritarian rule.

Although he remained a monarchist, politically Bergbom supported moderate liberalism and constitutional democracy. The ideology that became the most important to him was nationalism, with the idea that nations are formed inclusively, transgressing class boundaries, ideas he treated in his early plays,[7] including a Swedish-language verse drama *Pombal och jesuiterna* [Pombal and the Jesuits] which celebrates nationalism as a moderate, democratic political force.[8] Bergbom's friend and his elder sister implored him to switch to writing his literary works in Finnish instead of Swedish, as a part of the Fennoman goal of raising the status of the Finnish language. Bergbom attempted this, but his efforts did not pay off.[9]

In the spring of 1868, Bergbom completed his dissertation *Det historiska dramat i Tyskland* [German Historical Drama], where he first gave shape to his thoughts about the nature and quality of Shakespeare's works. First, he believed that an essential prerequisite for drama was the presumption of free will, which he thought was specifically found in Protestant Europe:

> [P]rotestantism leaves a lot of leeway for evil, since it so heavily emphasizes the corruption of human nature. English playwrights like to depict how passions demonically drive human actions. A Catholic will drive away evil temptations by making the sign of the cross, but a Protestant cannot do that as he knows that he carries the worst temptation of sin in his own heart; the heroes of Calderon cast themselves on the hands of mercy and allow outside forces to fight for them when guilt presses them down, but Shakespeare's heroes must wage their battles between heaven and hell in their own chests.[10]

As his source for interpreting Shakespeare, Bergbom mainly used Hermann Ulrici's *Ueber Shakespeare's dramatische Kunst* (1839) [*Shakespeare's Dramatic Art*, 1876], which was influential in

German circles and provided background to Elizabethan theatre and analysis of the plays. Following the Romantic tradition, Bergbom emphasizes powerful personalities and their actions:

> Historical heroes do not need to legitimize themselves through any religious or political ideals, as is the case with Spanish and French playwrights, or as bearers of general historical ideas, as the poets of our century love to do. Rather, their highest justification is that they exist in the first place. Only a free, strong and energetic personality is so entitled – the masses are treated with contemptuous irony.[11]

Bergbom interprets Shakespeare's characters as being typically aristocratic, masters of themselves and others, adroitly using their mental superiority over other characters:

> Shakespeare's predilection for these aristocratic, masterful characters who, with an arrogant sense of humour, play games with conventional morals meant for more limited and narrow souls, like Percy, Faulconbridge, Henry V; or those demonical characters such as Richard III or Cleopatra etc., whose boundless corruption is only equalled by their boundless willpower.[12]

The topic of Bergbom's doctoral dissertation, perhaps better described as a roughly 100-page essay-like contemplation, was German drama, so he bypassed Shakespeare's history plays and only considered as such the three Roman plays, *Coriolanus*, *Julius Caesar* and *Antony and Cleopatra*, in which 'purified, supreme mastery of form' in a historical play reached its 'highest possible poetic perfection' [sin högsta möjlighet av poetisk fulländning].[13]

Bergbom's professor Fredrik Cygnaeus (1807–1881) had concluded already in 1853 that writers of historical drama should be faithful to what we know about a given historical person while at the same time capturing their essence in a poetically workable form. According to Bergbom's dissertation, the author of a historical drama should not try to advance an agenda, creating characters whose opinions they agree or disagree with. Rather, it is more important for the plays to be as historically accurate as possible and every character allowed equally to defend their point of view. It must be said, however, that in his own play *Pombal och jesuiterna* Bergbom was partial towards some characters, as it was and is not so uncommon for authors to present their ideas through their characters in a morally selective way.

Bergbom as a critic of Shakespeare performance

A review by Bergbom on a Shakespeare performance provides a glimpse into both his theatrical aesthetics and his politics. In July 1865, accompanied by the Finnish author Aleksis Kivi, Bergbom saw a production of *Othello* performed by the private Swedish Theatre company of Georg Dahlqvist.[14] In *Helsingfors Tidningar* he praises the choice of play but criticizes the cuts (*Bühnenfassung*) used by Dahlqvist, though at the time theatres commonly used abbreviated versions:

> The form in which Othello was performed yesterday was a stage adaptation based on Hagberg's translation, and was therefore characterized – like all of the Skakespeare [*sic*] interpretations of this excellent translator – by a powerful poetic style and faithfulness to the original. The adaptation, however, cannot be said to have been done with similar reverence. That they had cut the role of the clown might be appropriate since Shakespeare's 'clowns' are rather unenjoyable to present day audiences. It is harder to explain, however, why the entire role of Bianca had been cut, seeing as how important it is in shedding light on the character of Cassio; and it is even more of a flaw that entire scenes have been cut which carry the plot.[15]

Bergbom's view that jesters' lines and even roles could be cut for 'present-day audiences' nicely summarizes the way Shakespeare was received in those days: jesters, comic figures such as gravediggers and other clown characters are better cut lest they slowdown plot developments or interfere with the audience's deep empathy towards the suffering of the protagonist or victim. Schiller does not include comical scenes or scenes from a contrasting point of view. Bergbom was a product of his times, representing both in this and in his future theatre an aesthetic of goodness, beauty and harmony, which could even be considered as representative of European Biedermeier or the early Victorian cultural heritage. The Fennomans were particularly loyal to the emperor who supported the rise of this new Finnish elite.[16]

A few years earlier in his tragedy *Kullervo* (1860/4), Aleksis Kivi had utilized Shakespearian contrast by mirroring the main plot with a comic subplot. Bergbom, by contrast, never wanted anything uncouth, overly confused or ambiguous onstage. He also loathed the cynical or ironic view of humans embraced by some dramaturgs. Bergbom followed these same principles later when he cut Kivi's verbose plays for productions at the FT.[17]

Bergbom's thoughts on an actor's work, specifically delivery, can be gleaned from the way he continues his review of *Othello*: even in the wildest eruptions the actor must retain control and integrity of expression. Sudden outbursts of great emotion were often admired as signs of the virtuosity of a Romantic star actor, but for Bergbom, unrestrained yelling only represented strained and exaggerated histrionic virtuosity. Neither should the depiction of pain be too excessive or 'naturalistic'. Bergbom believed the actor should construct a holistic and poetic human work of art, as in this analytical description:

> Without disparaging his declamation, the brilliant artist mostly, and quite correctly, emphasized faithful and well clarified portrayal of the role. A brave, loyal soldier; a straightforward, fearless man; a tender lover; and alongside all this a hot-blooded African with the serenity of a lion but the rage of a tiger – in brief, all the nuances of the character of Othello melted together into a single person in Mr. Dahlqvist's Othello. In addition to the brilliant rendering of these most characteristic features of the role, what we most admire in Mr. Dahlqvist's acting is the artistic sensibility and harmony he develops in the violent eruptions of Othello's rage; there is not a trace of that virtuosity of yelling and shouting often cultivated even by great actors who follow the example of Ira Aldridge.[18]

Bergbom also praises Dahlqvist's troupe for its ensemble acting, which since the 1850s had increasingly been seen as something to be valued. At the very least this meant the different actors needed to be performing the same play, and so that their actions came in response to a fellow actor's speech and action. The degree to which this was achieved was in direct proportion to the time spent in rehearsal: 'Most worthy of praise was the ensemble acting. No-one wished to shine at the expense of others. Everything was noble and even and attested to the greatest care having been taken at rehearsals.'[19]

During his three-decade career as director, Bergbom had the opportunity to fulfil, within certain boundaries, the ideals of his youth – at least in principle. However, a certain tension arose since Bergbom also had affinities to German Romanticism and its more exaggerated way of acting, though it was gradually going out of fashion. For example, he sent his promising young actress, Ida Aalberg, to be trained by an old German actress at the end of the 1870s.[20] These German influences could also be seen in the traditions being established by the FT, sometimes characterized by empty pathos and grandiosity. These came to be considered a more 'Finnish' form of expression than the more restrained Nordic style followed at the Swedish Theatre in Helsinki and its native Swedish actors who had been trained in Stockholm.

As a director, Bergbom did not always manage to achieve a balance between Romanticism's inner fire and Nordic-controlled external expression. The biggest problem was the lack of consistent theatre training in Helsinki during Bergbom's lifetime, but also the lack of discipline and cultural erudition of his star actors. Elsewhere in Europe as well, it was commonplace for the arrogance of the best actors – often having just risen to stardom – to easily run into conflicts with the rest of the ensemble, with the director's and even with the author's aims. Throughout Bergbom's career, there was tension between star actors and the ambition of the director for more even ensemble acting.

On the road to becoming a director

Producing Finnish-language Shakespeare at the FT was a long process due to the complete lack of a professional Finnish-speaking theatrical tradition. Towards the end of the 1860s, Kaarlo Bergbom was especially interested in opera as he and some of his friends believed Finnish-language theatre could be first developed through an opera unit connected to the Swedish-speaking Nya Teatern.[21] They thought that singing the roles in Finnish would be easier for performers drawn from the educated Swedish-speaking class, whose Finnish skills were not yet adequate for expression in fully spoken roles. A key early theatrical performance was in May 1869 of Aleksis Kivi's one-act play on a biblical theme *Lea*, the fictive daughter of Zacchaeus, performed in Finnish by Charlotte

Raa, a Swedish professional actress who did not know Finnish but managed to memorize her lines.

In 1871, Bergbom travelled to Berlin, where over a period of six months he saw performances, both theatre and opera, read widely and was apparently also writing an opera libretto. In the spring of 1872, after much heated debate in the press, the *Suomalainen Teatteri* (FT) was founded. The first actors came from a small partly bilingual group of theatre apprentices led by A. Westermarck, which had occasionally performed in Finnish in the provinces. Oskari Wilho (Gröneqvist) now began to lead this still small theatre company, directing most of the productions in Finnish. The actors had so little acting experience, and indeed general education, that performing Shakespeare was out of the question for a long time,[22] not to mention that at the time the only existing Finnish translation of a Shakespeare play was Kaarlo Slöör's *Macbeth* (1864).[23]

By contrast, the majority of the actors in Helsinki's Nya Teatern were professionals from Sweden, and there was nothing embarrassing about the Shakespeare offerings of this well-established professional theatre performing in Swedish and adhering to the more restrained Nordic tradition of expression.[24] Already the following year, in the fall of 1873, alongside the Finnish Spoken Theatre section a Singing section, that is, the Finnish Opera, was founded, with Bergbom directing its productions. By the time he took up his first Shakespeare play, *Romeo and Juliet* (1881), Bergbom had directed an astonishing twenty-seven operas, often to high acclaim.[25] For such a small organization, however, it became financially untenable to maintain such a large-scale opera division, which had to compete with Swedish opera performances in the still rather small city of Helsinki.

While performing Shakespeare was always a goal, programming needed to be gradually developed to enable the actors to develop their skills. The most important domestic work in this regard was J. J. Wecksell's *Daniel Hjort* (1862) which already in its time was recognized as an adaptation of *Hamlet*. Daniel, a student in service to the aristocracy in the castle of Turku (Åbo slott), hears a secret about his father's identity and is tasked by his mother to exact revenge 'on behalf of the people'. Translated into Finnish in 1877, Wecksell's fine play was to assume a significant position for decades as a Shakespearian drama depicting domestic history. Other plays leading up to Shakespeare included Victor Hugo's melodramas (*Marie*

Tudor, 1873; *Angelo*, 1878), which provided a vehicle for visits by Charlotte Raa, who after her second marriage took the name Hedvig Winterhjelm. Key plays of Friedrich Schiller were also included: *Kabale und Liebe* (1874), *Die Räuber* (1878) and *Maria Stuart* (1880). The demands of these plays helped the performers develop their acting skills, an important preparation for Shakespeare. Other classics were Sheridan's *The School for Scandal* (1879) and Molière's *The Miser* (1879). These two plays were presented partly because Oskari Wilho (prev. Gröneqvist) wished to act their lead roles.[26]

The FT begins to perform Shakespeare

The following table lists Finnish-language premieres of Shakespeare's plays at the Finnish Theatre in Bergbom's time (1872–1905), along with years of significant revivals and total number of performances by the end of Bergbom's era.

Year	Play
1881	*Romeo and Juliet* (1886, 1904), 38
1882	*The Merchant of Venice* (1892, 1902), 32
1883	*The Taming of the Shrew* (1890, 1897, 1902), 21
1884	*Hamlet* (1886, 1890, 1901), 34
1886	*King Lear* (1889, 1897, 1902), 27
1887	*Macbeth* (1894), 13
1889	*Othello*, 5
1889	*Julius Caesar* (1904), 16
1891	*A Midsummer Night's Dream* (1904), 14
1896	*The Winter's Tale* (1899), 11
1896	*Antony and Cleopatra*, 9
1897	*Richard III*, 6
1901	*Viola (Twelfth Night)*, 14
1902	*The Tempest*, 12

The selection of plays produced at the FT often paralleled those in the Swedish Theatre just a few blocks away[27] but was also determined in part in Bergbom's consultation with the translator Paavo Cajander and by the availability of actors. The first play selected was *Romeo and Juliet*, premiering in 1881. As discussed in Chapter 2, this play was mainly selected as a star vehicle for Ida Aalberg, but there might have been political considerations as well. A possible precedent is Bergbom's selection in 1870 of Verdi's *Il trovatore* as the first opera to be performed in Finnish. It depicts a feud between Conte di Luna and Manrico who turn out to be brothers but are only recognized in death. Similarly, the young lovers of *Romeo and Juliet*, whose deaths are the price of reconciliation of the 'two noble households', might be seen as representing feuds between Swedish- and Finnish-speaking Finns or indeed between the aristocracy and common people, with the message being that such feuds endanger national unity and should be settled amicably. Since the cultural and political significance of this production is discussed in Chapter 2, I will only add here that commentators lauded the staging, the exceptionally carefully crafted sets and medieval costumes, which were said to be the best the theatre had ever done.[28] Bergbom had hired Severin Falkman, a renowned historical painter, who also did the costume design.

The choice of the next Shakespeare production was dictated by the health and wishes of the actor and vice-director of the theatre, Oskari Wilho (Gröneqvist) (1840–1883). For two decades, he had dreamed of playing Shylock.[29] The role of a despised Jew (like the gypsies in *Preciosa* and *Il trovatore*) represented an oppressed people, a theme which resonated with Fennoman political concerns. Thus, the series continued with *Merchant of Venice*. Since the play required an elaborate set to portray Venice, it was decided to rehearse and perform it first in Vyborg (now in Russia), which had a suitable and newly renovated theatre building.

Vyborg was an interesting choice in this regard, as it was one of the cities in the Russian Empire where Jewish retirees of the Russian Army had often chosen to settle. The political position of Jews in Finland was complex, as there were constant changes in rights and restrictions, sometimes Russian, other times Finnish regulations prevailing. In 1882 the first proposal for granting Finnish citizenship to Jews was heard in the Diet, though I have been unable to determine whether there is a connection between the FT production and the proposed law. The proposal led to the founding of Jewish congregations in the largest cities, but equal rights were guaranteed only after independence in 1917.

Benjamin Leino's 'Jew' was considered 'a poignant, effective and carefully studied whole'.[30] Playing in Helsinki on 13 April 1883, the production was again praised for its sets, overall poetic atmosphere and especially Leino's Shylock for his 'sure, courageous and highly interesting character'.[31] In May 1883, the FT production of the *Merchant* was even performed as part of the Helsinki festivities celebrating to the coronation of Alexander III in Moscow.[32]

The performance was not free of the anti-semitic imagery of its time, but Bergbom had no reason to turn Shylock into a stage monster. One reviewer noted the ways his 'Jewish character' came out in his angry movements, apparently including rocking back and forth, for the reviewer mentions that this was done more effectively in an earlier performance though now it was more restrained. Shylock's conflicting emotions were most visible in the scene with Tubal, where he switched between the 'infinite despair shaped by greed' and his 'joy of revenge'. Especially impressive was his sharpening of the knife in the courtroom.[33] Over the next seven years, *Merchant of Venice* was performed 1–7 times per year and was revived in 1892, 1898 and 1902, for a total of 32 performances, so the play seems to have resonated with Fennoman concerns and audiences.

From a present-day perspective it is perhaps not surprising that the next play to be performed in Finnish was a comedy, *The Taming of the Shrew*, in a translation by the poet Kaarlo Kramsu. The play was performed in Vyborg on 19 October 1883 and in Helsinki on 23 April 1884. Kaarola Avellan played Kate with 'perfect understanding of the role' and Bruno Böök's Petrucchio was also said to be 'nimble and energetic and light, simply captivating'.[34] Nothing is mentioned in the reviews about how the battle of the sexes was received, but as such it was a mirror and certainly recognizable.[35] A new face in the company was Adolf Lindfors, who as the servant Gremio displayed his comedic skills. The choice of play may have had something to do with the woman question, as this was a decade when women's rights were increasingly being debated. It was clear, however, that audiences did not much care for the play: it was considered neither funny nor profound and lacked Shakespeare's customary depth. With such material, the actors did not reach anything out of the ordinary.[36] *Shrew* was performed only one season, 1883/4; including repeat performances, the total number of performances for *Shrew* during Bergbom's tenure was only twenty-one. Perhaps the play differed too much in spirit from the newer Nordic drama which the FT was also putting on despite in general wishing to differentiate itself from the Stockholm theatre scene. With modern Scandinavian drama, emphasizing strong women asserting their independence, Bergbom could secure his reputation in the eyes of the new generation.

The play everyone was waiting for was *Hamlet*, the classic test of a theatre company and necessary for fulfilling Fennomanian goals. In 1879 it was the first play published in Cajander's complete works translation project into Finnish.[37] A problem for the theatre, however, was that it did not have an actor capable of playing the lead role. Axel Ahlberg, who had played Romeo and was making progress in learning to interpret intellectual dramatic texts, remained hopelessly melodramatic and physically stiff in his delivery. A newcomer, Niilo Sala, was sufficiently intellectual, sensitive and frail enough to perform the role in the Romantic *Hamlet* tradition, where some of Hamlet's passivity and reticence could be interpreted as ambivalent sexuality. In a heteronormative world, this made it easier to understand his indecision, inability to take action and the abandonment of Ophelia. It was possible for audiences to understand Hamlet in this framework as both Ahlberg and Sala, who alternated in the role, were known for their homosexuality.[38] In addition, after her great success as Juliet, Ida Aalberg was available for the role of Ophelia. Without her, it would not have made sense to perform *Hamlet*, as she continued to be the theatre's biggest box-office draw.

This time, the idea was to preview the play in Turku (31 October 1884) and bring it the following spring to the capital (4 March 1885). Although the performance of *Hamlet* was considered a significant step in the series of inaugural Finnish-language Shakespeare productions, it was not met with equally clear praise. Exceptions to this were Ida Aalberg's Ophelia and Benjamin Leino's Claudius. 'Aalberg's Ophelia leaves a critic speechless.' The Queen, performed by Aurora Aspegrén, was neither a 'character role' nor a 'person of stature', implying that her characterization was overly folksy. Neither Ahlberg nor Sala were fully successful as Hamlet. Ahlberg built his performance too much on fluctuating and capricious moods, effects picked up 'from this role or that', and in the end was essentially just displaying his own theatrical chops. There was too much energy in his depiction; a Hamlet like that would have killed the King before the end of the third act.[39] Sala, for his part, had studied his role well but was more subdued and lyrical, and his gestures displayed no manliness or ability to take action of any kind. Sala thus remained a moonlight prince, devoid of any 'manly intentions', which would mean that the King could hardly be seen as being in any kind of mortal danger.[40]

Ida Aalberg's Ophelia also reveals ways that Shakespeare (among others) created opportunities for actors to circulate in the Nordic countries and more broadly in Europe. In the spring of 1885, Aalberg was enthusiastic and burning with ambition. In five years, she had risen to be the star of the company, and all major productions were now planned according to her whims. A few Finnish-born opera singers had already succeeded in transitioning to the Nordic and even more far-reaching 'singer markets' and now Aalberg wished to do what so many dramatic actors in central Europe were doing: touring in different cities performing starring roles – thus destroying any attempt at a coherent ensemble performance. After playing the role of the avenging abandoned 'gipsy girlfriend' Homsantuu in Minna Canth's *Työmiehen vaimo* (1885) [The Worker's Wife], Margareta in Goethe's *Faust* as well as her triumph as Ophelia, Ida Aalberg travelled to Stockholm and offered to perform at the Swedish Royal Theatre opposite the Italian actor Ernesto Rossi, who was on tour. Rossi liked her, and she was allowed to perform Ophelia in Finnish on 11 May 1885. Aalberg also made sure that the news reached the Finnish press, which for about ten days rehashed quotations from Stockholm newspapers.[41]

The era of the great tragedies: *King Lear*, *Macbeth*, *Othello* and *Julius Caesar*

In keeping with Fennoman cultural and political goals, the order in which Paavo Cajander translated Shakespeare's plays into Finnish progressed from the most famous and important to the less frequently performed. In the early 1880s, Cajander translated what were considered the great tragedies: *King Lear* (1883), *Othello* and *Julius Caesar* (1884), and *Macbeth* (1885). It was natural that these would be the next tragedies at the FT, although the theatre was still performing on the small stage of the old wooden Arkadia Theatre. The timing was dependent on how they fit in the rest of the programme and on the availability of suitable actors. Around these years the question of when Ida Aalberg would schedule herself to appear in Finland was becoming a major headache for Bergbom: Aalberg had refused a permanent contract and only wished to perform in Arkadia as a guest artist which also drove up her fees. Plays with one big male lead, such as *Lear* or *Macbeth*, were clear-cut: they could be undertaken with Benjamin Leino. Moreover, Leino's acting style had 'calmed down' to a degree so that in these great roles he now had a certain serenity of expression.

The female roles in *Lear* could be performed with local talent: Kaarola Avellan as Goneril, Inez Borg as Regan and Katri Rautio, a new face performing ingénue roles, as Cordelia. Adolf Lindfors, who had specialized in comic roles, was Lear's Fool, and Niilo Sala was Edgar. *King Lear* premiered on 12 March 1886 to mainly favourable reviews. The general sentiment was that this fifth Shakespeare production in every way met the cultural expectations that were placed on the theatre.[42] In these early years each new Finnish-language Shakespeare was eagerly tallied in the media, so readers would know how many had already been translated and performed. Interestingly in terms of the political situation, Axel Ahlberg's Edmund was criticized for being only the lover of Goneril and Regan without expressing enough of his fierce ambition to rule.[43]

Given the importance of female stars in drawing in audiences, it is worth considering the influence on programming of the FT's two most important female actors, Ida Aalberg, the ambitious daughter of a railway keeper, and Kaarola Avellan, the daughter of a civil servant. The contrasts between them tell much about the intersections of gender, class and status on the nineteenth-century Finnish stage. Aalberg had always been the bigger star, the most important box-office draw. Whenever she returned to Finland, it was possible to bring back both *Romeo and Juliet* and *Hamlet*. *Merchant* could be performed without having to consider Aalberg's schedule, since it rested on Benjamin Leino and Kaarola Avellan (Portia). In the early years, Aalberg was primarily known for playing ingénue roles, including Juliet and Ophelia, and later Desdemona in the 1889 production of *Othello*, still during the early part of Bergbom's tenure. As mentioned earlier, Aalberg resigned from the FT in 1885 and afterwards all of her contracts had to be individually negotiated. So Bergbom was forced to start putting together his programme, including Shakespeare, in such a way that the theatre would not be dependent on her.[44] The following winter season, Aalberg wished to conquer Copenhagen, but her Danish turned out to be wholly inadequate, and she came back home to lick her wounds. Her next attempts at European conquest targeted Paris, St Petersburg and Berlin.

The situation continued like this throughout the 1890s: whenever Aalberg came back to Finland or happened to be having financial difficulties, Bergbom would arrange for her to reprise her old roles and yet again bring in box-office revenue. Aalberg's strengths were good mastery of Finnish; great fieriness, intensity and dramatic effect; the ability to take nervous energy all the way to the breaking point; the richness with which she analysed her roles; and her nuanced acting alternating between opposite emotions. The other female lead actor, Kaarola Avellan, was from an upper-class family and had joined the theatre after training in Stockholm. Avellan soon came to see that she could not match the energy of Aalberg. As the daughter of a civil servant, Avellan could not compete with Aalberg's openly erotic and emotional acting, which was sometimes even considered vulgar.[45] Avellan was acclaimed for her strong performances of modern, strong-willed female roles in modern Scandinavian plays, but also got to play 'evil women' in classical plays. Among Shakespeare's female roles, Avellan played Portia in *MV*, Kate in *TS*, Goneril in *KL* and Lady Macbeth (premiere 11 March 1887). Avellan's performances were partly greeted more critically as her Finnish was not impeccable, but she was seen as an intelligent actress whose aristocratic delivery was sure and considered. Her sleepwalking scene as Lady Macbeth was especially praised, though some critics saw the performance as superficial. From the perspective of Bergbom's Shakespeare canon, it was a pity that Avellan resigned from the Finnish Theatre in the spring of 1887 and never returned. Lady Macbeth was to be her last big role. After that, she worked as a private acting teacher influencing generations to come.

Of the great tragedies, the next was *Othello* (5 April 1889), which was timed so that Ida Aalberg would be available for rehearsals. As in the previous productions, Bergbom spent time cutting and shaping the play before the beginning of rehearsals, sometimes using various *Bühnenfassungs*, ready-made practical stage adaptations from Germany. But he often cut plays himself, allowing him to get to know the play better and to adjust it for his actors. In *Othello*, the most interesting role was Iago, played by Benjamin Leino, while Othello was played by Axel Ahlberg and Desdemona by Ida Aalberg. Kaarle Halme, who was to become one of the leading figures of the next generation of important actors, played Cassio.

The acting styles were starting to change away from the Romantic and towards the modern. In 1889, especially Swedish-speaking critics criticized the FT's leading performances for being overly grandiose and declamatory in style. Critics hoped for even a few 'real' moments, such as when Axel Ahlberg's Othello began to exhibit jealousy. For Ida Aalberg's Desdemona, moments of 'naïve devotion' or 'suffering endurance' were felt to be less crafted compared to her performances of heroines with more willpower. According to one critic, Benjamin Leino's Iago was not sufficiently demonical, the actor did not 'milk his role to the fullest'. Leino was even described as smiling too much, being too mischievous in his feigned candidness, wholly lacking in dark undertones. Some critics also wondered whether the play had stood the test of time, Iago's motives being one of the great mysteries of the play.[46] There were only five performances of *Othello*, and it was never revived during the Bergbom era.

The last of the great tragedies that Bergbom took on was *Julius Caesar*, first performed in 1889 and revived in 1904, the latter during a particularly provocative period in Finnish history where the murder of an autocrat onstage might very well awaken political passions. Bergbom represented the generation then known as Old Fennomans who supported concessional politics, while the Young Fennomans were obstinately constitutional and demanded active resistance to protect old privileges. In 1889, Alexander III, one of the 'good tsars' for the Finns, was still on the throne. For the Old Fennomans, there was no reason to view the conspirators favourably. It was only eight years since the murder of his father Alexander II, the most liberal of the Grand Dukes of Finland. His murderers were perceived as radicals whose deeds only increased reactionary nationalism in Russia. The revival of *Julius Caesar*, by contrast, took place at a very different time, towards the end of the first period of Russification (1899–1904), during the reign of

Nicholas II who instigated strong measures to reduce the privileges of Finnish autonomy in order to unify the Russian Empire into a single cultural, political and economic system. This strengthened anti-Russian opinion in Finland and only five months later the Russian governor general N. L. Bobrikov, the executor of the Russification policy, was assassinated by a Finnish activist who first shot Bobrikov and then himself.

Strikingly, reviews and later assessments of the production focused not on the ethics of political violence, an issue which was increasingly dividing the country, but rather on aesthetic issues connected to staging, how well Bergbom managed crowd scenes (whether there were enough extras). In scholarship there is discussion on whether Bergbom had been influenced by performances he saw in 1889 by the theatre troupe of the Duke of Sachsen-Meiningen: some say that Bergbom's development as a theatre director took place long before he saw the Meiningen troupe, while others contend that he matured as a director only after he had seen the German company.[47] It is worth exploring these discussions for what they reveal about attitudes towards German influence both at the time and beyond.

In the summer of 1889 in Stockholm, the famous Sachsen-Meiningen troupe performed Schiller's *The Maid of Orleans*, the *Wallenstein* trilogy and *William Tell* plus Shakespeare's *The Winter's Tale* and *Merchant of Venice*, as well as their phenomenally successful *Julius Caesar*, which had premiered in 1874. On his prior European travels, Bergbom had not managed to cross paths with this famous theatre company. To understand the presumed influence or 'learning' of these two weeks in Stockholm, we must put them in the context of Bergbom's life. The man watching the Meiningen troupe that summer was a theatre professional with over twenty years of directing experience with well over 200 productions of plays and operas under his belt. He had also seen at least as many theatre performances in central Europe, where he had travelled almost every year since 1871. Moreover, Bergbom was already known for his meticulous crowd scenes, as, for example, in 1882 the second scene in Zacharias Topelius's drama *Regina von Emmeritz*, which depicts the conquest of a castle yard by Gustaf II Adolf's army,[48] and various choir scenes in opera performances. From the outset, the same was true for the Shakespeare series: reviewers regularly ended with praise for his sets and the mise en scène. Of the Meiningen performances, Bergbom shared the general rather critical sentiment that everything was 'impeccable', but the overall impression was somewhat mundane and tedious due to the lack of charismatic actors in key roles.

Before his visit to Stockholm, Bergbom had already decided to do *Julius Caesar* on his tiny stage at the Arkadia Theatre, premiering on 13 November 1889. Bergbom was assisted by Niilo Sala, his confidant and friend who also played Brutus, the close friend and hesitant murderer. The Meiningen production had been immortalized in an engraved newspaper illustration depicting the Forum scene, where Mark Antony is giving his speech next to the bier holding Caesar's body. On 13 November 1889 *Uusi Suometar* published a lengthy puff piece which knowledgeably described the events of the play and especially the tragic role of Brutus. It also anticipated an impressive crowd scene where the people would be yelling to see Caesar's will.[49]

Two days later, however, a critic writing for *Uusi Suometar* complained that there were not enough extras in the Forum scene:

> The effectiveness of the latter could, in our opinion, very easily be elevated further. Why can't all extras be brought onstage to fill it completely? As it is, our stage is very modest for these purposes, and if it is only half full how small does that render the population of Rome? We should also hear more of the male bass voices and less of the women's sopranos.[50]

A longer review was published in the Fennoman party newspaper *Uusi Suometar* on 19 November 1889, again focusing on issues of staging:

> Costumes, decorations and other sets are most satisfactory. One cannot say that anything is overly detailed, but everything needed to keep the illusion intact has been taken into account. . . . For instance, in the Forum scene, the main effect must be achieved with the crowd of men. . . . and now it has been achieved. . . . The extras have been well trained, and now at the third performance their movements were also somewhat freer. But we do think the stage makeup makes them look too young, especially the Roman Senators, as only a few seem to

have reached a more mature age. – It's doubtful whether *Julius Caesar* has ever been presented with such care, with the possible exception of the Meiningen troupe for whom staging is almost their chief objective. We have already mentioned the immense dramatic effect of the Forum scene, and we were also impressed with the gently poetic colouring of the scenes at Brutus' home and in his tent at Sardis. In the former, the thunderstorm and flashing sky very poignantly and powerfully accompany the formation and conclusion of the pact.[51]

Acting roles were in the familiar hands of Bergbom's Shakespeare group, but nevertheless some critical observations about their performance were recorded, such as Niilo Sala's Brutus ('delicately dreamy presentation') and Kaarle Halme's Cassius ('anxiously unclear diction'). Leino's Caesar was 'unfocused' and Ahlberg's Mark Antony continues to 'swallow or abbreviate the last syllables'.[52] The revival of *Julius Caesar* in 1903/4 was led by Jalmari Finne, then the assistant director. It took place in the new theatre building, home of the present Finnish National Theatre, which had been inaugurated in 1902. On its much larger stage, huge crowds of extras were able to shout louder than fifteen years earlier.

Shakespeare – A reservoir of consolation and lyricism

It is tempting to identify ideological or stylistic changes in Bergbom's Shakespeare productions during his mature period. In the 1880s it had been culturally and politically important to prove that the FT was capable of performing Shakespeare's works in Finnish to a respectable standard. Performances of the great tragedies and two comedies served as proof of this. During his last decade as director of the FT, Bergbom seems to have changed his approach to choosing repertoire. Staging new plays in Finnish had always been a primary obligation. As to foreign plays, he mostly followed the developments in Berlin with a close eye and picked important new plays from there. Actors likewise voiced their own wishes, for example, classic roles they wished to play. Among Shakespeare's plays, these included *Antony and Cleopatra* and *Richard III*, neither of which Bergbom had any obvious personal relationship to. *Coriolanus*, which Cajander had translated in 1887, had still not yet been performed, probably due to its many politically charged scenes between the social classes and conflicts between the rule of people and the rule of patricians. Never an easy topic during the long nineteenth century.[53]

A kind of turning point came in 1892, an annus horribilis in Bergbom's personal life, which included the tragic illness and suicide of Niilo Sala.[54] Afterwards, we see in Bergbom's repertoire a certain wistfulness, nostalgia and increasingly a need to stage plays expressing consolation – both for the audience and for himself. Since his status in the theatre was that of the Sun King, *le théâtre, c'est moi*, these choices may be interpreted from the perspective of Bergbom as director-auteur.

Paavo Cajander's next Shakespeare translations were a lyrical comedy, *A Midsummer Night's Dream* (1891) and two of the late romances, *The Tempest* (1892) and *The Winter's Tale* (1894). Approaching his fiftieth birthday, Bergbom focused on them. Bergbom had already long been planning to stage *A Midsummer Night's Dream*. Props had been acquired years earlier, most notably a donkey's head from Berlin.[55] Felix Mendelssohn's music would be used in the performance, played by Robert Kajanus's orchestra. The premiere was on 20 November 1891. A review captures a sense of the production: 'A magical Southern forest was created in the Arkadia Theatre, full of dancing fairies and impish pranks humorously entwined by the Bard with the romantic adventures of four love-struck youths in a land of illusion.'[56] The critic of *Nya Pressen* (21 November 1891) likewise gave the performance full marks. Of particular note was the music, which was seen as Romantically linking a series of 'unbelievable events happening in an ancient land'. Mendelssohn's music is indeed lively and youthful, the prelude being composed when the composer was just seventeen. The entire company was needed for the roles, and they enjoyed performing them. As Puck, Olga Finne was 'charmingly ethereal', and Adolf Lindfors (Bottom) displayed such 'nuanced and rich comic skills that he kept the audience in stitches of laughter'.[57] Cajander's Finnish translation was also praised, with the reviewer commenting that his poetry did not fall short compared to Swedish and German translations. *Uusi Suometar* describes the staging and also comments on how the play feels special, almost like a new genre:

> The eye derives great enjoyment from the magnificent scenes and the dances of the fairies, complete with moonlight and flowers. No expense or effort has been spared to heighten their effect, and it was done most successfully. Let us only mention those twenty or so fairies who looked so small one had to wonder whether they could already roll their r's, but nevertheless played their roles with astonishing conviction. . . . When one has been torn asunder by heart-breaking tragedies, weighed down by realistic plays depicting life as it is, or laughed until one's sides ache at a comedy, it is charming for a change to glide into this mythical world, refreshing if not realistic, giving free rein to fantasy. We cannot imagine a more pleasant experience for a child than being taken to see *A Midsummer Night's Dream*.[58]

There were only six performances at the time, but Bergbom would revive *Dream* in the spring of 1904 for eight more. He was always very fond of children and loved to play with his nieces and nephews, so now he could use available children as fairies. This was of course not exceptional in the nineteenth-century tradition of *Dream* productions.

There would be another five years before the premiere of a tenth play. Shakespeare continued to be performed in the 1890s but mainly in revivals of earlier productions as doing Shakespeare at the theatre always involved a lot of effort and necessitated time for rehearsals. Moreover, at the beginning of the 1890s the theatre was concentrating on presenting new Finnish drama on historical topics, for example medieval Finnish history. Beginning in 1893, large-scale plays based on themes from the Finnish national epic *Kalevala* were also produced annually. Both types tended to be long verse plays and included demanding crowd scenes. As large-scale spectacles, they occupied one slot in the repertoire. Thus, the turn towards Finnish history and folk poetry slowed down the pace of Shakespeare premieres.[59]

A final reason for this slowdown had to do with Bergbom's ideas about the suitability of Shakespeare's history plays for Finnish stages. He had already come to this conclusion in 1883 when he saw *Krieg der Rosen* in Vienna, the first German adaptation of the War of the Roses. In fact Bergbom chose not to produce works depicting kings who had ruled over Sweden and Finland, such as early work by Johan Börjesson, which had not been translated into Finnish. It was not until August Strindberg's history plays that the Swedish kings – familiar to Finnish audiences – found their way onstage, where they later thrived for several decades in such works as *Gustav Vasa*, *Erik XIV* or *Karl XII*. Another factor limiting the uptake of new Shakespeare plays in the early 1890s were a series of crises at the theatre,[60] and then later Bergbom's wish to direct some of the great works by his other favourite author, Friedrich Schiller, including *William Tell* (1892), *Don Carlos* (1897) and a repeat of *The Maid of Orleans* (1896). As far as the effort they called for from the theatre, these were comparable to performing Shakespeare.

While *A Midsummer Night's Dream* includes theatrical romp and fairy pranks, it is also a play about nature and the senses, hope, dreams and reconciliation, themes important to Bergbom during these years. After turning fifty in 1893, his repertoire started to feature plays which can be interpreted as reflecting his personal sentiments. Bergbom had lost his mother when he was only ten, and as a teenager he wrote a Romantic verse play where a mother rises from her sickbed and comes to meet her son.[61] Bergbom was also very close to his nieces and nephews as he had no children of his own. With the death of Niilo Sala in the summer of 1892, he lost his companion of ten years. At the theatre's twenty-fifth anniversary gala in 1897, contrary to his normal habit, he gave a speech reminiscing about the many friends of the theatre and his early actors who had passed away – often all too early.

In this frame of mind, the play that spoke to him was *The Winter's Tale*, which in the late nineteenth century was being performed a great deal in Europe and which premiered at the FT in 1896. This melodramatic, even sentimental, story about a man who in a fit of jealousy and stubborn rage destroys his marriage, leaves his wife and loses his children, but then through wondrous coincidences gets back almost all that he has lost is a veritable metaphor of life with its foundlings, forgiveness and a couple reunited. The statue coming to life has parallels with Bergbom's youthful play about a mother rising from her sickbed. In other regards as well, *The Winter's Tale* is a play about the passage of time and the growth of a new generation, and like many other plays from Shakespeare's last period, it ends in reconciliation and forgiveness.

Casting *The Winter's Tale* was not difficult. As Hermione – who delivers a magnificent speech defending herself against the slander against her – Bergbom could cast Katri Rautio who had risen in the ranks to become his most trusted actress.[62] After the first performance, Finnish-language newspapers mainly praised the production (one with mild reservations), again thanking the theatre (and its director) for having once more produced such a praiseworthy performance. It is interesting to read the critic's detailed description of the stage design:

> The stage presentation was done with particular care, and as far as we can understand, very successfully. A great deal of attention had been paid to costumes, and a large number of new ones had been acquired. Especially the women's clothes were beautiful with their stylish trimmings. The space had also been skilfully decorated in the Greek style, complete with columns and statues. The dance of the swords at the beginning was amusing and the sheering festival in the fourth act was sweet. The last act was especially beautiful, where Leontes and his companions are shown a statue of Hermione who turns out to be the living Hermione herself.[63]

Actors celebrating with and through Shakespeare – Cleopatra and Richard

Towards the end of the 1890s, some choices of repertoire were linked to key actors. Ida Aalberg continued to be a draw. Through marriage she had become the Baroness Aalberg-Uexküll-Gyllenband and getting the Baroness onstage required negotiations with her high-ranked husband even when Ida herself was eager to perform: she needed the theatre, and it needed her. Unusually for the FT, the spring of 1896 saw a second new Shakespeare production. Barely six weeks after *The Winter's Tale*, *Antony and Cleopatra* opened on 11 March 1896 – a larger spectacle than anything that had been attempted before. The choice of play was based on Bergbom having his A-cast available: Ida Aalberg-Uexküll-Gyllenband as

Cleopatra, Axel Ahlberg as Antony, Adolf Lindfors as Octavius and Benjamin Leino as Enobarbus. Reviewers especially praised the actors, foremost among them Aalberg's masterful and nuanced depiction of the seductive Cleopatra. It seems that the eroticism of the character was nevertheless subdued enough that a woman who now bore the title of Baroness could perform it:

> What we saw was more like Marguérite Gautier [Lady of the Camellias] in Egyptian clothes, but not Shakspere's [sic] Cleopatra. To put it bluntly, Mrs. Aalberg eliminated the brutal yet calculating lust, the full-blooded, intensely sensual streak in this strange female figure, with her yellow-brown skin and delicate, snake-like litheness of movement. All that remained was a loving woman with a checkered past, ennobled by a great passion for a man she looks up to.[64]

Judging by the reviews, these were the right roles for both Axel Ahlberg and especially Ida Aalberg and her 'grand style':[65]

> But it is in the third act where the acting is at its best. There are so many feelings fluctuating there, all depicted with wondrous skill and effectiveness. Unspeakable longing turns into the wildest fury when Cleopatra learns that Antony has married. In a rage, Cleopatra knocks the messenger to the ground, hits, kicks him. This is followed by depression, which then suddenly changes again, finally building up to wild joy and triumph when she learns her rival is no match for her.[66]

As many times before, the visual appearance of the production was especially commended:

> Without question, both in terms of stage design and acting, *Antony and Cleopatra* is one of the best productions done by the Finnish Theatre ... Mrs Aalberg's costumes, especially in the first act, were incredibly beautiful. The staging was the work of a master, to mention for example only the mausoleum, the fleet at the Battle of Actium with ships rocking on the waves, the battlefield etc. etc. In a word, the play was in all respects performed in a stately fashion, to the credit of the theatre and its brilliant director.[67]

Another reviewer notes many of the same details.[68] But in one instance, however, Bergbom's sense of style failed. When Cleopatra asks to hear music, for some reason the harpist had been given a banal ballroom piece to play: Moszkowski's 'Serenade'. It is possible that this might have been Ida's idea. The effect had been comical, but the piece could still be changed, advised one critic.[69] Aspelin-Haapkylä compares the premiere production of *Antony and Cleopatra* to other noteworthy successful productions at the FT, including *Faust*, Zacharias Topelius's *Regina von Emmeritz* and Gustaf von Numers's *Elinan surma* [The Death of Elina]. Sets for *Antony and Cleopatra* had been obtained from Grabow's scene painting studio in Stockholm.[70] Reviewers indicated there were around a hundred extras.[71] The glamour around the Baroness's visit lasted to the end of March 1896.

Adolf Lindfors had matured into an important comic asset for the FT, though his humour was often crude or 'beyond good taste' at least according to the Bergbom siblings. On the other hand, this guaranteed him the support and favour of what was known as the 'second balcony audience'. The next Shakespeare premiere, *Richard III* (1 December 1897), was clearly driven by Lindfors's ambition to get to play the famous villain. For Bergbom's audience it would be their first Shakespeare's history play and considering the intellectual and moral atmosphere of the Fennomans in the 1890s, an interesting choice: Bergbom had never favoured vile or evil main characters, and Richard's ruthless ambition might have been off-putting. However, in Lindfors's interpretation, Richard's deceit and manipulation were visible from the start. Indeed, sometimes his asides to the audience would break the theatrical illusion and were very exaggerated. According to one review, in the last act, Lindfors's acting was 'flailing and noisy', even comical.[72] Katri Rautio, by contrast, 'yet again convincingly hit the mark', this time as Lady Anne.[73] *Richard III* was thus not an unqualified success and was only performed six times. Writing to his sister Emilie, Bergbom admits he shared her and the critic's view:

> We do not need to wonder why *Richard* did not match the success of *Lear*. Partly it is because *Lear* is a more mature masterpiece, partly because it was better suited to our resources, and partly because *Lear* was more appropriate at the time. We

can be satisfied Lindfors managed as well as he did. Regarding the last act, I found him just as disagreeable as you did.⁷⁴

The remark on Lear as 'more appropriate at the time' is very interesting although we cannot know for sure what Bergbom had in mind. But at the same time, the letter does suggest that politics might have affected his choices of repertory.

Kaarlo Bergbom and Jalmari Finne – Two comedies and the art of directing

When we compare the Shakespeare programming at the FT to what was performed during these years at the Swedish-speaking Svenska Teatern, we notice that the ever popular and much performed *Twelfth Night* premiered at the latter theatre in 1884, but Bergbom does not seem to have even considered including it in his repertoire, as seen also in the fact that Cajander did not translate the play into Finnish until 1899. Bergbom's reasons for avoiding the play may well have been a mix of personal and political. A Romantic person like himself may have not liked a play which mocks love and the rhetoric of love. In addition, in keeping with Fennoman ideals he may not have liked the foul language the lower status characters use when speaking about their noble masters and ladies, nor the fact that the alcohol-consuming upper-class characters plot with the servants. The Malvolio subplot is long and indeed forms the main attraction of the play next to the rather mechanical upper-class love plots. It seems that especially Emilie and perhaps not even Kaarlo found the play 'at all funny'.

The relative lack of comedies among Bergbom's repertoire choices perhaps also says something about how Shakespeare's humour was seen in relation to the moral values and world view of the late nineteenth-century upper classes identifying with the Fennoman movement. The Fennomans were loyal to local authorities and especially the emperor. They were bent on upholding the social and political status quo, which required reverence towards one's superiors as long as the language was right (i.e. Finnish) and upheld Christian values. *Twelfth Night* is a painful kick in the shin to this kind of high-minded world view as it mocks the upper class, whose self-understanding in real life still idealized the Finnish-speaking lower classes and who were expected to show some gratitude to their leaders. The play also contains what we think of today as queer elements. At a fundamental level the question was whether it was desirable to put something onstage that could be morally unacceptable.

So it was not Bergbom but his new assistant director Jalmari Finne who directed *Twelfth Night* (called *Viola* in Finnish) in 1901. Bergbom made the casting decisions, but the rehearsal period was scheduled to take place in late December 1900 to early January 1901 when he himself would travel to Berlin, leaving Finne to oversee rehearsals. Afterwards when thinking about problems in the performance, Finne thought he had paid too much attention to the Duke's love plot at the expense of the comic subplot and thought it would have been better to approach the play through its comedy.[75] The audience, however, liked the play and it was performed fourteen times.

FT's 1901 production of *Twelfth Night* was also important for what it reveals about new ideas about scenery and the importance of European influences. Finne had seen performances in Europe and England, and was eager to try out practical and innovative staging solutions. He simplified stage sets: every detail did not need to be separately visible, and he used open set changes. One reviewer commented on these changes, which elsewhere he indicates were imported from England:

> With a bit of ingenuity, the theatre makes do with just three set changes. The performers enter from the same spot where they left, just from the other side perhaps, and the viewer can imagine the various places they might have been to and what they might have done. This was fully in accordance with the spirit of the piece and deserves our highest praise.[76]

In Finne's writing we also get a humorous sense of how important the Shakespeare traditions were to the FT's actors:

> I had to rehearse Shakespeare's *Twelfth Night* which had not been performed in a Finnish theatre before, so I could thankfully avoid having to listen to friendly comments by the actors on how things had always been done. Although usually well-intended,

this kind of advice is an impediment to independent work. These comments never target deeper issues, what is essential, but always something external.[77]

Bergbom had cast a second-class actor as Malvolio, which makes one wonder whether he realized the character's centrality and comic potential. Either Bergbom was unfamiliar with the play's performance tradition or he wished to use casting to direct the audience's focus and thus advance his own values and preferences. Similarly, in *The Winter's Tale* Paulina was given to an actress too young for the role. After 1906, *Twelfth Night* spread to different theatres around the country, and with its upstairs-downstairs theme became one of the most frequently performed Shakespeare comedies in Finland, at least up to the 1960s. For the 1908 performance of *Trettondagsafton* at Svenska Teatern, Jean Sibelius composed songs for Feste in Swedish verse.

Cajander had finished his translation of *The Tempest* ten years before it was produced. Maybe Kaarlo himself viewed it so clearly as a 'farewell play' that he did not want to take it up until he knew or felt that someday his own time would end. A natural time for staging *The Tempest* came in the spring of 1902 when the company moved to the new Finnish National Theatre, a stone structure in the National Romantic style built next to the main railway station. Jalmari Finne served as assistant director, once again showing his innovative stagecraft. Of the production, Finne recalls both Bergbom's mastery of the play as well as the performance of Axel Ahlberg as Prospero:

> That spring Bergbom created the greatest of his Shakespeare productions when he did *The Tempest*. Bergbom had explained the fundamental ideas behind Shakespeare's plays to me before, but never as brilliantly as now. He needed someone to explain his thoughts to, and in me he had an enthusiastic listener. I have since read many analyses of *The Tempest*, but no European scholar has ever been able to analyse everything so clearly and brilliantly. For once, Axel Ahlberg approached a part with humility, and learned it long before opening night. His strong intellectual bent came to the fore. The role gave him no opportunities to depict vigorous youth, something he usually desperately clung to, but instead the interpretation had to be intellectual. In some

places, especially towards the end where Prospero is making a reckoning with his life and prepares to leave the world of spirits he has ruled over, Ahlberg was almost shatteringly effective in his masculine simplicity.[78]

Ahlberg was the only conceivable choice for Prospero, for whom it surely was a dream role even if it forced him to confront his actual age. The cast included Olga Leino (Ariel), Lilli Högdahl, the current jeune premier (Miranda), Oskari Salo, reliable but no longer quite so young (Ferdinand), Adolf Lindfors (Stephano), Aleksis Rautio (Trinculo) and Otto Närhi (Caliban).

In a puff piece on *The Tempest*, the Finnish poet Eino Leino was inspired to write about Shakespeare's silence and his last work. His spirited cultural and literary historical essay fills two full columns, ending with the question: What is Caliban? He was also captivated by Ariel's flying:

> Mrs. Olga Leino as Ariel was most successful, sufficiently otherworldly to be a spirit, and sufficiently worldly to be of flesh and bone. Especially when aided by the flying machine, she glided and swayed over the stage as freely as a fairy, while retaining her full artistic dignity even in the most head-spinning aerial jumps. It was a charming sight.[79]

Bergbom was afraid of an accident with the flying machine and would have been happier without it and other fancy electrical gadgets, as reported by the actress Elli Tompuri.[80]

The critic (and Bergbom's friend) Hjalmar Lenning joined the chorus of praise.[81] A review signed E. K. in *Uusi Suometar* (13 May 1902) articulated the general sentiment of the times that it is indeed necessary to cut some of the crudities of Shakespeare's times. Also cut was the shipwreck at the beginning, which was replaced by a mute scene on a stormy sea:

> [We saw] a wordless prologue, a shipwreck in a gale and a thunderstorm Prospero had brought up by his magic. Indeed, the prologue gave a very impressive and enticing opening atmosphere, and the audience's enthusiastic applause brought a tempest of clapping over the tempest.[82]

In his memoirs Finne characterized Otto Närhi (Caliban) as an actor who was 'worse than average if he needed to depict an ordinary person, but all the more marvellous if the character to be performed was outside of the realm of reality'. During rehearsals, Bergbom had had one of his uncontrolled fits of rage at Närhi. Finne managed to calm him down and promised to direct Närhi himself.[83] Since some critics complained that the performance was overly 'naturalistic', we may guess that perhaps the argument between Bergbom and Närhi had been over the intensity of his expression:

> Mr. Närhi performed the part of the misshapen Caliban, a monstrosity, with truly frightening naturalness which at times bordered on what's possible on stage. Maybe a little less would have sufficed to serve as a wild counterpoint to the play's tenderly poetic moments.[84]

In *Päivälehti*, Eino Leino called for a return to poetry, imagination and fantasy to the arts after a period of realism and interpreted Caliban through drives and instincts:

> The laurels this time rightfully go to Mr. Närhi as Caliban, who performed the role with all the fresh originality this talented actor possesses. His depiction of Caliban's animalistic drive towards Miranda in the scene where Prospero admonishes him for his failed rape attempt was masterful, as were the drunken scenes which he performed with wild fury.[85]

For music Bergbom used 'pieces by Sullivan and Taubert'. The English Arthur Sullivan had composed very popular stage music for *The Tempest* in 1861 and the German Wilhelm Taubert two operas on Shakespearean themes. Although we cannot be sure, it is likely that such an event would have been attended by Jean Sibelius and his family. But what we know for sure is that in 1925, Sibelius, who had composed several incidental music scores for theatre, accepted the invitation of the Royal Theatre in Copenhagen to compose music for *The Tempest*. *Stormen* is now considered one of his late masterpieces. And when *The Tempest* was revived in 1927 in Helsinki with his music, it was his daughter Ruth Snellman who played Ariel. Another person inspired by the production was

Wilho Ilmari Sundberg, a schoolboy for whom seeing Bergbom's *Tempest* defined his choice of career. Under the name Wilho Ilmari he became the most important Shakespeare director in Finland for the first half of the twentieth century.

On his trip to Italy in June 1903, Kaarlo Bergbom had a stroke in Genoa and fell gravely ill. That autumn while still abroad he turned sixty, not returning to Finland until early 1904. That spring, although his capacity for work had crucially weakened, he nevertheless wanted to revive *A Midsummer Night's Dream* for the new theatre building. So the fairy forest was reconstructed on the stage of the new theatre with the help of Finne and others. This was Bergbom's last Shakespeare in his new theatre building.

Bergbom and his sister Emilie ended their long tenure at the theatre in the spring of 1905, some thirty-three years after the theatre was founded. Emilie died the following autumn. *The Tempest* was to be Kaarlo's last Shakespeare production, but *A Midsummer Night's Dream* was his farewell to the theatre. Throughout his life, music was at least as important to Bergbom as theatre, and in the spring of 1904 he got to see the production again with Mendelssohn's music. Bergbom died in January 1906, two weeks after seeing his favourite play as a youth, Schiller's *Don Carlos*.

Concluding thoughts

As has become clear, the construction of a Finnish-language Shakespeare tradition at the Finnish Theatre (later Finnish National Theatre) depended on a wide range of factors, ranging from the cultural and political imperatives of the Fennomans to the influences of German Romanticism, the personnel and practical resources of a young theatre and the personal wishes of its director. It was made possible by the Finnish translations of Paavo Cajander, whose complete works project encompassed thirty-six Shakespeare plays (1879–1911). Cajander's Shakespeare translations were considered cultural milestones, as were their first performances at the Finnish Theatre. In the early years, each new production was eagerly added up, creating a running total of new Shakespeares, attesting to the cultural importance of performing Shakespeare. In the Swedish-language press as well, the FT was commended for its efforts to elevate Finnish culture and language. For the actors, Shakespeare provided an avenue for 'deepening their understanding of the arts', their ways of thinking about these demanding roles and learning the oral delivery needed to perform them. Sometimes a role took years to fully mature, or at least Axel Ahlberg was still playing Romeo at age fifty, an age which requires friendly spectators. Nearly every review remarked on the great care Bergbom showed in constructing the mise en scènes, which were seen as harmonious and beautiful.

In terms of his repertoire, at first Bergbom focused on the most well-known works of Shakespeare, but in later years, his choices became more personal, reflecting his own unique emotions. He was well-educated, very well-read, cultured and talented in literature, music and the visual arts. He was an intellectual with a keen eye with a bent towards sarcasm and irony. All of this meant he could be impatient and indeed intemperate when confronted with artistic efforts he considered half-hearted or less intellectual, and could break into uncontrollable fits of rage or other infantile behaviour. He was a deeply Romantic, emotional and idealistic person who believed in or consistently tried to maintain his belief in beauty and goodness. In keeping with the old school of theatre aesthetics, all gestures onstage had to be beautiful.[86]

In terms of genre, Bergbom mainly focused on Shakespeare's tragedies and lyrical comedies. Absent were the plays on English kings, as well as some of Shakespeare's middle comedies. Bergbom shied away from plays built around intelligent female characters whose wit, irony and sarcasm allow them to get their way with their lovers. Ever the Romantic, Bergbom seems not to have liked plays where the audience is asked to laugh at the pathos of Romantic love.

Bergbom also believed that 'the second balcony audience', consisting of lower-class workers, should not be incited or provoked in any way. Therefore, he avoided Shakespeare's more grotesque and burlesque elements, as these were considered off-putting in late nineteenth-century Europe. Shakespeare was simply not always 'suitable for present tastes'. Joking about death, making fun of the nobility and sexual punning were not part of the public image of Europe's cultured bourgeoisie of the time, nor did these fit in with upper-class Fennoman ideology. But Bergbom was not naïve and, as we have seen, always aware of the context of domestic policy in which the plays were taken up.

For decades after Bergbom, his Shakespeare performances at the Finnish Theatre were considered ideal models and his traditions were maintained, so in a very real sense 'Shakespeare' became 'Bergbom's Shakespeare' for Finnish-speaking audiences. But by the end of the Second World War, Cajander's translations started to be hard for audiences to understand, and new generations of theatre practitioners tried to free themselves of the pathos-filled grandeur and to look for more modern angles from which to approach the plays. A few later directors, such as Wilho Ilmari, Glory Leppänen and Jouko Paavola, dedicated themselves to Shakespeare, seizing any opportunity to direct a Shakespeare play.

But in Finland it was not really until the 1960s that the performance tradition rooted in central European Romanticism started to crumble – as it did elsewhere.[87] There were, of course, differences between the Nordic countries, but one milestone influential in all of them was Jan Kott's *Shakespeare Our Contemporary* (1961). In Finland the real turning point was Kalle Holmberg's direction of *Richard III* (1969, Helsinki City Theatre), which in one fell swoop made away with men in tights and cardboard sets and turned Shakespeare into 'our contemporary'.

Notes

1 In 1881–1902, these Shakespeare productions mainly took place at the Arkadia Theatre (1861–1908), located in central Helsinki. Designed by C. L. Engel, the wooden building originally served as the Esplanade Theatre (1827–1861) and was expanded and repaired many times. In 1902, the Finnish Theatre changed its name to the Finnish National Theatre and moved to its current location next to the Central Railway Station.

2 For discussion of the Norwegian context, see the chapters by Myklebost and Sandhaug in the present volume.

3 The cultured classes also knew French, but the use of English was for a long time limited to professions involving trade and marine traffic.

4 Lanier, 'Shakespearean Rhizomatics', 33.

5 On the rivalry of Swedish and Finnish opera, see Paavolainen, 'Two Operas'.

6 For information on Bergbom's early years, see Paavolainen, *Nuori Bergbom*. Prior to 1860, Helsinki had seen productions (in Swedish) of *Ham*, *Oth*, *RJ*, *Mac*, *KL*, *TS*, *MA* and *MV*.

7 In 1858, this Romantic teenager wrote *Ljuxalas ros* [The Rose of Ljuxala], inspired by historical plays by Johan Börjesson on the Vasa dynasty (Paavolainen, *Nuori Bergbom*, 92–5).

8 See Paavolainen, *Nuori Bergbom*, 190–5, 248–50, 268–71, 282–92, 685–92.

9 Jaakko Forsman, the brother of the Fennoman leader Yrjö Koskinen, together with Emilie Bergbom managed to change Bergbom's mind. Kaarlo published a few melodramatic Finnish-language short stories and a two-act play *Paola Moroni* (1870), an adaptation of the German historical drama *Pietra*. See Paavolainen, *Nuori Bergbom*, 267, 365, 436–45, 505, 506.

10 Bergbom, *Det historiska dramat*, 10.

11 Bergbom, *Det historiska dramat*, 11.

12 Bergbom, *Det historiska dramat*, 11.

13 Bergbom, *Det historiska dramat*, 12.

14 Paavolainen, *Nuori Bergbom*, 289–95.

15 *Helsingfors Tidningar*, 3 July 1865.

16 These remarks are condensed from my three-volume biography (Paavolainen, *Nuori Bergbom*; *Arkadian arki*; *Kriisit ja kaipuu*), which examines Bergbom's correspondence for information on his preferred and actual aesthetic choices.

17 See the SKS Aleksis Kivi *Critical Editions*, which include articles on the staging history of each play.

18 *Helsingfors Tidningar*, 3 July 1865. For Aldridge and *Othello*, see also Sivefors, 'A Blot'.

19 *Helsingfors Tidningar*, 3 July 1865.

20 See Keinänen's chapter in this volume.

21 The spelling and name of the theatre changed over time. From the season 1870/1 the name was modernized to Nya Teatern whereas from January 1887 it was called Svenska Teatern (Lüchou, *Svenska teatern*). The latter year was the first term in office of Harald Molander.

22 Though Charlotte Raa had performed as set pieces Ophelia's and Lady Macbeth's mad scenes in Finnish, the first complete Finnish-language professional performances in Finland were still in the future. See Keinänen's chapter in this volume.

23 Bergbom seems not to have noticed or paid attention to Lagervall's *Ruunulinna* (1834), for which see Nummi et al., 'The Poetics of Adaptation'.

24 Before the Nya Teatern's first building (1860–1863) was destroyed by fire, the only Shakespeare production was *MV* (1863). In the second stone theatre (1866–) there were productions of many of the central plays, including *TS* (1866), *RJ* (1867), *KL* (1867). *Ham* was performed in 1866, with Charlotte Raa as Ophelia. Charlotte and her husband Frithiof Raa played Desdemona and Iago in *Oth* (1868), and Beatrice and Benedict in *MA* (1869). During these years the couple were the main stars of the Helsinki theatre scene. Frithjof's final role before his death in 1872 was Oberon in *MND* (1871). The production was very successful, and it was the first time Mendelssohn's music was heard in Finland. The dance sequences were choreographed by Alina Frasa.

25 The list of operas Bergbom directed from 1873 to 1879 is impressive: *Lucia di Lammermoor, Norma, La sonnambula, Les Huguenots, La juive, Roméo et Juliette* (Gounod), *Robert le diable, Dinorah, Faust, Il Trovatore, Lucrezia Borgia, Ernani, La Traviata, Die Zauberflöte, Don Giovanni, Fidelio, Der Freischütz, Alessandro Stradella, Fra Diavolo, Le domino noir, Martha, Linda di Chamounix, Zar und Zimmermann, La Fille du Régiment, Il barbiere di Seviglia, Don Pasquale, Les noces de Jeannette.*

26 Other historical plays (in prose) before the first Shakespeare included B. Björnsson's *Maria Stuart in Scotland* (1880), A. E. Brachvogel's *Narcisse Rameau* (1875) and C. Birch-Pfeiffer's adaptation of Charlotte Brontë's *Jane Eyre* (1879).

27 All of these and others following remained in the repertoire for decades. With few exceptions the lists of plays are almost identical. New Shakespeare productions included *Mac* (1872) and *WT* (1873). After this the favourite plays were revived, but there were fewer new productions: *Cym* (1882), in an adaptation by Wilhelm Bolin, *TN* (1884, under the title *Viola/Trettondagsafton*) and *MW* (1891). The FT and the Swedish-language theatre (called, as previously noted, Nya Teatern from 1870 and Svenska Teatern from 1886) were competitors. In terms of theatre history, the Swedish side is especially interesting for the work done by its director Harald Molander, who challenged Bergbom and who later became a well-known director in Sweden. For Molander, see Per Ringby's extensive *Författarens dröm på scenen.*

28 As, for example, in *Hufvudstadsbladet*, 4 May 1881, and *Helsingfors Dagblad*, 4 May 1881; *Suomen Wirallinen Lehti*, 5 May 1881, said Ahlberg's best scene as Romeo was when he pulled out his dagger in Friar Lawrence's cell. Böök's Mercutio would only have needed to remember to speak and move in a more aristocratic

way (*Suomen Wirallinen Lehti*, 5 May 1881, and *Morgonbladet*, 14 May 1881).

29 Gröneqvist (1840–1883) had been an apprentice in a production of *Merchant* at Nya Teatern in 1863 and decided on a career in the theatre. Since there were no acting schools in Finland at the time, he travelled to Stockholm to study acting. Already in the 1860s he became enamoured of Shakespeare and decided to study English in the hopes of one day being able to translate Shakespeare's plays into Finnish ('since the Hagberg translations deviate from the original') and to act in them.

30 *Ilmarinen*, 7 December and 12 December 1882.

31 *Morgonbladet*, 14 April 1883. See also *Suomen Wirallinen Lehti*, 14 April 1883; *Uusi Suometar*, 17 April 1883; *Hufvudstadsbladet*, 24 April 1883; *Ilmarinen*, 3 November 1883; *Östra Finland*, 3 November 1883.

32 This information *passim* in Paavolainen, *Arkadian arki*; on the Jews in Finland, https://fi.wikipedia.org/wiki/Suomen_juutalaiset, accessed 23 May 2022.

33 *Uusi Suometar*, 17 April 1883.

34 *Ilmarinen*, 20 October 1883 and 25 October 1883 (correction).

35 Laughter and/or plotting against the male conservativity appears in many of the domestic plays which Bergbom was midwifing for the stage.

36 *Suomen Wirallinen Lehti*, 29 April 1884; *Uusi Suometar*, 30 April 1884 (explains some of the cuts).

37 For the cultural significance of this first translation, see Keinänen, 'The Role'.

38 The issue of homosexuality was not discussed in the press, however. At the FT there were much more queer constellations than has been previously thought, not least because Bergbom himself was homosexual. In Finland, homosexuality was not criminalized until 1894.

39 *Suomen Wirallinen Lehti*, 10 March 1885. The reviewer was also of the opinion that a prince would not crawl on the floor as Ahlberg did to see whether the Mousetrap play was having an effect on the king.

40 *Helsingfors Dagblad*, 23 March 1885; *Finland*, 6 and 7 March 1885; *Hufvudstadsbladet*, 8 March 1885; *Suomen Wirallinen Lehti*, 10 March 1885; *Finland*, 10 March 1885, said Sala's gesturing was 'weak'; *Finlands Allmänna Tidning*, 14 March 1885, analysed

Ahlberg's and Sala's performances in detail, and said of the latter that such a young person should never have been given the role. *Suomen Wirallinen Lehti*, 19 March 1885, also compares the two, with Sala coming in second.

41 Stockholm reviewers are referred to and cited: *Finland*, 13 May 1885; *Åbo Underrättelser*, 15 May 1885; *Suomen Wirallinen Lehti*, 15 May 1885; *Hufvudstadsbladet*, 16 May 1885 (mentions that the King [Oscar II of Sweden], Crown Prince [later Gustav V of Sweden], Crown Princess and Prince Oscar attended the second half of the performance); *Finland*, 16 May 1885; *Helsingfors Dagblad*, 16 May 1885; *Suomen Wirallinen Lehti*, 16 May 1885; *Uusi Suometar*, 16 May 1885; *Finland*, 17 May 1885; *Wiborgsbladet*, 19 May 1885; *Tampereen Sanomat*, 19 May 1885; and for about a week in smaller papers in both Finnish and Swedish. On her Norwegian visit, for example, *Uusi Suometar*, 30 May 1885, and other newspapers on the same day.

42 *Helsingfors Dagblad*, 13 March 1886; *Uusi Suometar*, 13 March 1886; *Finland*, 3 March 1886 and 21 March 1886; *Uusi Suometar*, 17 March 1886.

43 *Finland* 21.3.1886.

44 Although it was well known that in practice 'only Ida Aalberg will draw a crowd'.

45 See Keinänen's chapter in this volume.

46 *Hufvudstadsbladet*, 6 April, 1889; *Uusi Suometar*, 6 April 1889 and 13 April 1889 (a longer analysis); *Nya Pressen*, 6 April 1889.

47 This view is presented in Tiusanen, *Teatterimme hahmottuu*, 119–21, and has been repeated by several writers.

48 Aspelin describes the production in *Valvoja*, no. 3, 92, 1888, and repeats it in Aspelin-Haapkylä, *Suomalaisen teatterin historia*, iii, 291.

49 *Uusi Suometar*, 13 November 1889, declared: 'This is a very hard piece to perform . . . keeping in mind our small stage compared to the large Roman forum, where thousands hungry for food and freedom shout "the will, the will". The effectiveness of this scene depends on the crowd of men. We say this not to demand the impossible, only enough to create the proper illusion. The Finnish Theatre has never disappointed its audience when performing these great plays.' The classic technique is to divide the extras into groups where the leader provides the correct reactions which those standing nearby mimic at right moments.

50 *Uusi Suometar*, 15 November 1889. The reviewer also remarks: 'Then there's the word *säännös* ["provision"], which in our opinion is very

abstract and mild. Why don't they use the word *testamentti* ["will"], which would give a much better effect and be more intelligible? We bring this up because we think it would be a very easy way to improve things a lot.'

51 *Uusi Suometar*, 19 November 1889.

52 *Uusi Suometar*, 19 November 1889.

53 *Coriolanus* was first staged in 1912–1913 in the National Theatre, in a new political constellation between Finnish and Russian ambitions. Since that only in 1934 and 1970. The concept of the Long Nineteenth Century refers to the time from the French Revolution to the outbreak of the First World War (1789–1914).

54 Two other disappointments were a copyright and authorship feud with Gustaf von Numers; and Minna Canth's decision to write for Harald Molander in the Swedish Theatre as a protest against the conservative Old Fennomans.

55 Emilie Bergbom writes to her brother about it: 23 July 1891 (45:1:214), Kaarlo Bergbom archive, Literature Archive, SKS.

56 Aspelin-Haapkylä, *Suomalaisen teatterin historia*, iii, 416.

57 *Nya Pressen*, 21 November 1891. In his translation, for the name 'Bottom', Cajander chose *Pulma* [Problem], which is a bit misleading as it loses the reference to the buttocks. There would have been other possibilities, such as *Pohja* or *Perä*, which would have preserved the connotation and been perfectly reasonable as names (and indeed were chosen by later translators).

58 *Uusi Suometar*, 21 November 1891.

59 J. H. Erkko's *Aino* (1893) and *Kullervo* (1895), Zacharias Topelius's *Prinsessan av Cypern* (on the Kalevala character Lemminkäinen) (1896), Aleksi Kivi's *Kullervo* (1897), Eino Leino's *Sota valosta* (1901), J. H. Erkko's *Pohjan neiti* (1902) and Juhani Aho's *Panu* (1903).

60 See note 55 on the *annus horribilis* of 1892.

61 Paavolainen, *Nuori Bergbom*, 90–7.

62 Maiju Rängman played Paulina. According to a review, her personality was well suited to the role, but she was too young to wield the necessary power against Leontes or to believably manage Hermione's escape and hiding. *Uusi Suometar*, 28 January 1896.

63 *Uusi Suometar*, 28 January 1896.

64 *Nya Pressen*, 13 March 1896.

65 *Päivälehti*, 14 March 1896.

66 *Uusi Suometar*, 14 March 1896.

67 *Päivälehti*, 14 March 1896.
68 O. R[elander], *Uusi Suometar*, 14 March 1896. He writes: 'When we remember that the play has ten scenes, and in addition to the numerous actors onstage there are hundreds of extras, you understand how much care and genius is demanded from the director for everything to go smoothly, naturally. The production design was superb, and all departments succeeded very well. Here we will only highlight the royal palace in the first scene with its exquisite colonnade, the peninsula of Actium with its ships and masts in the sixth, and the mausoleum with its sphinx in the last act.'
69 *Nya Pressen*, 13 March 1896.
70 Aspelin-Haapkylä, *Suomalaisen teatterin historia*, iv, 66.
71 O. R[elander], *Uusi Suometar*, 14 March 1896.
72 'Over here, everything has been quiet and smooth. Richard was performed 6 times, but with only average success. Lindfors's extremely noisy, even comical manner in the last act ruined the good impression from the previous acts' (Emilie Bergbom to Kaarlo Bergbom, 20 December 1897, 45:1:238, Kaarlo Bergbom archive, Literature Archive, SKS).
73 R. R., *Uusi Suometar*, 3 December 1897 (analysis of the play) and 8 December 1897 (analysis of the actors).
74 Kaarlo Bergbom to Emilie Bergbom, 26–27 December 1897, 46:1:247, Emilie Bergbom archive, Literature Archive, SKS.
75 'What a colossal mistake! This play is organized to give joy. The Duke's love story is there mainly to hold the play together, and it's in fact Sir Toby and his gang who bring people into the theatre. I had the theatre's best resources for them: Lindfors, Rautio and Hemmo Kallio. They did their best, but I wasn't able to direct them in such a way as to bring out their best' (Finne, *Ihmeellinen seikkailu*, 98).
76 *Uusi Suometar*, 26 January 1901.
77 Finne, *Ihmeellinen seikkailu*, 97–8.
78 Finne, *Ihmeellinen seikkailu*, 115.
79 *Päivälehti*, 13 May 1902.
80 Tompuri, *Etu- taka- ja syrjähyppyjä*, 266.
81 *Hufvudstadsbladet*, 13 May 1902.
82 *Uusi Suometar*, 13 April 1902.
83 Finne, *Ihmeellinen seikkailu*, 116.
84 *Uusi Suometar*, 13 May 1901.

85 *Päivälehti*, 13 May 1901.
86 Ruth Snellman (*Tuokio sieltä*, 49–50) recalls how around 1910 the actress and drama teacher Katri Rautio was still insisting on the beauty of (balletic-like) movement.
87 My PhD thesis on social change and theatre in Finland shows that between 1959 and 1971 the most commonly played were *TS* (324), *TN* (300), *MW*, *MND* and *RJ*, each seeing more than 100 performances during that decade and 75 performances of *Ham*. The rest include: *MA*, *R3*, *Tem*, *AYL* and *Mac*. Even *TC* was produced, as were *Oth*, *Cor*, *JC* and *AW* (Paavolainen, *Teatteri ja suuri muutto*, 314–15).

Works cited

Aspelin-Haapkylä, Eliel, *Suomalaisen teatterin historia*, i: *Teatterin esihistoria ja perustaminen* (Helsinki, 1906).
Aspelin-Haapkylä, Eliel, *Suomalaisen teatterin historia*, ii: *Puhenäyttämön alkuvuodet ja Suomalainen ooppera, 1872–79* (Helsinki, 1907).
Aspelin-Haapkylä, Eliel, *Suomalaisen teatterin historia*, iii: *Nousuaika, 1879–93* (Helsinki, 1909).
Aspelin-Haapkylä, Eliel, *Suomalaisen teatterin historia*, iv: *Bergbomin loppukausi: Kansallisteatteri sekä Liitteitä ja nimiluettelo* (Helsinki, 1910).
Bergbom, Kaarlo, *Kaarlo Bergbomin kirjoitukset*, i: *Näytelmät ja kertomukset*, eds E. Aspelin-Haapkylä and P. Cajander (Helsinki, 1908).
Bergbom, Kaarlo, *Kaarlo Bergbomin kirjoitukset.*, ii: *Tutkimukset ja arvostelut*, eds E. Aspelin-Haapkylä and P. Cajander (Helsinki, 1909).
Bergbom, Karl, *Det historiska dramat i Tyskland* (Helsingfors, 1868).
Cygnaeus, Fredrik, 'Konung Erik XIV som dramatisk karaktär', in Fredrik Cygnaeus, *Samlade Arbeten*, iii, *Literatur-historiska och blandade arbeten* (1853; Helsingfors, 1882), 3–91.
Finne, Jalmari, *Ihmeellinen seikkailu: Ihmisiä, elämyksiä, mietteitä* (Jyväskylä, 1939).
Hirn, Sven, *Alati kiertueella: Teatterimme varhaisvaiheita vuoteen 1870* (Helsinki, 1998).
Ilmari, Wilho, *Teatterimiehen lokikirja*, ed. Aino Räty-Hämäläinen (Helsinki, 1971).
Keinänen, Nely, ed., *Shakespeare Suomessa* (Helsinki, 2010).
Keinänen, Nely, 'Suomalaisen Shakespeare-perinteen syntyvaiheista', in Nely Keinänen, ed., *Shakespeare Suomessa* (Helsinki, 2010), 15–35.

Keinänen, Nely, 'The Role of *Hamlet* in Finnish Nation-Building, 1879–84', in Márta Minier and Lily Kahn, eds, *Hamlet Translations: Prisms of Cultural Encounters Across the Globe* (Cambridge, 2021), 81–100.

Kott, Jan, *Shakespeare tänään*, trans. Salla Hirvinen (Helsinki, 1984).

Lanier, Douglas, 'Shakespearean Rhizomatics: Adaptation, Ethics, Value', in Alexa Huang and Elizabeth Rivlin, eds, *Shakespeare and the Ethics of Appropriation* (New York, 2014), 21–40.

Lüchou, Marianne, *Svenska Teatern i Helsingfors: Repertoar, styrelser och teaterchefer, konstnärlig personal 1860–1975* (Helsingfors, 1977).

Nummi, Jyrki, Eeva-Liisa Bastman, and Erika Laamanen, 'The Poetics of Adaptation and Politics of Domestication: *Macbeth* and J. F. Lagervall's *Ruunulinna*', in Nely Keinänen and Per Sivefors, eds, *Disseminating Shakespeare in the Nordic Countries: Shifting Centres and Peripheries in the Nineteenth Century* (London, 2022), 117–56.

Paavolainen, Pentti, *Teatteri ja suuri muutto: Ohjelmistot sosiaalisen murroksen osana 1959–1971*. Diss., University of Helsinki, Helsinki, 1992.

Paavolainen, Pentti, 'Two Operas or One – Or None. Crucial Moments in the Competition of Operatic Audiences in Helsinki in the 1870s', in Anne Sivuoja, Owe Ander, Ulla-Britta Broman-Kananen, and Jens Hesselager, eds, *Opera on the Move in the Nordic Countries during the Long 19th Century*, Docmus Research Publications, 4, Sibelius Academy (Helsinki, 2012), 125–54.

Paavolainen, Pentti, *Nuori Bergbom: Kaarlo Bergbomin elämä ja työ*, i: *1843–1872*, Teatterikorkeakoulun julkaisusarja, 43 (Helsinki, 2014).

Paavolainen, Pentti, *Arkadian arki: Kaarlo Bergbomin elämä ja työ*, ii: *1872–1887*, Teatterikorkeakoulun julkaisusarja, 51 (Helsinki, 2016).

Paavolainen, Pentti, *Kriisit ja kaipuu: Kaarlo Bergbomin elämä ja työ*, iii: *1888–1906*, Teatterikorkeakoulun julkaisusarja, 64 (Helsinki, 2018).

Ringby, Per, *Författarens dröm på scenen: Harald Molanders regi och författarskap* (Umeå, 1987).

Sivefors, Per, '"A blot on Swedish hospitality": Ira Aldridge's Visit to Stockholm in 1857', in Nely Keinänen and Per Sivefors, eds, *Disseminating Shakespeare in the Nordic Countries: Shifting Centres and Peripheries in the Nineteenth Century* (Bloomsbury, 2022), 189–210.

Snellman, Ruth, *Tuokio sieltä, tuokio täältä* (Helsinki, 1970).

Tiusanen, Timo, *Teatterimme hahmottuu: Näyttämötaiteemme kehitystie kansanrunoudesta itsenäisyyden ajan alkuun* (Helsinki, 1969).

Tompuri, Elli, *Etu- taka- ja syrjähyppyjä: Muistelmia Arkadiasta Kansalliseen* (Helsinki, 1952).

4

Shakespeare and the Norwegian National Theatre, 1899–1914

Christina Sandhaug

This chapter explores Norwegian Shakespeare dissemination in the late nineteenth and early twentieth centuries, focusing on the Norwegian National Theatre (Nationaltheatret), where eight productions of plays by Shakespeare were staged during the fifteen years from the theatre's opening in 1899 to the outbreak of the Great War in 1914: *Twelfth Night* (1899), *The Taming of the Shrew* (1900), *A Midsummer Night's Dream* (1903), *The Merchant of Venice* (1906), *Hamlet* (1907), *Othello* (1908), *Henry IV* (1910) and *As You Like It* (1912).[1] Norwegian plays form the overwhelming majority of productions in this period, and possible reasons are not hard to find: the nation had fostered two major playwrights in the nineteenth century, Bjørnstjerne Bjørnson (1832–1910) and Henrik Ibsen (1828–1906), whose plays were extensively performed at the National Theatre. The National Romantic movement of the mid-nineteenth century was on the wane, but cultural nationalism was still surging in the young Norwegian nation, whose liberation from almost four centuries of Danish rule dated back to 1814 and whose union with Sweden was under increasing pressure, dissolving in 1905.

In this period of transition from National Romantic provincialism to a more modern, cosmopolitan view of the nation, Shakespeare resonates loudly, but indirectly, with the nation-building project of which the National Theatre was part: as a master of high art whose works cultivate the audience's tastes and provide ultimate tests for a theatre's artistic might; as a prophet of eternal human truths and values for the edification of a people; and as a model of a cultural hero, whose firm grasp of human nature promotes progress and enlightenment. Shakespeare at the National Theatre in the period 1899–1914 is a tale of adaptation and reception that traverses the boundaries of the theatre and challenges any coherent narrative of a 'Norwegian Shakespeare' or 'staging the nation'. To explore this 'tale', the chapter embraces two entangled perspectives: it explores contextual and historical perspectives by examining how the National Theatre was conceived (in both senses of the word) as a cultural institution and by mapping Shakespeare's presence in Norwegian public discourse. Zooming more closely in on the Shakespeare plays staged at the National Theatre in the period, it also explores adaptation and reception in relation to the wider conception of 'Shakespeare' that emerges in this public discourse, with the aim of discovering what role Shakespeare might have played in Norwegian national theatrical discourse more broadly defined.

'National Theatre' may refer to the products of the dramatic arts, the practice of theatrical activity and the site at which this practice takes place. Theatre as *site* and *product* may be counted, measured and assigned market value, and hence traded, owned and stolen, as is the case with Shakespeare in the global market.[2] The metaphor of culture as product is prevalent in Norwegian theatrical discourse of the nineteenth century, connected to capitalist and nationalist ideas of importation and exportation, smuggling and contraband goods.[3] This product metaphor is germane to the discourse of adaptation and reception, central concepts when looking at theatre as *practice*. In global Shakespeare, a performance site is constructed 'by the artists' effort in creating a local habitat for the fabula of the play and a cultural location' for the imported wares.[4] The site thus becomes inseparable from product and practice, and is no longer contained in the building, as the agents of production and reception transcend and expand the site: a national theatre 'not only appears at designated theatres but comprises a complex nexus of theatrical activity'.⁵ Indeed, the notion of a national theatre was debated in Norwegian public discourse long before the National Theatre was even thought feasible.⁶ 'Shakespeare at the National Theatre', therefore, implies the adaptation and reception of individual plays within a broad network of dissemination that goes far beyond the National Theatre.

Focusing on the theatre as a site or a building relies on facts, figures and drawings. Focusing on the theatre as a product adds the support of textual editions of plays, actors' scripts, perhaps also footage and film of performance. Focusing on theatre as a practice, however, the critic is at the mercy of reception. According to Paul Menzer, theatre history is one of absences and performance studies depends on recollection. To fill the absence, and flesh out the recollection, trace-based theatre history relies on architectural, political and economic 'affiliations and transactions' relating to sites and products.⁷ Ironically, such archival traces of performance are about everything but performance:

> [T]heatrical traces are usually deliberately – and therefore credibly – not about performance but about the material circumstances of theatrical production. This creates a peculiar paradox: it is the fact that these traces are peripheral to performance that makes them so trustworthy. (The other buried paradox here is that the closer archives get to performance, the less trustworthy they become.)⁸

Anecdotes, however, 'capture' performance too well to be credible, but what they *do* show is that they *were* believed: 'Anecdotes tell us what people believed, or were happy to believe, or, even when they were unbelieving, what they wanted or even needed to be true.'⁹

In short, anecdotes are the stuff of reception, suggesting to us the experiences of and beliefs about play-going. This chapter fuses perspectives of adaptation and reception by relying on both archives and anecdotes to explore Shakespeare at the National Theatre. If we wish to understand why *Twelfth Night* (1899) flopped on its opening night (as we shall see), we must search beyond the archives of production, which suggest the play was a triumph, and venture into the world of reception, which reveals that the performance fell flat. Relational or horizontal conceptualizations of adaptation have redefined the object of study from Shakespeare's texts to Shakespeare adaptations, 'the aggregated web of cultural forces and productions that in some fashion lay claim to the label "Shakespearean"'.[10] This chapter adds popular reception to this aggregated web. Translations, theatre histories, play texts and prompt books cannot sufficiently explain why the 'performance did not manage to inspire the audience, in spite of handsome stage machinery and scenography as well as respectable acting by individual actors'.[11] For that, we need a wider backdrop of national culture, theatrical discourse and popular dissemination and reception.

Norway, national culture and National Theatre, 1890–1914

When the National Theatre opened in Christiania in September 1899, it was not inevitable that the theatre as cultural institution should, could and would contribute to the ongoing national revival.[12] The two playwrights Ibsen and Bjørnson had achieved international renown, and their works were considered national-cultural treasures, Bjørnson having even penned the words of the national anthem. *Poetry*, however, was not synonymous with *theatre*, and the latter was more often associated with entertainment and circus-like frivolity than with serious intellectual and cultural advancement. Indeed, government representatives suggested placing the new theatre in an area already dedicated to amusement, called 'Tivoli'.[13] Besides, Norway had other feats with which to pride herself, in comparison with which drama and theatre paled, such as Nansen's Fram expedition to the North Pole, which had successfully returned in 1896.[14] Such feats boosted nationalist sentiments, which had swelled from the mid-nineteenth century. If national identity is 'the meeting point between the individual and the collective conception of the nation',[15] between the lived experience of national identity and the conscious, political national efforts, then two unions were hampering Norwegian national identity: the political union with Sweden and the cultural union with Denmark. The political emancipation signalled by the dissolution of the union in 1905 was paralleled by a movement towards cultural 'emancipation' of the Norwegian people,[16] which stimulated the development of a new, Norwegian theatre that could represent and shape 'Norwegiandom'.

The idea of a national theatre was not new. There was already a theatre in the city of Bergen called the National Stage (Den Nationale Scene), established in 1876 as a continuation of the Norwegian theatre (Det Norske Theater, est. 1850). Some, most famously Bjørnstjerne Bjørnson, claimed that a national theatre belonged in the capital, Christiania.[17] In 1850, though, the location in Bergen made more sense. Ole Bull wanted a stage for the Norwegian language, and Christiania was culturally Danified and politically Swedish. There *were* theatres in the capital from the early nineteenth century: the Christiania Theatre (established 1837) where Danish actors performed predominantly Danish plays in the Danish language, and the rival Kristiania Norwegian Theatre (established 1852), where Norwegian actors performed in Norwegian.[18] Christiania had grown explosively during the nineteenth century and with it grew the idea that a new theatre of national significance should be built.[19]

A national theatre (uncapitalized) is 'a space for shared civil discourse, entertainment, creativity, pleasure and intellectual stimulation'.[20] Of course, newspapers and other communicative infrastructure (letters, magazines, pamphlets, church and school) played a crucial role in scaffolding and extending the horizon of this space.[21] One material condition for nationhood is communication. People in the north of Norway or the marginal or impoverished strata of society would need to know that they *are* Norwegian and be *able* to participate in this space. Theatre can play a role in this process of nationhood, Nadine Holdsworth suggests, as a 'creative space' for exploring and representing nationhood on an imaginative level, generating a 'creative dialogue with tensions in the national fabric'.[22] One example is the religious discussions that followed in the wake of Bjørnson's *Beyond Our Power* in the opening season. The play's blasphemous content sparked fears of a godless future, but, as one commentator reassures his readers, 'the destiny of Christianity in Norway is not decided in the theatre, not even the National Theatre'.[23]

A National Theatre (capitalized) is a 'high-profile building in a capital city brimming with civic pride and cultural prominence, producing works by national playwrights and theatre-makers in shows that exude high production values because of their sizable government subsidies'.[24] In Norway, however, at the end of the nineteenth century, a new theatre in the capital was not on the political and financial agenda. Power was in other hands and concerned with other things, and so money had to be found elsewhere: the National Theatre was initially funded by selling shares and some contributions from the capital's bankers and spirits league, as well as income from a national lottery.[25] The continually precarious financial situation of the theatre until 1927, when state funding was awarded, is also part of the network of dissemination of Shakespeare at the time, influencing both choice of plays and strategies of scenography and stagecraft.

It was on the wave of national pride swelled by the expeditions of Nansen that the completion of the National Theatre could surf: the lottery that gave much needed cash came about by a joint venture to collect money for the nation's scientific and artistic institutions, led and secured by the recently established Nansen Fund. This affair managed to turn the National Theatre from a 'cause' of interest only to the capital into a cause of interest for the entire nation, representing national values and fostering national pride.[26] Significantly, this is also when the National Theatre project was granted its location among the institutions of Monarchy, Parliament and University. The committee for the building project spoke to this national pride in their appeals to potential investors. They claimed that 'a national stage is one of the most crucial vehicles of culture for an enlightened and progressive people', insisted that it must be of national interest and asked 'any Norwegian with an eye for the importance of the scenic arts for the people's culture and capabilities to sacrifice something for the promotion of [the theatre]'.[27] The daily and weekly press supported the building of what they considered a national cause. One magazine insisted that 'art and science could represent considerable national values' that could occasion a 'national refinement of our country'.[28] The newspapers shared these great expectations, and by the time of the opening, the theatre had had sufficient publicity to make the tag 'near the National Theatre' a geographical indicator and a selling point.[29]

There were diverging views of the role of the National Theatre in the nation. For example, Bjørnson stressed the nation-building capacity of the theatre.[30] In his eyes, the theatre was any nation's primary guard against the foreign,[31] and a National Theatre should be in the nation's capital. This view implies the tension between centralizing forces that resulted from nationalism and the idea of finding the real Norway in the regions, and an antagonistic opposition to 'the foreign' that often lead to isolationism. A commentator in *Morgenbladet* reveals another perspective when complaining about the excess of actors in the two largest cities (Bergen and Christiania). His suggested solution is interesting: for the scenic arts to become truly national, these superfluous actors should be sent to the regions to establish regional, Norwegian theatres. This would kill two birds with one stone, as it would give these hapless people something to do and rid the regions of the Danish troupes that still roamed those parts.[32] The irony is that although national culture is seemingly built on rural and local traditions, it is now only staged in the large cities, showcasing the complex negotiations of periphery and centre that global Shakespeare is also subject to. The same tension extends to the relation between national and foreign. Later in life, Bjørnson modified his ideas of the theatre as a guard against the foreign, to a *mediator* between the national and the foreign.[33] The very same development occurred in many emerging nations in the late nineteenth and early twentieth centuries, for instance on Iceland, where a hankering for an identity as sophisticated, European cosmopolitans replaced the National Romantic ideal of the rural, authentic peasant.[34] The National Theatre was thus established on a threshold between two overlapping outlooks. On the one hand, the National Romantic project of recovering the folkloric, rural or historical, mythic past and representing it in nationally produced drama in the vernacular, and, on the other hand, the cosmopolitan idea of staging foreign classics as a way of demonstrating artistic prowess on an international level, with concomitant challenges of translation, adaptation and reception. These pressures, of adaptation and reception, archives and anecdotes, art and finance, local and global impulses, shape the reception of Shakespeare and his plays in Norway.

Shakespeare in Norway

The migration and adaptation of Shakespeare across time and space are part of the international, European, now global spread of Shakespeare, which is what brought Shakespeare's plays to the Norwegian stage in the first place. Though fuelled by such international currents, nationalism is often isolationist and exclusivist rather than expansionist. This paradox is evident in nineteenth-century theatre discourse. Opera, it was said, being a foreign article, had no 'national right' to be staged at the National Theatre as long as there were no esteemed Norwegian writers of opera, to which a rather global response was given:

> What about drama? Is it invented in Norway? And our dramatic literature, where does it have its roots? I think it stems from the common culture that nourishes all nations and belongs exclusively to no one. Through this culture, mankind's great spirits belong to all countries. We let Shakespeare, Göthe and Molière onto our stage with as much right as other nations let Bjørnson and Ibsen onto theirs. Likewise, Mozart's operas are not created only for Austria, Weber's not for Germany, Verdi's not for Italy, and the French opera comique's masterpieces not only for France – luckily, they belong to mankind and have a home everywhere.[35]

Acknowledging the cosmopolitan nature of great art does not make the theatre less 'national', they conclude, revealing an awareness of this tension between cultural nationalism and globalization, and the possibility that plays can be at home everywhere, locally actualized and topical, and nowhere, universal and 'for all mankind'. As Anston Bosman points out, a 'hallmark of Shakespeare's intercultural entanglements is this tension between the apparently universal values of a story and the local motivations of its staging'.[36] Instead of regarding this tension in terms of a dichotomy, Bosman suggests, studying Shakespeare dissemination in terms of theatrical and textual networks teases out the entangled relation, and simultaneity, of global and local impulses.[37]

The concept of rhizomatics illustrates the fungal ways in which such networks operate, spread, morph and manifest themselves,[38] the mushroom perhaps incarnating the duality, or glocality,[39] of the travelling (in time and space) Shakespeare as at once global and local, universal and topical. The late nineteenth and early twentieth century is a period in which this duality was acutely felt. The forces of nationalism manifested themselves in a celebration of all things Norwegian, but national pride also accommodated the cosmopolitan urge to rise to the standards of other nations. Alexa Huang and Elizabeth Rivlin take such conceptualizations of global

Shakespeares to imply that the 'ethical responsibility of the critics shifts from delimiting the boundaries of Shakespeare to tracing the ever-changing potential of "Shakespeare"'.[40] Distinguishing global and national concerns is a false dichotomy even in 1899, and 'Norwegian Shakespeare' is not limited to or contained in the National Theatre but is rather to be found in the networks of Norwegian national theatre. We cannot, according to Douglas Lanier, fully understand an adaptation 'without being attentive to the particular historical "Shakespeare" with which it is engaged'.[41] A brief discussion of the theatrical and textual networks which produce this 'Shakespeare' will be useful for the ensuing exploration of the National Theatre productions of Shakespeare's plays.

Newspapers were concerned with European cultural life ['Aandsliv'] as witnessed by articles on foreign art, literature and music. Interest in English culture, history and news was emerging in late nineteenth-century Norway, after years of French and German cultural influence. Reviewing a translation of *The Merchant of Venice* in 1880, one writer claims that the new translation is proof that the desire to familiarize oneself with Shakespeare has awakened.[42] Familiarity with England was stimulated by, among other sources, Robert Blatchford's *Merrie England* (1893), which was translated into Norwegian in 1899 and was extensively reviewed. The Danish scholar Georg Brandes's massive *William Shakespeare: A Critical Study* was published in Danish and German in 1896 and was heavily marketed in most Norwegian newspapers. In 1899, his book was issued in a 'people's edition', suggesting a wider and more popular reach.[43] Brandes's psychobiographical method did much to influence popular conceptions of Shakespeare as a divinely inspired genius, but there were other voices in Shakespeare discourse, such as Theodor Bierfreund, whose *William Shakespeare and His Art* painted a more sober picture of a hard-working word-smith. Controversy, too, could sell newspapers. In February 1895, *Dagbladet* ran a series of articles called 'The Battle of Shakespeare', about the (already then) old theory that Francis Bacon wrote Shakespeare's plays.[44] In late November 1906, papers all over the country reported that the 'old battle over Shakespeare's authorship has been rekindled'[45] by the German nationalist Karl Bleibtreu, who suggested that Shakespeare was the Earl of Rutland – a suggestion dismissed by Dr Furnivall as 'utterly childish'.[46] Critical dissemination also happened outside of print, such as public and private lectures. In January 1899, after an annual political meeting in the south-eastern town of Halden, there was a party 'with lectures about Iceland and Shakespeare/ Macbeth'.[47] Such dissemination is suggestive of the market value of 'Shakespeare'.

Shakespeare's plays were read and staged mostly in Danish translation. A trickle of Norwegian translations appeared in the early twentieth century, as part of the development of New Norwegian, and thus had nationalist motivations.[48] The author Arne Garborg repeatedly claims that, though it can manage both 'Bible and Shakespeare', the New Norwegian language will never be a cultural language until it is also used in schools.[49] *Macbeth* and *The Merchant of Venice* both came in New Norwegian translations in 1906. Mostly, however, Norwegian readers, to the extent that they did read Shakespeare, relied on Dano-Norwegian translations.[50] Theatres also used Danish translations, though often with a Norwegianized pronunciation, first Peter Foersom's (publ. 1803–1818), then the translations of Edvard Lembcke (publ. 1861–1873), in addition to the less successful, though very popular, adaptations of Sille Beyer in the middle of the century.[51] Not until the 1920s did any significant Norwegian translations appear.[52]

Printing translations does not necessarily equal widespread reading. Commenting on a new edition of Holberg's comedies, a writer compares Holberg with Shakespeare and Goethe, whose works are 'readily available for people who have more will to read than money to buy books', suggesting that titles were available but expensive.[53] Of course, libraries were multiplying in the nineteenth century. In 1840 there were 240 public libraries in Norway, and, after state funding was established in 1876, the number soared to 650 by 1901.[54] Yet, it does not seem that Shakespeare was much taken out. The city librarian of the coastal town of Fredrikstad laments that 'among foreign, translated literature, which is much sought after, I have to mention a few that rarely or never leave the shelves: Byron, Shakespeare, Goethe, Molière, Dante, Manzoni'.[55] Another interview with a librarian, entitled 'What People Read', reveals that lenders' inclinations change over time: 'I have often observed a worker begin with Marryat [novels about life at sea, mostly] and end up reading all of Shakespeare's works.' Sadly, he has also seen readers begin with Shakespeare and end up reading Karl Olsen (biographical stories of seafaring and gold digging).[56] Inevitably, though, what lenders borrow from the library is not always what they read. Audiences at recitals, however, are likely to hear what is read. *Morgenbladet* reports on the rising popularity of literary recitations, and they refer specifically to Shakespeare,[57] suggesting that familiarity with Shakespeare's works was spread via such channels, too: the 'renowned Shakespeare-reader Herman Linde' reportedly gave five readings in Christiania in 1880.[58]

The name of Shakespeare also appears in the Norwegian press in contexts that have little to do with literature or theatre. He is listed in regular posts on birthdays and holidays, and his life is frequently commented on, as in the brief note in a regional paper, about how, without any apparent explanation to anyone, Shakespeare suddenly left house and home, wife and kids, to go to London and write plays.[59] Some stories claim historical authenticity, such as the much-printed brief report on the remarkable glove collection in the Ashmolean Museum, which contained gloves reputedly having belonged to Mary Stuart, Elizabeth I, Henry VIII – and Shakespeare.[60] Others appeal to science: an extensively circulated report on the physiognomy of eye colour capitalizes on Shakespeare, who apparently had nut-brown eyes, which indicates a tender heart, good head and gentlemanly behaviour.[61] Anecdotes appear frequently, both about Shakespeare's life and about Shakespeare reception in theatres and elsewhere. Several papers delight in a story of Shakespeare's fathers' beer test: sitting in beer clad in leather breeches could determine the stickiness, hence quality, of the beer.[62] The alleged duel that took place in Paris, between the poet Catulle Mendez and one M. Vanor, caused by a dispute over Hamlet's girth, was also broadly circulated.[63] By the time of the opening of the National Theatre, Shakespeare's name was familiar enough to be the subject of jokes.[64]

'Shakespeare' was also a catchphrase and frame of reference. Concluding an exposition with 'as Shakespeare said' is ubiquitous, and writers frequently call for 'a Shakespeare' when tragedy looms: writing about the attack on Alexander II of Russia, *Morgenbladet* claims that it would 'require a Shakespeare to render the House of Romanoff's great tragedy in all its measures'.[65] Shakespeare not only entered the language, he was also a reference *for* language. According to a piece on English vocabulary, printed in many papers, it was 'Shakespeare, considered the greatest English Poet, who employed the largest vocabulary', though he only used 16,000 of the available 200,000 words.[66] Shakespeare likewise serves as measure for the standards of other writers. The author Arne Garborg is favourably compared to Shakespeare: 'Garborg is the thinker in our literature. One thinks of Nietzsche and Shakespeare.'[67] In an article called 'Goethe and Women', the writer claims that 'no other poet, except Shakespeare, knew women so well'.[68] An advertisement for Tolstoy's *War and Peace* uses Shakespeare as a selling point by asserting that 'Not since the days of Shakespeare has any poet managed to render such a diverse and colourful image of life as this one'.[69] Such comparisons are occasionally unfavourable. A review of Hamsun's play *At the Gate of the Kingdom* points to a blemish in the plot concerning the female character's 'self-deprecation' and dismisses the young Hamsun by claiming that Shakespeare and Ibsen would never make such a mistake.[70] 'Shakespeare' was often used about great men generally, from Count Bismarck, who is characterized as Shakespeare incorporated,[71] to the 'Indian Shakespeare' King Sudraka, the author of the play *Vasantasena*.[72] The German poet Schiller is simply introduced as 'Germany's Shakespeare',[73] testifying to the status conferred upon events, objects or people by the Shakespearean tag.

Norwegian theatrical discourse often linked Shakespeare to divine, universal truth. The following is typical, if a little elaborate: 'We have Homer and Socrates, we have Rafael and the sculptor Thorvaldsen, we have the poets Shakespeare and Göthe, and many, many such stars, which rose from God's hands from pole to pole across the eternal firmament of memory, and who have caught their light from the sun, each in his own way.'[74] The ancient poets, as well as Shakespeare, Racine and Molière, knew how to make use of 'le document humain' in their poetry, so that through 'long centuries, mankind has seen itself mirrored in their work and thought there to recover their feelings and passions'.[75] Marking the Goethe jubilee in 1899, the German is repeatedly juxtaposed to Shakespeare as one of the greatest poets of modern times.[76] The Danish poet Holger Drachmann lists Shakespeare among men touched by divine fire, along with such men as Galilei and Dante,[77] and he is said to 'mingle in brotherly unity' with Sophocles, Holberg, Oehlenschläger and Ibsen at the Danish Royal Theatre.[78] Even the Norwegians' own Wergeland and Ibsen had the grace of Shakespeare bestowed upon them.[79] In a speech given on the national holiday, 17 May 1899, Shakespeare enters the Norwegian national discourse side by side with Ibsen, Nansen, Luther and, last but not least, Jesus of Nazareth.[80]

Small wonder, then, that Norwegians considered Shakespeare as formative to English identity. Only the English cricket hero Gilbert Grace could stir an outburst of national excitement so great that 'not even Shakespeare, Darwin or Cayle together could have inspired it'.[81] Papers often report on Shakespearean events in England, in particular the Shakespeare Festival in Stratford and performances in London, and on what Shakespeare means to England.[82] There is also a growing sense of Shakespeare as a European and global phenomenon, with lengthy articles on Shakespeare abroad, for instance regarding the challenges of performing *Othello* in the American south.[83] There is, however, little effort to make him 'Norwegian', beyond translation and stage production.

Shakespeare on the Norwegian stage

As artistic director of Christiania Theater (1857–1862), Bjørnstjerne Bjørnson had mounted a successful campaign to promote Norwegian theatrical culture by introducing classics such as Shakespeare's plays.[84] Shakespeare's plays were frequently staged at Christiania Theatre, and at the smaller Central Theatre (Centraltheatret) and Second Theatre (Secondtheatret), in the latter half of the nineteenth century.[85] The general reception of 'this not unknown author Shakespeare'[86] is characterized by, on the one hand, an endless fascination with and admiration for his skill in looking into the human soul and his plays' ability to speak to audiences across time, and, on the other hand, increasing frustration with inconsiderate cutting, inadequate acting and misguided scenography, as well as an uneducated spectatorship.[87]

Morgenbladet (1903) refers to the German theatre critic Alfred von Berger, who had recently claimed that after the naturalism and symbolism of the last decade of the nineteenth century, there was again a desire for the 'simple, true and great . . . primarily Shakespeare, this radiant sun, which always anew spreads light and warmth over the theatre'.[88] This mystified conception of Shakespeare is ubiquitous in criticism and reviews. Shakespeare is referred to as the great dramatic master, enthralling his audiences with the magic of his genius, and the plays are described as playfulness, imagination and mystery incarnate, his poetry divinely infused and inspired to the utmost perfection of human creativity. Johanne Dybwad's Puck embodied this Shakespearean spirit in her 'festive union of elfish jesting and the natural mysticism of fairy tales. The spring of a natural force, the feathery lightness of a fairy, the sparkling glee of a pixie, the mighty magic swing of the slumber-rose, a perpetuum mobile of twitching and delicate, steady hopping – it was all there'.[89] This adoration of Shakespeare's genius and work is contrasted with the enormity of the challenge of performing a Shakespeare play. In *Hamlet*, for instance, Shakespeare demands of the Danish prince 'the extraordinary, the marvellous'.[90]

Partly because of this mystified conception, Shakespeare productions were considered fraught with difficulty.[91] The first challenge has to do with adaptation: the many elements suitable for his time, such as 'the forced witticisms, the empty puns, the many obscenities and especially the naïve and artless that often emerge in the structure of the plays', cannot simply be cut, and it would take a clever hand to give us good artistic adaptations.[92] The second difficulty has to do with reception: in Shakespeare's subjective world view, the person is all and the environment nothing, they claim, so the setting of the play needed only the slightest hint. Our world view considers the individual as a product of its surroundings, which is why illusion has replaced imagination on stage, with audiences demanding to be completely transported in time and place by illusionistic stagecraft.[93] Such scenography cannot handle the many changes in Shakespeare's plays, which will therefore have to be restricted, which again could impact the coherence of the performance. It is also vulnerable to 'mean anachronisms' that may disturb the illusion, such as turning 'the foolish butler' Malvolio into a pietist: 'The puritans were the dark backdrop to the life and joy of Elizabeth's merry, cheerful England, but the Pietists were not yet at home neither in the Queen's realm nor in the poet's imagination.'[94]

Reviews often stress the difficulty of mounting a production of a Shakespeare play. Shakespeare's plays are often considered too demanding for Norwegian companies, a verdict used both as an excuse for a poor performance and as discouragement to future performances. *Bergens Aftenblad* accused the Central Theatre for 'aiming too high' when they attempted to incorporate Shakespeare into their repertory, an accusation with roots in regional rivalry.[95] Likewise, *Ørebladet* warns Christiania Theatre not to 'overstretch on Shakespeare' in their last season before they close down.[96] Poor productions were also blamed on adaptation and cutting. Plays were cut for performance, of course, but misshaping of plays did not go down well.[97] In the years before the National Theatre opened, staging plays in disfigured form was apparently becoming a habit: 'These days we are unfortunately used to getting Shakespeare in a more or less mutilated form.'[98] Performances of Shakespeare's plays at the National Theatre must be explored against this background of reception.

Shakespeare at the Norwegian National Theatre, 1899–1914

The early choices of repertoire at the Norwegian National Theatre contrast with those of the other Nordic countries, where the first Shakespearean plays tended to be tragedies.[99] Director Bjørn Bjørnson's primary concern was finance and the first years were characterized by popular comedy, and the first four Shakespeare plays at the National Theatre were comedies.[100] Not receiving state funding, the theatre had to balance the books, and comedies tended to draw larger audiences.[101] Under the next director, Vilhelm Krag (dir. 1907–1911), Shakespeare was the only foreign playwright on offer, and Krag managed to show the audience that 'the great Brit was more than a comedian'.[102]

Twelfth Night was the first Shakespeare play on stage at the National Theatre, about a month after opening in 1899, under the direction of Bjørn Bjørnson. It was considered a grand occasion, to which was attached great expectations that were thoroughly disappointed. In spite of a very able ensemble and state-of-the-art technology, the performance was unmoving and the audience were disinterested. The next play fared better, with a racy *Taming of the Shrew* keeping audiences rapt and cash flowing in. With *Midsummer Night's Dream* (1903), victory was proclaimed, much to the credit of Johanne Dybwad, who played a 'completely Shakespearean' Puck.[103] *The Merchant of Venice* (1906) was another success, though unfortunately not enough to convince the authorities to approve the theatre's application for state funding, submitted that very year. The first *Hamlet* (1907), and the first tragedy, was a 'cultivated, but average' performance,[104] whereas the following year's *Othello* managed to combine the cultivated and contained style with intensity and nerve. *Henry IV* (1910) failed because it used Bjørnson's reworking, which should rightly be called 'Falstaff' (and in fact is, in one review).[105] The last play in our period was, however, a complete success: in *As You Like It* (1912), adaptation and revision, acting styles and scenography, as well as a perfect balance of universal, eternal themes in topical garb, conspired to make the production a triumph of the Norwegian scenic arts.[106] In a sense, then, this performance overcame all the challenges and obstacles of adapting a Shakespeare play.

Adaptation, in the Darwinian sense of 'change', is key to survival in a changing environment, also for stories on stage.[107] It is as a result of the dual pressures of universality and actuality that adaptation happens. Global Shakespeare, today as in the early twentieth century, does not present 'a frozen Shakespeare from four hundred years ago, fit for consumption today after reheating in the microwave'.[108] For instance, *Romeo and Juliet* at Kristiania Norwegian Theatre in 1899 'incarnated' the play, not because it performed the play in 'Shakespeare's spirit and style', but because it was 'artistically reborn' in a language and tone closer to our own time.[109] Johanne Dybwad, who played Juliet in this production and became the National Theatre's most successful actress in the early years, is described as particularly adept in accessing the universal content of the classics and making them feel contemporary.[110] Successful adaptation embraces innovation and shies away from permanence. Shakespeare is universal *because* adaptable, or as John Forster and Andrew Murphy put it, he is 'peerlessly mutable . . . his plays are both historical documents and contemporary talking points'.[111]

While adaptation may offer salvation, it is also potentially a curse. The reception of *Henry IV* (1910) and *As You Like It* (1912) illustrates this contrast. Both performances were based on texts in Dano-Norwegian translation that, according to Ruud, were so heavily adapted that they could not rightly be called Shakespeare.[112] *Henry IV* (1910) used Bjørnson's contraction and reworking of the two plays from 1867, which was based on Lembcke's Danish translation and adapted even further for the 1910 production. This adaptation was not well received. The 'Purgatory of Adaptation has been more painful than cleansing' to the play.[113] In his quest to 'improve' Shakespeare, one review notes, Bjørnson 'has killed the play's women and crippled the men'.[114] To make matters worse, this specific 1910 production has mutilated the play even further.[115] Commentators, in 1910 as in 1867, suggest that the play should be renamed 'Falstaff', and they question the right to attribute the resulting play to Shakespeare: 'Should Shakespeare rise from the grave he would protest loudly against having his name put on it!'[116]

Critics and historians take two main issues with this adaptation, both in 1867 and in 1910. First, the text is said to be a 'heavily cut mash-up of scenes from the two parts', concentrating on Falstaff.[117] The main flaw is that it makes Falstaff foreground, instead of the background for Prince Henry's development, and hence misses the whole point of the play.[118] Second, and relatedly, the reviewers accused the author of having 'butchered' Shakespeare's text and the National Theatre of having 'molested' Shakespeare's play.[119] Several reviews acknowledge the necessity of cutting any play for the stage, but a contraction of two plays into one cannot but fail to maintain the integrity of the plays' structure. The crucial development of Prince Henry's character unfolds gradually against the background of his relation to Falstaff, the reviewers claim. For instance, the parts that shed light on Henry's attitude to the robbery (i.e. Part 1, Act 1), in which we gradually glean a better side to his character, are cut, which makes his decision to go against Percy later seem sudden. The contrasts are gone: 'this Henry has never run wild and lusty through the streets of London'.[120] And the parts treating of Percy's rebellion are so massively cut as to be unintelligible without recourse to the 'original' play: 'Glendower has barely left the stage before the letter arrives to tell Percy that help is not forthcoming.'[121] The character of Percy himself is scaled down to 'a peculiar, bellowing creature which shows itself on stage in a single scene'.[122] Yet, this scathing reception occludes a more complex network of reception. According to Ruud, the resulting play, 'chaotic as it seems, makes no ineffective play', which, with the help of the genius actor Johannes Brun, was favourably received in 1867.[123] Bjørnson's purpose, he claims, was to secure the success for Christiania Theatre he knew would result from Brun's Falstaff, and 'the nature of the cutting reveals the purpose at every step'.[124] The actor playing Falstaff in 1910, Johan Løvaas, did not have the gravity to pull the resulting, loosely connected scenes and characters together.[125]

As You Like It (1912) used a commissioned adaptation by the poet Herman Wildenvey, who had also taken considerable liberties with the original text 'but without insulting its spirit or meaning'.[126]

Wildenvey's text was a 'brilliant translation and an extraordinary free adaptation'.[127] Regarding the structure of the play, Wildenvey has cut and moved scenes and inserted parts of his own invention. He has, for instance, reduced five acts to four and contracted Act 2 to one scene, but these adaptations do 'no great violence to the fable nor to the characters'.[128] When it comes to treatment of the text, however, he has given remarkably free translations and reworkings: 'Shakespeare is mercilessly cut and mangled.'[129] He has turned speeches into dialogues by letting silent characters insert comments and introduced dialogue of his own making, such as an opening conversation between the duke and Amiens, 'fully in Shakespeare's tone, but Wildenvey's own invention'.[130] He has turned prose into rhymed poetry – for instance the brief prose dialogue between Jaques and the lords in 4.2, which Wildenvey turns into iambic tetrameter.[131] This 'needlessly free' translation, though not Shakespeare, is 'good poetry in itself', according to Ruud.[132]

Like Bjørnson's *Henry IV* adaptation, Wildenwey's *As You Like It* was also adapted to suit a certain actor, Johanne Dybwad.[133] In fact, *she* chose this play with which to celebrate her twenty-fifth anniversary as an actor, and the translation was commissioned for this occasion.[134] It was truly an occasion, marked in the papers with interviews, reportage and odes to Dybwad, in addition to the usual reviews, and celebrated with a banquet in her honour on opening night, also widely reported. It was an evening where 'the spirit of humankind [sat] spellbound by the revelation of genius'.[135] Wildenvey's translation was published the very same day, and it sports a photo of Dybwad on the dust jacket and a dedicatory poem to her by the translator (see Figure 4.1).

Theatre reviews were infected with the spirit of these celebrations and appear more concerned with her genius than with Shakespeare's or the play. 'Shakespeare and Johanne Dybwad – the two geniuses – the two stage-wise geniuses – let the theatre unfold all its might', opens one review.[136] 'We never saw a better Shakespeare-evening on any stage', enthuses another.[137] 'It is remarkable that this graceful, daring play, this rainbow of jollity, has been so gloriously presented in our drab surroundings', remarks a third.[138] Dybwad's genius, as demonstrated over the previous years, is so great, claims one commentator, that the poets themselves owe her gratitude.[139] In fact, another concludes, this was the second time in history this play fulfilled its destiny, the first being in Shakespeare's own time.[140]

FIGURE 4.1 *Johanne Dybwad as Rosalind in* As You Like It, eller Livet i Skogen *(The National Theatre, 1912). Photo: Photographer unknown. The National Theatre Picture Archive/National Library of Norway.*

In order to fully appreciate these adaptations of *Henry IV* and *As You Like It*, one must therefore look beyond the play texts. We must move beyond a limited perspective on adaptation as relating only to an 'original' authority, to a more complex relational perspective that takes into account how the national theatrical network or fabric inflects the adaptation and reception of both performances. Bjørnson's adaptation of *Henry IV* was tailored to Johannes Brun in 1867 in order to promote Christiania Theatre, and could not work its magic without the actor for whom it was adapted, whereas Wildenvey's *As You Like It* was prepared for Johanne Dybwad in 1912 and given lustre by the above-mentioned celebrations. Yet, both plays were popular successes. Ruud suggests that changes could be tolerated by Norwegian audiences that would cause outrage in a more established and cultivated environment, suggesting that being 'peripheral' in this sense might have its perks, at least for the translator-adapter.[141] Norwegian audiences were not generally familiar with Shakespeare in 'original' garb, and they were on the whole not concerned with the accuracy of English history or matters of philology. Besides, they were more likely to be dazzled by stagecraft, costumes and decorations, and star-struck by some of the actors, than annoyed with the cutting of parts of a text with which they were not familiar.[142]

Theatre critics and reviewers, too, were often more concerned with acting and scenography than with the translation and adaptation of the play text itself. *Twelfth Night* was a 'fiasco' because the actors 'stomped about on heavy wooden clogs, and tore to pieces the fresh, delightful veil the poet has drawn over his Sunday children!'[143] Such Romanticized conceptions of Shakespeare's plays reverberate through the entire reception, as we have seen earlier, and form the unattainable ideal against which acting and scenography are measured. *Twelfth Night* is one of Shakespeare's most

> delightful plays, conceived while the poet was in harmonious equilibrium and the poet's eye looked brightly on the marvellous destiny of man on earth. The god of love in this play is the delightful, mischievous Amor, whose arrows glimmer on their flight through the sunny, Attic summer air. And Bacchus himself, who directs the comedy's comedic elements, is wearing a wreath of ivy and wine leaves in his hair – he is not down

with drink. Lightly and playfully are the threads of the intrigue spun.[144]

Translated to Dano-Norwegian and played by us northerners this magic evaporates, another paper laments.[145] The festive odes to beauty and blazing poetry of love often sound 'so oddly dry, so artificial and untrue', laments another, and blames it on the style of acting currently prevalent at the theatres, especially the National Theatre.[146]

The 'cold and stern art of realism' and 'classical' declamation dominated the current acting style,[147] and 'verse, and flowing and elegant diction in general, remains a weakness at the National Theatre'.[148] This 'restrained and realistic' style of acting is unable to deliver the lyrical or grotesque, tragic or comic, or the 'lightest and most fragile poetry'.[149] *Twelfth Night*, 'with all its rich poetry, fell powerless to the ground, because one sat cold and listened in vain for some living feeling behind the splendour of the words'.[150] *The Taming of the Shrew*, however, was successfully acted because it broke with this style, being 'lively and natural, free from all misunderstood, classical rigidity'.[151] Bluster and affectation, however, were not tolerated. In *Twelfth Night*, there was more noise than poetry and merriment.[152] The same was said about *Henry IV*.[153] In both cases, there was a failure of extremes – cold rigidity and plainness thwarting naturalness and blustering noise masquerading as liveliness. The actor playing Hamlet in 1907, however, in spite of the lukewarm reception of the performance, was praised for speaking his lines as they should be, free of stagy posing, 'as sudden ideas and thinking aloud, and not as grand occasions'.[154]

Theatre performances, however, *were* grand occasions. Contrary to the critic von Berger, reviewers and audiences were mostly pleased with the scenography and stagecraft. Even the 'fiasco' of *Twelfth Night* could boast handsome costumes, stylish decorations and technologically advanced staging. *A Midsummer Night's Dream* (1903) in particular moved critics to wax lyrical: 'Light flows from the crown of a yellowish red tree – a beautiful effect. Plump hollyhocks shoot up, pink peonies erupt, creepers drape from the ceiling . . . everything is magnificent and brilliant.'[155] Another critic was so taken with the spectacular that all meaning became redundant: 'Meaning! What meaning is there in the playful swirling dance of the fog through the midsummer night, or in the moonshine that charms dewdrops into diamonds?'[156] Such rhapsody forms the backdrop for much of the criticism aimed at actors whose art could not 'measure up to the standards set by the poetry'.[157] However, the scenic presentation can be too ostentatious, according to some who recommend looking to the scenic conditions under which the plays were originally conceived and performed. Shakespeare 'must be played simply, because he himself is simple'.[158] Interestingly, to this verdict is appended an appeal for state funding of the theatre, to alleviate the pressure to dazzle an audience with operatic spectacle and to edify rather than simply entertain.

Appropriations within translation, adapting, acting and staging usually aim to make the foreign Shakespeare more familiar to an audience. Contemporary reception, too, is caught in the tension between topicality and universality, local and global. Several comments on audience reception relate to the foreignness of the plays' setting, plots and poetry. *Twelfth Night*, according to one critic, 'seemed somewhat foreign to the audience',[159] perhaps, as another critic suggested, because 'our audiences are not yet fully charmed by the great Renaissance master's magic, whatever the reason may be'.[160] The 'adventure-romantic plot' of *The Merchant of Venice*, for instance, 'might seem blunt and naïve, and the linguistic tapestry artificial and silly' to a contemporary audience.[161] The 'morals' of *The Taming of the Shrew* were considered 'incredibly odd for present-day people'.[162] Occasionally, critics also call for some recognizable feature to make Shakespeare hit closer to home. One reviewer of *A Midsummer Night's Dream* was impressed by the staging, but he missed 'something of the Nordic summer night's pale, blonde stillness'.[163] Domesticating changes, such as the previously mentioned turning Malvolio into a pietist, proceeds from a wish to make the character take root in Norwegian soil. Linguistic domestication, too, aims to give the language a local flavour. In *As You Like It*, 'shepherd' is repeatedly translated to 'dreng' (i.e. 'boy', in for example 3.5), perhaps because the Norwegian alternatives for 'shepherd' would carry too spiritual ('hyrde') or too agrarian ('gjeter') connotations. Oberon's reference to 'the Athenian' in *A Midsummer Night's Dream* (3.2.41) is rendered 'Atheneren' in Lembcke's Danish translation, but an actor's script from the National Theatre's 1903 production replaces the printed word with a scribbled 'mannen' (i.e. 'the man'), perhaps to loosen the ties to foreign lands.[164]

What makes Shakespeare performable in spite of distances in time, space and language is, in contemporary reception, the eternal and universal qualities of his plays. *The Taming of the Shrew* 'amuses now as it amused London's population 300 years ago', because the 'woman's delight in finding someone stronger than herself is still alive today', in spite of the oddity of some of its morals.[165] Such appeal to eternal and universal qualities abound: 'A play's life force lies in the fact that it, even in a time when man's emotional and intellectual life has taken new forms, can seem immediate, because a basic human feeling has been given strong, rich, deep or powerful expression.'[166] *Othello* and *Hamlet* in particular are often taken to speak across time and space. A review of *Othello* claims Shakespeare for the European stage. 'Thanks mostly to the German Romantics, Shakespeare was once more pulled from oblivion and turned into the living property of the European stage'.[167] Another accentuated the geographical and historical relations: 'it took a Shakespearean genius to make dramas from the English Elizabethan theatre able to live on through the centuries'.[168] They also call attention to migration across theatre traditions and styles, claiming that on the Elizabethan stage the broad epic unfolded, whereas the present theatrical form demands dramatic concentration à la Ibsen. Shakespeare nevertheless traverses traditions and forms because he 'infused eternal values in his work, and therefore they will prevail, however much form and taste change'.[169] *Hamlet*, too, speaks to our time. One critic even claims that it is *written* to speak to the future:

> The Danish Prince, who roamed about in his own ponderings – who saw the world's evils through the looking glass of his pain and wit – what else is he, than a prototype of the sick Genius, which three centuries after Shakespeare's death enflames the literature of our time? . . . Modern science will immediately discover the seeds of our times' most dangerous illness. It will in Hamlet find answers to one of its most difficult questions about the relationship of Genius to what the doctors call neurosis. This is why Hamlet affects the modern audience so forcefully, this is why this grandiose and unique person stands so close to us – this dithering, sovereign spirit, created several centuries before Nietzsche and Sterner had preached their new gospel.[170]

If *Hamlet* was written in tune with the future, *As You Like It* (1912) was written for this very production: 'When Shakespeare in his bright happy period let Rosalind sing, in the forest of Arden, her hymn in honour of all fresh and natural women's love, he undoubtedly had Johanne Dybwad's art in mind.'[171] Dybwad had previously played Puck to great acclaim, and here, she is said to illustrate and heighten Shakespeare's text, and his words 'are given new value by her looks and smiles'.[172] These raptures are informed by the celebrations discussed earlier, but they do suggest a belief in the contemporaneity of Shakespeare. She was 'Shakespeare's contemporary, and she was our contemporary, there was a whisper of eternity above her head'.[173] Praise indeed, for a performance of a play that, according to Ruud, could not rightly be called Shakespeare at all.[174]

It thus took more than *just* 'Shakespearean genius' to make Elizabethan dramas survive travels in time and space – it took adaptation in the form of translation, acting and scenography to make this play strike a happy balance between eternal universality and timely topicality. One commentator muses on the impulse to compare foreign and domestic theatre experiences, comparisons

FIGURE 4.2 As You Like It, eller Livet i Skogen *(The National Theatre, 1912)*. *From left, front: Gunnar Tolnæs (Le Beau), Ingolf Schanche (Jacques), Agnethe Schibsted-Hansson (Phoebe), Johan Løvaas (Sylvius), Aagot Didriksen (Celia), David Knudsen (Oliver), Stub Wiberg (The Duke), August Oddvar (Orlando), Johanne Dybwad (Rosalind), Hauk Aabel (Touchstone), Signe Heide Steen (Audrey). Photo: Photographer unknown. The National Theatre Picture Archive/The National Library of Norway.*

that are sometimes to the detriment, but often to the benefit, of Norwegian theatre: 'where life is at stake, faith, hate, love – where we must look into primal causes to find explanations – there we have seen Norwegian interpretations that fully meet the measures and requirements of the greatest poets'.[175] *As You Like It* demonstrated to most critics the prowess of the Norwegian stage, made even more impressive in the light of the enormity of the challenge: 'So high can the Norwegian scenic arts reach when a genius kindles the spark in all part-takers. So high, that we can proudly brave the claim that no one does it better.'[176] 'It might be that what we saw yesterday was the utmost of the land in which theatre lives', one impressed critic proposed, and it seemed, at least at the time, that this land could be Norway, if only by indirection (Figure 4.2).[177]

Conclusions: Shakespeare and/in the nation

Shakespeare's works could help edify the uncultivated portions of Norwegian theatre audiences, act as an acid test for the theatre's artistic capacities and model artistic influence. Shakespeare's plays could help the theatre fulfil its obligation to edify the audience's tastes,[178] but in order for that to fully succeed the theatre needed a stable source of income that would reduce the need to entertain with farce, popular comedy and spectacle.[179] Another way Shakespeare's plays could indirectly support the National Theatre in its national cause was to demonstrate the theatre's prowess. Considering the conceived difficulties of putting on a Shakespeare play, a successful performance would testify to the theatre's artistic capacities, as when *A Midsummer Night's Dream* had the National Theatre gather a great 'artistic might' for a 'high artistic task',[180] and *As You Like It* brought the Norwegian scenic arts to perfection in 1912.[181] Finally, if Shakespeare was never to be to Norway what he was to England, he was certainly considered a model for Norway's own great dramatists, being to Wellington what Ibsen was to Nansen:

> It wasn't only his father's and his own home Shakespeare built. He also built the great house of English literature ['bokheimen']. Here, he shows English youth how to live in order to be men.

The English have learnt from their great educator. One of many examples of this is the renowned Wellington, the great Napoleon's conqueror. He once said, 'The history I know I have learnt from Shakespeare'. These words make us think of Ibsen, and Nansen's polar expedition. As we know, Nansen said that it was Henrik Ibsen who had taught him to set high goals for himself and to not give up until they were reached.[182]

The explorations of this chapter suggest that in order to fully appreciate the role of Shakespeare at the National Theatre, we must broaden our base of evidence to comprise networks of theatrical practices and discourses and include anecdotal evidence of reception as well as archival evidence of adaptation. The entire field, web or network (or rhizome) of 'Shakespeare at the national theatre' affects Shakespeare dissemination, as any adaptation serves many 'masters', only one of which is the 'original' Shakespearean text. Shakespeare adaptation at the Norwegian National Theatre responds not only to the network of adaptations that constitute 'Shakespeare' but also to the wider discourse of national theatre. Seen through the lenses of Shakespeare adaptation alone, where, historically, local reception has been measured against an unattainable ideal of an 'original', our view of Shakespeare's role in Norwegian National Theatre becomes narrow and limited. Taking on board reception expands the picture and allows us to grasp the nuanced, conflicted and often contradictory role of Shakespeare in Norwegian National Theatre.

Notes

1 There were two main theatres in Christiania in the latter half of the nineteenth century, Christiania Theatre (Christiania Theater, est. 1837) and the Christiania Norwegian Theatre (Christiania Norske Theater, est. 1852, as the Christiania Norwegian Dramatic School). These two theatres merged in 1863, after several years of newspaper debates on the subject. The Christiania Norwegian Theatre went bankrupt in 1862, and the new, merged theatre lived on as Christiania Theatre, until it, too, closed down in June 1899, only three months before the opening of the National Theatre. Several actors and artists transferred from Christiania Theatre to the National Theatre. At the same time, there were also smaller theatres in Christiania, primarily the Central Theatre (Centraltheatret, est. 1897) and the smaller, and

short-lived, Second Theatre (Secondtheatret, est. August 1899, closed 1901). The city of Bergen was the primary cultural hub in the early to mid-nineteenth century, where Ole Bull founded the Norwegian Theatre (Det norske Theater) in 1850, later renamed the National Stage (Den Nationale Scene, 1876). Trondheim also had a permanent theatre building, at which several theatre companies performed, and from 1911 there was a company called Trondheim's National Stage (Trondheims Nationale Scene). Shakespeare plays were only sporadically given, due to the perceived cost and difficulty of the undertaking (Ruud, *An Essay*, 197). The National Stage in Bergen only gave one Shakespeare play in the period 1899–1914, namely *A Winter's Tale* in the season 1902–1903 (Ruud, *An Essay*, 199).

2 Joubin, 'Global Shakespeares', 4.
3 Schmiesing, 'The Christiania Theater', 323.
4 Huang, 'Global Shakespeare Criticism', 326.
5 Holdsworth, *Theatre and Nation*, 8.
6 Schmiesing, 'The Christiania Theater', 329.
7 Menzer, 'Archives and Anecdotes', 221.
8 Menzer, 'Archives and Anecdotes', 221.
9 Menzer, 'Archives and Anecdotes', 229.
10 Lanier, 'Shakespearean Rhizomatics', 27.
11 *Aftenposten*, 6 October 1899.
12 Oslo was named Christiania from 1624 to 1924, but from 1897 the name was officially spelled Kristiania. This chapter adopts the former spelling, except where the name is part of a title or quotation.
13 Ringdal, *Nationaltheatrets Historie*, 13.
14 Roald Amundsen would make the same journey seven years later and then to the South Pole in 1910–1911.
15 Holdsworth, *Theatre and Nation*, 21.
16 Steine, 'Ut av unionene', n.p. The ensuing sketch is in large part based on this article.
17 Wilmer, *National Theatres in a Changing Europe*, 16.
18 Schmiesing, 'The Christiania Theater', 326.
19 Ringdal, *Nationaltheatrets Historie*, 16.
20 Holdsworth, *Theatre and Nation*, 6.
21 The Norwegian newspaper industry grew explosively towards the end of the nineteenth century, and a plethora of papers with diverse

political affiliations made for a nuanced media discourse when taken as a whole. Individual papers, though, had their individual agendas and biases (Solheim and Syvertsen, 'Norsk pressehistorie', n.p.). Literacy, too, was extending to increasing parts of the population, with the introduction in 1889 of a common Folkeskole ('people's school') for all children aged seven to fourteen (Thune, 'Norsk Utdanningshistorie', n.p.)

22 Holdsworth, *Theatre and Nation*, 6–7.
23 *Aftenposten,* 7 December 1899.
24 *Aftenposten,* 7 December 1899, 27.
25 *Folkebladet*, No 16, 1899, 239.
26 *Folkebladet*, No 16, 1899, 241.
27 'Indbydelse til fornyet aktietegning til "Selskabet for opførelse af et nyt theater i Kristiania"', 1891.
28 *Folkebladet*, No. 16, 1899, 241.
29 For example, *Aftenposten*, 4 October 1899 (an advertisement for a room to let boasts proximity to the new theatre).
30 Schmiesing, 'The Christiania Theater', 318.
31 Schmiesing, 'The Christiania Theater',317.
32 *Morgenbladet*, 21 February 1901.
33 Schmiesing, 'The Christiania Theater', 319.
34 Þorgrimsson, 'Being European', 30.
35 *Aftenposten*, 8 December 1898.
36 Bosman, 'Shakespeare and Globalization', 289.
37 Bosman, 'Shakespeare and Globalization', 286. He refers to the digital network, too, which is irrelevant for the period under scrutiny, though essential to the work on this current chapter.
38 Lanier, 'Shakespearean Rhizomatics'.
39 For example Orkin, 'Local, Global, and "Glocal"'.
40 Huang and Rivlin, 'Shakespeare and the Ethics of Appropriation', 9.
41 Lanier, 'Shakespearean Rhizomatics', 33.
42 *Stavanger Amtstidende og Adresseavis*, 4 March 1880.
43 Advertised and reviewed in many papers, for example *Fedrelandsvennen*, 28 February 1899; *Bergens Tidende*, 21 April 1899.
44 *Dagbladet*, 28 July, 3 August and 8 August 1895. The gist of this was repeated in many papers, for example *Trondhjems Adresseavis*, 8 August.

45 *Oplandenes avis*, 1 December 1906.
46 *Fredrikstad Tilskuer*, 30 November 1906.
47 *Halden*, 30 January 1899.
48 Ruud, *An Essay*, 116.
49 For example *Nordlands Folkeblad*, 20 September 1906 (where he refers back to 'ten years ago', when he first wrote this).
50 See Per Sivefors and Nely Keinänen, 'Introduction', 25–9, for a discussion of Shakespeare translations in the Nordic countries in the nineteenth century.
51 Smidt, *Shakespeare i Norsk oversettelse*, 3.
52 See Svenn-Arve Myklebost's chapter in the present volume for a discussion of the translator Henrik Rytter.
53 *Aftenposten*, 28 November 1899.
54 The National Library, 'Library History', n.p.
55 *Fredrikstad Tilskuer*, 14 March 1895.
56 *Stavanger Aftenblad*, 3 October 1906.
57 *Morgenbladet*, 4 January 1880.
58 *Dagbladet*, 27 March 1880.
59 *Bodø-tidende*, 1 December 1899.
60 For example *Morgenbladet*, 15 September 1899.
61 For example *Akershus Amtstidende*, 31 July 1895.
62 For example *Social-Demokraten*, 8 March 1899.
63 For example *Morgenbladet*, 28 May 1899. Apparently, the duel was called off at the last minute, though the *NYT* claims Mendez was wounded.
64 For example 'Writer: I've just had a brilliant idea for a drama! Friend: Then, why don't you just start writing? Writer: Well, you see, the cursed thing is, that Shakespeare had the exact same idea before me!', *Buskeruds Blad*, 29 August 1899.
65 *Morgenbladet*, 25 February 1880.
66 For example *Trondhjems Adresseavis*, 22 May 1895.
67 *Bergens Tidende*, 15 November 1899.
68 *Romsdals Amtstidende*, 13 November 1899.
69 For example *Dagbladet*, 14 December 1899.
70 This scathing comparison would have aggravated Hamsun's already negative attitude to Shakespeare and to *be* a Shakespeare was

perhaps an honour that Hamsun was happy to forego. See Humpál, 'Knut Hamsun's Criticism of Shakespeare'.
71 For example *Bergens Aftenblad*, 8 April 1895.
72 *Morgenbladet*, 14 April 1895.
73 *Ringerikes Blad*, 2 May 1895.
74 *Fedraheimen*, 20 March 1880.
75 *Morgenbladet*, 26 January 1880.
76 For example *Trondhjems Adresseavis*, 28 August 1899.
77 *Dagbladet*, 21 February 1880. 'Ewald' refers to the Danish dramatist Johannes Ewald.
78 *Morgenbladet*, 3 January 1895.
79 For example *Avisen*, 12 July 1895.
80 *Social-Demokraten*, 19 May 1899.
81 *Trondhjems Adresseavis*, 1 July 1895.
82 For example *Morgenbladet*, 27 June 1899; *Trondhjems Adresseavis*, 21 May 1895.
83 For example *Aftenposten*, 21 May 1899; *Kristiansundsposten*, 29 April.
84 Schmiesing, 'Bjørnson and the Inner Plot', 466. See Keinänen and Sivefors's introduction to *Disseminating Shakespeare* for a discussion of critiques of stage machinery and language politics in connection with Bjørnson's *A Midsummer Night's Dream* at the Christiania Theatre in 1865.
85 See note 1 for an overview of theatres in Norway in the period.
86 *Dagbladet*, 15 January 1899.
87 The review of *Othello* in *Trondhjems Adresseavis*, 16 February 1895, is a good example of this dual conception of Shakespeare on the Norwegian stage.
88 *Morgenbladet*, 7 January 1903.
89 *Morgenbladet*, 17 January 1903.
90 *Morgenbladet*, 6 November 1907.
91 *Social-Demokraten*, 27 December 1900.
92 *Morgenbladet*, 7 January 1903.
93 *Morgenbladet*, 7 January 1903.
94 *Aftenposten*, 6 October 1899.
95 *Bergens Aftenblad*, 12 January 1899.

96 *Ørebladet*, 15 March 1899.
97 *Bergens Aftenblad*, 19 April 1895, on a production of *The Taming of the Shrew*.
98 *Bergens Aftenblad*, 2 May 1895.
99 See Keinänen and Sivefors's introduction to *Disseminating Shakespeare* for a discussion of early repertory in Nordic theatres.
100 Rønneberg, *Nationaltheatret gjennom femti år*, 34. Bjørn Bjørnson (1859–1942) was the son of Bjørnstjerne Bjørnson (1832–1910).
101 *Morgenbladet*, 14 June 1901.
102 Rønneberg, *Nationaltheatret gjennom femti år*, 45.
103 *Morgenbladet*, 17 January 1903.
104 Rønneberg, *Nationaltheatret gjennom femti år*, 45.
105 *Morgenbladet*, 11 February 1910.
106 *Morgenbladet*, 8 November 1912.
107 Hutcheon, *A Theory of Adaptation*, 31.
108 Joubin, 'Global Shakespeares in World Markets', 4.
109 *Dagbladet*, 14 March 1899.
110 Rønneberg, *Nationaltheatret gjennom femti år*, 61.
111 Foster and Murphy, 'Shakespeare, Ethnicity, and Nationalism', 188.
112 Ruud, *An Essay*, 144. Bjørnson and Wildenwey both translated Shakespeare into the Dano-Norwegian 'Riksmål' and not the 'new' Norwegian 'Landsmål'. See Svenn-Arve Myklebost's essay in the present collection for a discussion of the issue of Norwegian linguistic varieties.
113 *Morgenbladet*, 25 February 1910.
114 *Social-Demokraten*, 14 February 1910.
115 *Social-Demokraten*, 14 February 1910.
116 *Morgenbladet*, 17 February 1867; *Ørebladet*, 14 February, 1910.
117 Ruud, *An Essay*, 189.
118 *Morgenbladet*, 17 February 1967; *Social-Demokraten*, 14 February 1910.
119 *Social-Demokraten*, 13 February 1910; *Dagbladet*, 11 February 1910.
120 *Social-Demokraten*, 14 February 1910.
121 *Morgenbladet*, 17 February 1867.
122 *Morgenbladet*, 25 February 1910.

123 Ruud, *An Essay*, 189.
124 Ruud, *An Essay*, 192.
125 Rønneberg, *Nationaltheatret gjennom femti år*, 45.
126 *Morgenbladet*, 8 November 1912.
127 Wiers-Jenssen, *Nationalteatret Gjennem 25 Aar*, 255.
128 Ruud, *An Essay*, 138.
129 Ruud, *An Essay*, 138.
130 Ruud, *An Essay*, 138.
131 Shakespeare, *As You Like It, eller Livet i Skogen*, 122.
132 Ruud, *An Essay*, 141.
133 The square in which the National Theatre is situated was given the name 'Johanne Dybwads Plass' in 1989, which testifies to her place in the history of the theatre.
134 *Aftenposten*, 6 November 1912.
135 *Dagbladet*, 8 November 1912.
136 *Social-Demokraten*, 8 November 1912.
137 *Morgenbladet*, 8 November 1912.
138 *Social-Demokraten*, 11 November 1912.
139 *Morgenbladet*, 7 November 1912.
140 *Afternposten*, 8 November 1912.
141 Ruud, *An Essay*, 191.
142 Ruud, *An Essay*, 141, 193.
143 *Trondhjems Folkeblad*, 10 October 1899.
144 *Trondhjems Folkeblad*, 10 October 1899.
145 *Den 17de Mai*, 6 October 1899.
146 *Trondhjems Adresseavis*, 28 March 1900.
147 *Trondhjems Adresseavis*, 28 March 1900; *Trondhjems Folkeblad*, 10 October 1899.
148 *Morgenbladet*, 14 June 1901.
149 *Aftenposten*, 6 October 1899; *Tronshjems Folkeblad*, 10 October 1899.
150 *Trondhjems Adresseavis*, 28 March 1900.
151 *Morgenbladet*, 14 June 1901.
152 Rønneberg, *Nationaltheatret gjennom femti år*, 36.
153 *Morgenbladet*, 11 February 1910.

154 *Social-Demokraten*, 1 November 1907.
155 *Morgenbladet*, 13 January 1903.
156 *Morgenbladet*, 16 January 1903.
157 *Bergens Aftenblad*, 1 November 1907.
158 *Morgenbladet*, 12 September 1906.
159 *Morgenbladet*, 10 October 1899.
160 *Social-Demokraten*, 6 October 1899.
161 *Aftenposten*, 6 October 1906.
162 *Social-Demokraten*, 27 December 1900. What they found odd was the actual 'taming', although they hasten to add that the thrall of meeting your match was still highly recognizable at the time. See note 165.
163 *Morgenbladet*, 13 January 1903.
164 Simpler than prompt books, and containing less theatrical information, the scripts each actor used for studying and rehearsing their roles are preserved for many of the National Theatre productions.
165 *Social-Demokraten*, 27 December 1900. Such sentiments are of course considered offensive in 2021, as they would have been among the progressive egalitarians whose work resulted in gradual female suffrage in the period 1901–1913.
166 *Dagbladet*, 21 October 1908.
167 *Morgenbladet*, 20 October 1908.
168 *Landsbladet*, 23 October 1908.
169 *Landsbladet*, 23 October 1908.
170 *Morgenbladet*, 1 November 1907.
171 *Dagbladet*, 8 November 1912.
172 *Arbeidet*, 8 February 1912.
173 *Arbeidet*, 8 November 1912.
174 Ruud, *An Essay*, 144.
175 *Morgenbladet*, 7 November 1912.
176 *Morgenbladet*, 8 November 1912.
177 *Social-Demokraten*, 8 November 1912.
178 *Morgenbladet*, 14 June 1901.
179 *Morgenbladet*, 12 September 1906.
180 *Morgenbladet*, 17 January 1903.
181 *Morgenbladet*, 8 November 1912.
182 *Den 17de Mai*, 3 March 1900.

Work Cited

Newspapers:

All referenced newspapers can be found in the searchable, digital archive at the National Library. Older editions of all Norwegian newspapers are freely available here: https://www.nb.no/search?mediatype=aviser

From the archives, National Library, TSark 14 A:

'Indbydelse til fornyet aktietegning til 'Selskabet for opførelse af et nyt theatre i Kristiania', 1891.
'Nationaltheatret' [Renewal of the invitation from 1891], 1895.
Actor's script for *A Midsummer Night's Dream*, 1903.

Other sources

Bosman, Anston, 'Shakespeare and Globalization', in Margreta De Grazia and Stanley Wells, eds, *The New Cambridge Companion to Shakespeare* (Cambridge, 2010), 285–302.

Foster, John, and Andrew Murphy, 'Shakespeare, Ethnicity, and Nationalism: Introduction', in John Foster and Andrew Murphy, eds, *Studies in Ethnicity and Nationalism*, 16/2 (2016), 186–8.

Hansen, Niels B., 'Observations on Georg Brandes' Contribution to the Study of Shakespeare', in Gunnar Sorelius, ed., *Shakespeare and Scandinavia: A Collection of Nordic Studies* (Newark, 2002), 148–67.

Hemstad, Ruth, 'Skandinavisme og Skandinavisk samarbeid', at *Norgeshistorie. Fra steinalederen til i dag. Fortalt av fagfolk* (n.d./n.p.), retrieved from https://www.norgeshistorie.no/bygging-av-stat-og-nasjon/1412-skandinavisme-og-skandinavisk-samarbeid.html, 25 September 2021.

Holdsworth, Nadine, *Theatre and Nation* (Basingstoke, 2010).

Huang, Alexa, 'Global Shakespeare Criticism Beyond the Nation State', in James C. Bulman, ed., *The Oxford Handbook of Shakespeare and Performance* (Oxford, 2017), 423–40.

Huang, Alexa, and Elizabeth Rivlin, 'Shakespeare and the Ethics of Appropriation', in Alexa Huang and Elizabeth Rivling, eds, *Shakespeare and the Ethics of Appropriation* (Basingstoke, 2014), 1–20.

Humpál, Martin, 'Knut Hamsun's Criticism of Shakespeare', in Nely Keinänen and Per Sivefors, eds, *Disseminating Shakespeare in the Nordic Countries: Shifting Centres and Peripheries in the Nineteenth Century* (London, 2022), 319–42.

Hutcheon, Linda, *A Theory of Adaptation* (New York, 2006).

Joubin, Alexa Alice, 'Global Shakespeares in World Markets and Archives: An Introduction to the Special Issue', *Borrowers and Lenders*, 11/1 (2017), n.p.

Keinänen, Nely, and Per Sivefors, eds, *Disseminating Shakespeare in the Nordic Countries: Shifting Centres and Peripheries in the Nineteenth Century* (London, 2022).

Keinänen, Nely, and Per Sivefors, 'Introduction', in Nely Keinänen and Per Sivefors, eds, *Disseminating Shakespeare in the Nordic Countries: Shifting Centres and Peripheries in the Nineteenth Century* (London, 2022), 16–48.

Lanier, Douglas, 'Shakespearean Rhizomatics: Adaptation, Ethics, Value', in Alexa Huang and Elizabeth Rivlin, eds, *Shakespeare and the Ethics of Appropriation* (Basingstoke, 2014), 21–40.

Menzer, Paul, 'Archives and Anecdotes', in James C. Bulman, ed., *The Oxford Handbook of Shakespeare and Performance* [Digital Edition] (Oxford, 2017), 218–30.

Nasjonalbiblioteket, 'Library History' [Digital resource; n.d, n.p.], retrieved from https://www.nb.no/nbdigital/bibliotekhistorie/, 25 September 2021.

Orkin, Martin, 'Local, Global, and "Glocal"', in Bruce R. Smith and Katherine Rowe, eds, *The Cambridge Guide to the Worlds of Shakespeare* (New York, 2016), 1070–7.

Ringdal, Nils Johan, *Nationaltheatrets Historie: 1899–1999* (Oslo, 2000).

Rønneberg, Anton, *Nationaltheatret gjennom femti år* (Oslo, 1949).

Ruud, Martin, *An Essay Toward a History of Shakespeare in Norway* (Minneapolis, 1917).

Schmiesing, Ann, 'Bjørnson and the Inner Plot of "A Midsummer Night's Dream"', *Scandinavian Studies*, 74/4 (2002), 465–82.

Schmiesing, Ann, 'The Christiania Theater and Norwegian Nationalism: Bjørnson's Defence of the 1856 Whistle Concerts in "Pibernes Program"', *Scandinavian Studies*, 76/3 (2004), 317–40.

Shakespeare, William, *En Skjærsommernatsdrøm*, trans. Edvard Lembcke (København, 1896).

Shakespeare, William, *As You Like It, eller Livet i Skogen*, trans. and adaptation for the National Theatre by Herman Wildenwey (Kristiania, 1912).

Shakespeare, William, *A Midsummer Night's Dream*, eds Gary Taylor, John Jowett, Terri Bourus, and Gabriel Egan, The New Oxford Shakespeare (Oxford, 2016).

Smidt, Kristian, *Shakespeare i norsk oversettelse: En situasjonsrapport* (Oslo, 1994).

Solheim, John, and Trine Syvertsen, 'Norsk pressehistorie', at *Store Norske Leksikon* (n.d./n.p.), retreived from https://snl.no/norsk _presses_historie, 30 September 2021.

Sørensen, Øystein, 'Nordmennene blir norske for alvor', at *Norgeshistorie. Fre steinalederen til i dag. Fortalt av fagfolk* (n.d./n.p.), retreived from https://www.norgeshistorie.no/industrialisering-og-demokrati/1539 -nordmennene-blir-norske-for-alvor.html, 25 September 2021.

Steine, Bjørn Arne, 'Ut av unionene!'. at *Norgeshistorie. Fre steinalederen til i dag. Fortalt av fagfolk* (n.d./n.p.), retreived from https://www .norgeshistorie.no/industrialisering-og-demokrati/1513-ut-av-unionene .html, 25 September 2021.

Þorbergsson, Magnús Þor, 'Being European: Staging the Nation in 1920s Icelandic Theatre', *Nordic Theatre Studies*, 25/1 (2018), 22–33.

Thune, Taran, 'Norsk utdanningshistorie', at *Store Norske Leksikon* (n.d./n.p.), retreived from https://snl.no/norsk_utdanningshistorie, 30 September 2021.

Wiers-Jenssen, H., *Nationaltheatret Gjennem 25 Aar: 1899–1924* (Kristiania, 1924).

Wilmer, S. E., ed., *National Theatres in a Changing Europe: Studies in International Performance* (Houndmills, 2008).

5

Commemoration and conflict at Hamlet's Castle

The 1916 'Shakespeare *Mindefest*' in Elsinore

Anne Sophie Refskou

In the archives of the Danish Film Institute is an eight-minute silent documentary filmed on a windy summer's day in Elsinore in 1916.[1] The monochrome footage shows scenes of bustling excitement at what appears to be an important event: groups of people gather on audience podiums and sprawl on chairs and blankets on the grass at the easternmost bastion of Elsinore's Kronborg Castle next to the waves of the narrow sound that separates the Danish and Swedish coastlines.[2] Some look at the camera and smile a bit self-consciously – clearly unaccustomed to the novel technology – while holding on to their hats in the insistent breeze. Others direct their attention to a small theatre stage in front of Kronborg's impressive walls and towers. The camera captures a figure in a black costume walking across the stage. Elegantly dressed guests arrive in motor cars and horse-drawn carriages, including the Danish King Christian X and Queen Alexandrine, who are greeted by uniformed officials and dignitaries with flowers and handshakes. In another sequence, more people come out of Elsinore's characteristic Neo-Renaissance train station and walk along the harbour area next to ships and cranes. New arrivals push through the crowded station entrance, men in bowler hats blow great clouds of cigar smoke and little boys in sailor suits stop and grin cheekily at the camera. As with so much early film footage, these ghostly figures are comical, touching and a bit uncanny, manifesting such 'lively' traces of those who have long been dead.

The day immortalized in the documentary was 24 June, a Danish feast day known as *Sankt Hans* (St John's Day, after John the Baptist), mostly associated with popular celebrations of summer solstice. The evening before, many of those in the Elsinore crowds would have celebrated midsummer with bonfires traditionally believed to ward off evil creatures and spirits on the many beaches along the Danish coastline, as is still the custom today. However, the 1916 event captured by the camera was not to do with local customs but with the English playwright who had brought international fame to Elsinore and its magnificent fortified castle, built by King Frederik II in the late sixteenth century and still inauthentically – but inextricably – associated with the setting of *Hamlet*.[3] The occasion was referred to in Danish as a *Mindefest*, a commemorative celebration, to mark the tercentenary of Shakespeare's death. As indicated by the royal presence and the large audience, it was an event of considerable importance. A Danish newspaper at the time described it as a truly remarkable occasion which would no doubt attract attention beyond Danish borders.[4] Even if this prediction was an overestimation, the ambitious scale of the celebration is clear: the programme featured extracts from *Hamlet* performed by leading actors of the Danish Royal Theatre, and there were contributions by some of the most prominent Danes of the day, including the composer Carl Nielsen, the literary critic and Shakespeare biographer Georg Brandes and the poet and debater Helge Rode. In the audience were Danish official and cultural figures, while Denmark's Nordic neighbours were represented by two renowned Shakespearean actors: Johanne Dybwad from Norway and Anders de Wahl from Sweden.

Nothing in the cheerful scenes and faces in the documentary footage suggests that Europe – and the world – was in the middle of a geopolitical crisis on an unimaginable scale. Yet the guests at the *Mindefest* could hardly have been oblivious to the fact that a world war was going on, even if Denmark itself had managed to avoid direct involvement in the fighting and officially remained neutral. The same national and local newspapers that covered the *Mindefest* were filled with reports from the fronts, and earlier that same month gunfire between British and German ships during the Battle of Jutland had made windows rattle in towns along the Danish west coast. Ambiguous sentiments about Denmark's neutral position were also being expressed internally, partly in relation to the Danes making fortunes by selling canned foods to the German army (the so-called 'goulash barons') but perhaps most famously in a 1916 poem by the Danish writer Jeppe Aakjær. Aakjær's poem, originally entitled 'Song of History' (*Historiens Sang*), is a pacifist paean to Danish cultural history but also includes the still oft-quoted lines: 'You little country, furtively contented, while all the world is burning about your cradle.'[5] This description of Denmark as a country shutting its eyes to a world in flames and going about its small business implies that Danish pacifism was not unrelated to a shunning of political responsibility and a habit of avoiding the outside world. It also exemplifies the kind of ambiguity and mixed messages that characterize the content and context of the 1916 Elsinore *Mindefest* and its appropriation and celebration of Shakespeare.

What I want to suggest in this chapter is that the *Mindefest* represents an ambiguous tension between a Danish wish to stage a Shakespearean celebration as nostalgically and intrinsically Nordic while almost wilfully avoiding references to contemporaneous international politics and an outward-looking mindset which was prepared to be more politically explicit. Like other tercentenary celebrations in 1916, the *Mindefest* could not ignore the ongoing war, but, as I will demonstrate, it may have been in the organizers' diplomatic interest to avoid contentious content as much as possible, and keeping the theme intrinsically and slightly quaint was one way to do so. Thus, I read the *Mindefest*'s engagement with Shakespeare partly as Nordic cultural self-assertion and partly as a shying away from world events but also, almost paradoxically, as the least offensive and therefore most neutral course of action.

Shakespearean commemoration has attracted a significant amount of critical writing, not least immediately before and in the wake of worldwide celebrations of the 2016 Quatercentenary, which also prompted renewed interest in 1916 events.[6] However, although critics have shown very clearly that 1916 Shakespearean commemoration included a wide global spectrum of events, little attention has been paid to contributions from – and in – the Nordic countries. As these new collections edited by Keinänen and Sivefors demonstrate, there are various reasons for the continuously peripheral position of Nordic Shakespeares in Shakespeare studies and on the global Shakespeare map in general, ranging from geography to linguistic accessibility. Yet, as the collections also demonstrate, Shakespeare has had a long-standing presence and influence in the Nordic nations, and his status gained an ever-increasing currency throughout the nineteenth and early twentieth centuries. Sir Israel Gollancz's monumental commemorative anthology *A Book of Homage to Shakespeare*, issued in 1916 and reissued in 2016, features a good number of Nordic contributions among its impressive collection of global homage-payers, with five from Denmark alone, even if these are placed towards the end of the volume after their presumably more prominent fellow European contributors such as those from France and Italy.[7] In 1916, the Shakespearean world map was, not surprisingly, organized according to a 'centre and periphery' principle with England's imperial power at the centre, even if this was in the process of being displaced, as scholars like Coppélia Kahn, Gordon McMullan and Philip Mead have shown.[8]

The Nordic countries would inevitably be on the margins of that map, but the Nordic contributors to *A Book of Homage* are clearly still keen to document and share the influence of Shakespeare on their respective literary and theatrical traditions. Christian Collin's contribution in English, entitled 'Shakespeare and the Norwegian Drama', traces the Shakespearean influence on famous Norwegian writers, including Henrik Ibsen and Bjørnstjerne Bjørnson, while also praising the Shakespearean performances of the great Norwegian actress, Johanne Dybwad (who, as noted, was present at the Elsinore *Mindefest*). More significantly, Collin demonstrates an integration of Shakespeare with a Norwegian assertion of national-cultural identity, which is also present in some of the Finnish contributions, as Nely Keinänen has recently demonstrated.[9] This is exemplified in Collin's opening reference to the nineteenth-century Norwegian poet Henrik Wergeland, who is associated with the re-establishing of Norwegian culture after four centuries of Danish rule and who was a great admirer of Shakespeare.[10] Collin's homage to Shakespeare from a Norwegian perspective is simultaneously a homage to Wergeland, and both are presented as freedom-loving liberators from rules and restrictions – both literary, educational and political. As Collin writes,

> The name of William Shakespeare is thus to Norsemen associated with the vernal awakening of Neo-Norwegian poetry, a springtide of lyric enthusiasm which the nation looks back upon with feelings similar to those with which we witness the recurring miracle of early anemones, lifting their sweet blue eyes from amidst the snow.[11]

Nordic contributions to *A Book of Homage* also show residue of nineteenth-century National Romanticism and its medievalist reverence for Nordic history, myth and folklore combined with depictions of Nordic nature. This was not least the case in Denmark where *Hamlet* and to some extent Shakespeare were integrated into a widespread enthusiasm for a glorified past by Romantic writers. The poet Adam Oehlenschläger was a key proponent of Danish National Romanticism and a 'nordicized', heroic Hamlet appears in his play *Amleth* (1847) based on the medieval tale by Saxo Grammaticus in *Gesta Danorum*.[12] In Oehlenschläger's poem *Kronborg*, first published in 1834 and depicting an evening visit to the castle in Elsinore, he infuses the castle and its surroundings with the spirit of a Hamlet figure who, together with the ghost of his father (here cast as a spirit of an inextinguishably glorious past), wanders about the castle grounds in moonlight. In the final stanza of the poem, the poet identifies with this Hamlet figure, whom he sees as a childlike lover of old legends, and ends with the hope that children of the future will find similar occasion to revere the past glories of the North.

In *A Book of Homage*, Danish poet Niels Møller's 'On the Way to Shakespeare' ('Paa vej til Shakespeare') seems at first glance to channel Oehlenschläger in its poetic recollection of a first encounter with Shakespeare, full of childlike enthusiasm and set in a golden age of innocence.[13] However, the final stanza makes it clear that Møller sets his recollections of past joys in contrast to the present situation, which he, in a slightly cryptic metaphor, compares with living in the land of Kedar, while the Assyrian army 'pedantically' oppresses the earth. He concludes by expressing his gratitude that he at least was first able to hear Shakespeare's voice in English: 'I give my deepest thanks, that I have heard his voice in his own language, that I have known how sweet and rich is its song, that I have felt his fair soul, home-born on the white coast of an Englishman', thus offering a veiled statement of support for Britain but without directly alluding to the war.[14] Indeed, another significant aspect of the Nordic contributions to *A Book of Homage* is how they include, or exclude, any mention of the concurrent crisis, to which they were in different ways peripheral and neutral but by which they were nonetheless affected.

As scholars such as Clara Calvo have demonstrated, the Great War unleashed a series of antagonistic and patriotic appropriations of Shakespeare's symbolic value. In her important essay on wartime celebrations of the 1916 Tercentenary, Calvo outlines several cultural battle-lines in the fight over Shakespeare, most importantly the British-German quarrel which mirrored the political situation and included simultaneous use of Shakespearean references by the two countries in their respective war propaganda.[15] The long-standing appropriation of Shakespeare by the German Romantics and their successors – with significant contributions to Shakespearean scholarship and a prolific theatre tradition – was well known and provided some justification for the German dramatist and novelist Gerhart Hauptmann to state in 1915 that 'even if England was where Shakespeare was born, Germany was where he was truly alive'.[16] Andreas Höfele, who quotes Hauptmann's statement, finds an English retort in Henry Arthur Jones's short volume *Shakespeare and Germany* (written during the Battle of Verdun), published in 1916, which vehemently refutes any German claims to Shakespeare and asserts Shakespeare as wholly and patriotically English while also (albeit not very convincingly) reading anti-German sentiment into several of the plays.[17] Thus, in 1916, Shakespeare was at once perceived, promoted and fought over as the cultural representative of nationalism(s), internationalism, imperialism, multiculturalism and universalism, depending on different geopolitical and ideological positions. The 1916 *Mindefest* in Elsinore should be seen against the backdrop of these contradictory expressions and conflicts, not least because Denmark, as we shall see, found itself uneasily positioned between British and German interests. Like Møller's poem in *A Book of Homage*, the *Mindefest* contained expressions of sympathy with Shakespeare's native country – some direct and some indirect – but in other respects it steered carefully clear of anything that might be interpreted as political content.[18] Denmark's position in respect of the Great War was something like a Rosencrantz-and-Guildenstern-inspired approach to diplomacy. Having been badly bruised in antagonistic encounters with both Britain and Germany in the previous century, Denmark was painfully aware of the need to be cautious and avoid taking sides.[19] An important event in this context was the so-called Minelaying crisis (*Mineudlægningskrise*), which occurred at the outbreak of the war in August 1914 when the Danish government received a German request to lay mines in the 'Great Belt' strait between the Danish islands of Zealand and Funen to block British navy access to the Baltic and to the important German navy base of Kiel. This placed Denmark in a difficult dilemma: it risked offending either Germany or Britain or even presenting itself as a potential ally, which might bring about a crisis like those of the previous century (which had seen Denmark lose land to Germany). The Danish King Christian X, who was to be guest of honour at the Elsinore *Mindefest* two years later, took an active interest in the situation, which resulted in a slightly unexpected course of action. The king encouraged the government to comply with the German request but, without the government's knowledge, secretly informed his cousin in London, King George V, that although mines would be laid out in the Danish strait, they would not be armed. The responsible navy admiral, however, had not been informed of these exchanges *en famille* and was later somewhat surprised to find that he had been unwittingly disobedient, while the king was equally surprised (and displeased) to find that the mines were indeed armed. In the end, the severity of the situation was overestimated and Britain showed itself graciously understanding, so Denmark fared better than Hamlet's two schoolfellows and remained neutral after all, but the event did underline Denmark's difficult position and complicated the country's self-understanding in relation to the two fighting sides.[20]

In this context, it is perhaps not surprising that at first glance the Elsinore *Mindefest* seems to have staged its celebration of Shakespeare wholly detached from the war. The event had been an initiative of the Danish Writers' Association, led by the writer and dramatist Sophus Michaëlis in collaboration with Johannes Nielsen, director of the Danish Royal Theatre in Copenhagen. In an essay subsequently published in a Danish theatre review, Michaëlis defensively addresses some unidentified critics – indicating that some must have thought the aspirations of the *Mindefest* somewhat too grand – and lists his reasons why it was considered appropriate for Elsinore to host such an event:

> If it is idiotic to celebrate Hamlet in the town which through him has gained worldwide fame, then all celebration of spirit, genius, history and tradition must be silly. So it is ridiculous to travel to Weimar to celebrate Goethe, to remember Othello in Venice or to visit Juliet's house in Verona. So we should laugh at all the foreign visitors who come to Elsinore for Hamlet's sake. Ask not if such celebration be historically justified; let the question of whether Shakespeare ever visited Elsinore remain unanswered. But let the human spirit keep its fantasies.[21]

Michaëlis's justification for the *Mindefest* clearly rests on an understanding of Elsinore as belonging to a group of locations with intangible connection to Shakespeare and the assumed right to pay spiritual homage to his genius. His subsequent description of the various elements of the *Mindefest* focuses almost exclusively on the aesthetic and artistic qualities of the actors, the music and the set design, except for a few more defensive lines which again claim the right to pay homage to Shakespeare when others are doing the same despite the war: 'When a world-renowned name is associated with a town in our small and insignificant country, should we not light a sacrificial light for his genius in this place, when the world, even in its current dissolution, finds occasion to commemorate him?'[22] Although Michaëlis finally makes an explicit reference to the war, his insistence on Denmark as 'small and insignificant' implies a certain Danish detachment from world events and geopolitics: since Denmark is so small and insignificant, what difference would its presence make on the world stage? But modesty might also work as an excuse for sticking one's head in the sand, as implied in the lines by Jeppe Aakjær I cited at the beginning of this chapter. Clearly, defining the motive and purpose for the *Mindefest* was an uneasy business.

The centrepiece of the *Mindefest* was a set of *Hamlet* extracts performed by leading actors from the Danish Royal Theatre, preceded by a prologue in the form of a short cantata written by the poet Helge Rode and set to music by Carl Nielsen, who conducted the performance himself. The prologue itself was preceded by an opening speech by Georg Brandes. As Michelle Assay and David Fanning have shown in a recent article which also provides a helpfully detailed analysis of each of the *Mindefest* cantata's five songs, there were certain tensions between these three leading figures in Danish cultural life – Rode, Nielsen and Brandes.[23] Rode and Brandes especially had been in direct intellectual opposition for some years before the *Mindefest* which, I will suggest in what follows, further contributed to the mixed messages of the event.

Rode, who was a professed Neo-Romantic, wrote lyrics for the prologue cantata that quite clearly recall previous-century National Romanticism and the spirit of Adam Oehlenschläger.[24] This is particularly evident in the lyrics for the first song of the cantata, ending with 'Hail thee, proud swan of Avon, the sons of the North hail thee' and 'O great wooer, the daughters of the North say yes!' The stage design seems to have accentuated the Romanticism of Rode's lyrics by consisting of a medieval-looking façade with Romanesque arches, which rather clashed with the Renaissance architecture of Kronborg itself but channelled the Nordic National Romantic fondness for medievalism. The first song of the cantata was followed by 'Caliban's and Ariel's songs' and a final homage march which celebrates Shakespeare as the highest representative of poetry. As Assay and Fanning also note, the final march was initially to be played to the tune of *God Save the King*, but this was stopped in order to avoid a potential political impasse.[25] In a letter to his wife on 28 May 1916, Carl Nielsen recounts how Rode visited him and requested the composition of a new melody for the march because political reasons prevented the use of the British anthem at the Shakespeare commemoration.[26] Nielsen does not elaborate, but the reference makes it quite evident that the *Mindefest* organizers were trying to steer clear of any explicit homage-paying to Britain that might offend their German neighbours and that they were aware of the need for careful diplomatic manoeuvring.[27]

Nielsen's music appears to comply largely with Rode's content; the arrangements are simple, presumably also because, as the Danish newspaper *Nationaltidende* suggests in a review of the whole programme, they were designed for outdoor performance.[28] The same review also describes the music as highly pleasing and accessible to the popular ear and makes a reference to Nielsen's former teacher, the National Romantic composer Niels W. Gade. As Assay and Fanning write, Nielsen's recently finished Fourth Symphony (*The Inextinguishable*) also features quasi-folkloristic elements, and he was engaged in an ongoing project of composing folk-popular songs.[29] The simplicity, serenity and folkloristic qualities of the music might suggest that Nielsen was writing in accordance with the deliberately non-political tendencies of the *Mindefest*. Yet we know that Nielsen was strongly affected by the war and what he was seeing in Europe. As early as 1914, he wrote the following passage in a letter to his friend, the Swedish composer Bror Beckmann:

> But it is as if the whole world is dissolving. What will be the end of this? It is bad enough that the material world is destroyed and people are murdering each other, but even worse is the terrible fact that European men of thought and spirituality have lost their minds. National sentiment, which until now was considered valuable and beautiful, has become like a spiritual syphilis which has eaten the brains and now laughs from empty eye sockets in crazed hatred.[30]

Apart from the striking metaphorical language of the passage, it is interesting to note that Nielsen particularly renounces national sentiment, which makes his involvement with the sentiment expressed in aspects of the *Mindefest* slightly ambiguous. In other letters written shortly before the event, he expresses reluctance at the assignment and suggests that he has only agreed because of the remuneration.[31] This is not to suggest that his reluctance might necessarily have been politically motivated, only to emphasize that he did not express particular enthusiasm about taking part in the *Mindefest*. Nonetheless, it contributes to the impression of unease behind the scenes.

Another key element of the *Mindefest* programme more explicitly increases the sense of an event at odds with itself: Georg Brandes's opening speech. Brandes, who in 1916 was in his mid-seventies, was a controversial figure in Danish cultural circles and, as I have noted, a respected literary critic outside of Denmark. His biographical Shakespeare study had been published to widespread recognition on the European continent in 1898 and was subsequently translated into English by William Archer.[32] It is therefore no surprise that he should be invited to give the opening speech at the *Mindefest*, especially since Sophus Michaëlis was his former student and longstanding admirer. Michaëlis's previously quoted account of the event also includes an adulatory description of Brandes in front of the crowd and royals as the leading representative of the Danish *intelligentsia*, braving the wind with his piercing words, although, given Michaëlis's apparent attempt to steer the event away from potentially vexed content, inviting Brandes was not the safest choice, considering the critic's frequent outspokenness in both cultural and political debates. It is in fact slightly surprising that Brandes's short piece in *A Book of Homage* makes no mention of the war at all but is simply a somewhat casual note on literary interpretation. Even if the wider international audience of Gollancz's publication might have warranted a more careful treading on political ground, Brandes was not usually in the habit of biting his tongue.

Brandes's speech at the Kronborg bastion on 24 June 1916 begins by outlining various potential interpretations of *Hamlet*, but he intersperses these with a strong critique of past Danish attempts to repeat or appropriate Shakespeare's play – including Oehlenschläger's *Amleth*, which he dismisses as a poor attempt and, significantly, too Germanic in its language. In fact, Brandes claims, 'Hamlet is not particularly Danish at all' ['Hamlet er for så vidt ikke særlig dansk']. If anyone in the tragedy can be considered Danish, he continues, it might be 'the old fool, Polonius' ['det gamle Vrøvl Polonius'].[33] Such statements jar with the nationally inflected lyrics of Rode's prologue, which is not surprising given the general intellectual and critical differences between Rode and Brandes. In fact, well-informed audience members might have wondered at the sight of these two adversaries alongside each other in the programme.[34]

Brandes ends his speech with a strongly worded refutation of the politics of the war by claiming that (A)rt will ultimately survive politics, just 'as the bronze medal survives the emperor depicted on it'[35]. Brandes's Danish 'Kejser' possibly alludes to Kaiser Wilhelm II, and the impression of a dig at Germany and the Triple Alliance is strengthened by his final insistence that the *Mindefest*'s homage to Shakespeare and to (A)rt should be understood as a homage to England with Denmark's gratitude.[36] Yet Brandes should not necessarily be seen as expressing political allegiance to England as such; his speech fundamentally condemns the war and those who cause it, which is consistent with his views expressed elsewhere.[37] What makes his speech stand out is the fact that he so explicitly addresses the topic of the war, when the rest of the *Mindefest* programme seems to tiptoe around it.

Brandes's main message – his insistence on a quasi-sacred status for Shakespeare as a representative of art, genius and civilization in spite of the devastations of war – places his speech and the rest of the Elsinore *Mindefest* at the end of an era but still just about inside it. Later post-war voices would definitively shatter such views on human achievement. In Paul Valéry's oft-quoted 1919 'Letters from France', we find a European Hamlet figure, who looks out '[f]rom an immense terrace of Elsinore which extends from Basle to Cologne, and touches the sands of Nieuport, the marshes of the Somme, the chalk of Champagne, and the granite of Alsace' only to see 'millions of ghosts'.[38] Valéry's 'Hamlet of Europe', who is uncertain what his role should be, if indeed he has a role at all, was not yet manifest in the real Elsinore of 1916. But certainly Brandes's unequivocal dismissal of the *Hamlet* appropriations and interpretations largely belonging to – or inspired by – the Romantics as well as his sombre reminder to the audience that '[w]e live in a time of explosives' ['Vi lever i sprængstoffernes tid'] can still be read alongside the cultural markers that were bringing 'the long nineteenth century' to an end.

For some of those attending the 1916 *Mindefest* for Shakespeare in Elsinore, the event may have been mainly a celebration and a jolly midsummer's day out, but others may have experienced it as an insistent, perhaps uncomfortable, reminder of a world outside the comparatively safe confines of little Denmark. As I have suggested, it invoked a series of tensions between neutrality and active expression of political interest, between inward and outward-looking perspectives, between a Romanticized Hamlet figure of the past – now seemingly recovered to present a pleasing and unthreatening image – and a foreshadowing of Valéry's Hamlet as the powerless representative of a broken Europe.

At the same time, it prepared the ground for Elsinore's – and Denmark's – position on the global Shakespeare map and for its international theatre festival held at Kronborg Castle, which, to this day, implicitly reorganizes that map by becoming a local platform for sharing Shakespeare globally – what we might call, somewhat paradoxically, a peripheral centre.[39] On the one hand the international aspirations of the *Mindefest* have been more than fulfilled, but it could be argued that some of its underlying tension and ambiguities are still present, albeit in different ways, in Elsinore's unique ongoing relationship with Shakespeare. The Hamlet figure whom Elsinore has in several ways (re)adopted as a long-standing marker of identity for the town is also inevitably a point of intersection with the wider world, with globalization and foreign cultures. To repeat the words of Sophus Michaëlis, it ought to be straightforward to celebrate Hamlet in the town which through him has gained worldwide fame but, as we have seen, who or what Hamlet is to Elsinore was a point of contention in 1916, and it remains an ongoing conversation in this small corner of Northern Europe.

Notes

1 *Mindefesten paa Kronborg* (1916) [Documentary film], Denmark: Nordisk Film Kompagni. I am grateful to the editors of this volume for their helpful comments and suggestions on drafts of this chapter. I am also grateful to Carl Nielsen scholar Niels Krabbe for reading it and providing helpful comments on (especially) Nielsen-related content.

2 Elsinore is situated on the Danish coast north-east of Copenhagen and facing its Swedish neighbours across the narrow strait of Øresund. Kronborg Castle is built on the fifteenth-century foundations of *Krogen*, a strategically situated fortress controlling the sound, where, for centuries, the Danish crown extracted sound duties from passing merchant ships, and Elsinore consequently grew extremely prosperous and somewhat infamous throughout Europe.

3 For Kronborg as a Shakespearean site of 'fake authenticity', see Joubin, 'Site-Specific Hamlets'. I have also explored authenticity and Kronborg's Hamlet and Shakespeare associations elsewhere: see Refskou, 'Whose Castle'.

4 *Nationaltidende*, 25 June 1916.

5 Aakjær, *Historiens Sang*. The Danish original reads: 'Du pusling-land, som hygger dig i smug/mens hele verden brænder om din vugge' (all translations mine).

6 See, for example, Calvo, 'Fighting over Shakespeare'; Calvo and Kahn, *Celebrating Shakespeare*; Calvo and Hoenselaars, *Shakespeare and Commemoration*; Kahn, 'Remembering Shakespeare Imperially';

McMullan, 'Introduction'; McMullan and Mead, 'Introduction'; and, very recently, Bigliazzi, *Shakespeare and Crisis*; and King and Smialkowska, *Memorialising Shakespeare*.

7 In addition to the Nordic contributions mentioned in this chapter, *A Book of Homage* includes a contribution from the Swedish literature professor Karl Warburg and three contributions from Finland by the poet Eino Leino, literature professor Yrjö Hirn and writer Juhani Aho. As Keinänen, '*Commemoration*', 3, notes, the Finnish contributions are not grouped together with the other Nordic countries but constitute the last European group after a section with contributions from Russia and other Eastern European countries, which, as she writes, places Finland far in the periphery in relation to the organization of the contents. See also note 9.

8 McMullan and Mead argue that although many of the events and initiatives to celebrate Shakespeare during the 1916 Tercentenary – including some aspects of Gollancz's *Book of Homage* – can undoubtedly be read as underwritten by 'imperial values and aspirations', this was also the beginning of 'the process through which global Shakespeare came to displace imperial Shakespeare', *Antipodal Shakespeare*, 14. This echoes Coppélia Kahn's analysis of *A Book of Homage* as representing a vision of English imperial power and history, but, at the same time, that vision is unsettled by some of the individual contributions to the book by existing and former colonies, 'Remembering Shakespeare Imperially'. See also McMullan on *A Book of Homage* as a complex expression of two Shakespeares at a pivotal moment in history: 'the poet both of empire and of a world emerging into a new, very different global order', 'Introduction', 1–2.

9 Keinänen's essay represents a rare engagement with Nordic Shakespeare commemoration and focuses on the contribution to *A Book of Homage* by Finnish poet Eino Leino. She demonstrates how Leino's poem and its subsequent afterlife in translation and censured reprints show a significant, if complicated, harnessing of Shakespeare in the context of Finland's struggle for autonomy from Russia. This, together with the Norwegian contribution by Collin, suggests that another frequently overlooked aspect of Nordic Shakespeares is the potential for Nordic contributions to the study of politicized appropriation of Shakespeare in the context of nation building and independence struggles.

10 Denmark and Norway existed as a unified kingdom (but under Danish monarchy) between 1536 and 1814. After 1814, Norway was subject to Sweden but had home rule and gained its final independence in 1905.

11 Collin, 'Shakespeare and the Norwegian Drama', 499.

12 Oehlenschläger had also translated *A Midsummer Night's Dream* in 1816, the play appealing to his understanding of what Romantic comedy should be.

13 *A Book of Homage* also includes 'An Eddic Homage to William Shakespeare' by Icelandic scholar Jón Stefánsson, which, rather remarkably, fuses Shakespearean homage with a resurrection of Iceland's proud tradition of medieval poetry and sagas, but also seems to echo something of Nordic Romanticism.

14 Møller, 'Paa vej til Shakespeare (On the Way to Shakespeare)', 487–9.

15 Calvo, 'Fighting over Shakespeare', 55–65. To Gollancz's regret, Germany was also left out in *A Book of Homage*, but the German contribution to Shakespearean scholarship was acknowledged in an essay contributed to the anthology by C. H. Herford, demonstrating a sense of scholarly fair play and in tune with the universalist aspirations of the project.

16 From Hauptmann's 'Deutschland und Shakespeare' printed in the 1915 *Jahrbuch der Deutschen Shakespeare-Gesellschaft*, qtd. in Höfele, *No Hamlets*, 2–3.

17 See also Calvo, 'Fighting over Shakespeare', 55–6, or Hendley, 'Cultural Mobilization'.

18 For an interesting comparative European case, see Bigliazzi on 1916 Shakespearean commemoration discourse in Italy, which, as Bigliazzi shows, was influenced by the country's 'delicate change of alliance from the Central Powers (Germany and Austria) to Britain and France', 29.

19 Denmark chose to side with the coalition against Britain during the Napoleonic wars, which resulted in the battles of Copenhagen in 1801 and 1807, where Denmark suffered defeat and lost most of her fleet. In 1864, Denmark's miscalculated Second Schleswig War against Prussia and Austria resulted in an even more humiliating defeat and loss of lives and territory, and has often been read as a deeply traumatic cultural memory with direct and indirect influence on Danish identity and subsequent foreign policy.

20 For an analysis of Denmark's dilemma in relation to British and German interests in 1914, see Due-Nielsen, 'The Beginning of a Beautiful Friendship', 193–4.

21 Michaëlis, 'Shakespearefesten paa Kronborg', 138.

22 Michaëlis, 'Shakespearefesten paa Kronborg', 138. Michaëlis also has a possible slip when he refers to critique of the surroundings as too

large for the performance: 'Some thought the surroundings too large. But it was precisely here that the battle would be fought.' Describing the performance as a 'battle' may be rhetorical, but it is hard to overlook in view of the context.

23 Assay and Fanning, 'Nielsen, Shakespeare and the Flute Concerto', 70–1.

24 It is also worth noting that Sophus Michaëlis wrote a poem entitled *Kronborg* and dated precisely on 24 June 1916, which contains plentiful echoes of National Romanticism. The poem very much follows the pattern of Oehlenschläger's earlier poem of the same title and depicts a dreamlike evening atmosphere at the castle – which is described as 'a diadem on the brow of Denmark' – abound with ghosts of the glorious past and with Prince Hamlet suddenly appearing on the bastion.

25 Assay and Fanning, 'Nielsen, Shakespeare and the Flute Concerto', 79.

26 Nielsen, *Dagbøger og brevveksling*, 409.

27 It is not clear that information about the *Mindefest* programme would reach German, or indeed British, authorities (or that they would pay much attention to it), but in view of the Danish newspapers' expectation of international attention and the request to Nielsen to avoid the British national anthem, this must have been seen as a possibility.

28 *Nationaltidende*, 25 June 1916.

29 Assay and Fanning, 'Nielsen, Shakespeare and the Flute Concerto', 74.

30 Nielsen, *Carl Nielsens breve*, 144.

31 Nielsen, *Dagbøger og brevveksling*, 408. I am grateful to Niels Krabbe for explaining to me that Nielsen agreed to a number of minor commissions for incidental music because of the remuneration but with a degree of reluctance.

32 Brandes's engagement with Shakespeare has attracted fairly substantial scholarly attention and has been considered influential on, among others, James Joyce, who was an admirer of the critic (see Boysen, 'Brandes' Skygge'). For an overview and analysis of Brandes's Shakespeare study and its contribution to Shakespearean scholarship more widely, see, for example, Hansen, 'Observations' or 'The Prince, the Poet and the Critic'.

33 Brandes, 'Tale paa Kronborg Søbatteri', 236.

34 Rode opposed Brandes's influential concept known as 'The Modern Breakthrough' in literature, which stressed the need for literature to spark debate and break with what Brandes saw as Romantic

single-mindedness. Moreover, as Assay and Fanning write, 'Where Brandes had stressed the virtues of Darwinist realism, common sense and rational scientific explanation, Rode's priorities were Christian idealism and mysticism' ('Nielsen, Shakespeare and the Flute Concerto', 71).

35 Brandes, 'Tale paa Kronborg Søbatteri', 237.

36 Brandes, 'Tale paa Kronborg Søbatteri', 237.

37 In May 1916, Brandes had written an 'appeal' for peace, calling out what he saw as the hypocrisy of all the fighting nations. See Brandes, *Verdenskrigen*, 254–61.

38 Valéry's passage which refers to *Hamlet* is quoted in Höfele, 'Elsinore – Berlin', 1.

39 Elsinore's international theatre tradition began with the arrival of *Hamlet* productions from abroad (the first by the Old Vic in 1937 starring Laurence Olivier and Vivien Leigh) and continues to this day, where HamletScenen, the resident theatre at Kronborg Castle, hosts an annual international Shakespeare Festival and produces its own shows with Danish and international casts. I discuss the international theatre and festival tradition in Elsinore in Refskou, 'Whose Castle' and 'Unhomely Shakespeares'.

Works cited

Aakjær, Jeppe, *Historiens Sang in Digte 1908 –1918* (København, 1916), 161–2.
Assay, Michelle, and David Fanning, 'Nielsen, Shakespeare and the Flute Concerto: From Character to Archetype', *Carl Nielsen Studies*, 6 (2020), 68–93.
Bigliazzi, Silvia, '1916: Italian Narratives of the Tercentenary Crisis', in Silvia Bigliazzi, ed., *Shakespeare and Crisis: One Hundred Years of Italian Narratives* (Amsterdam and Philadelphia, 2020), 25–50.
Boysen, Benjamin Jon, 'Brandes' Skygge', in Steen Klitgaard Povlsen and Ida Klitgaard, eds, *Joyce og Danmark* (Aarhus, 2006), 27–39.
Brandes, Georg, *Verdenskrigen* (København, 1916).
Brandes, Georg, 'Tale paa Kronborg Søbatteri (St Hans dag 1916)', in Georg Brandes, *Taler* (1916; Copenhagen, 2017), 233–7.
Calvo, Clara, 'Fighting over Shakespeare: Commemorating the 1916 Tercentenary in Wartime', *Critical Survey*, 24/3 (2012), 48–72.
Calvo, Clara, and Coppélia Kahn, eds, *Celebrating Shakespeare: Commemoration and Cultural Memory* (Cambridge, 2015).

Calvo, Clara, and Ton Hoenselaars, eds, *Shakespeare and Commemoration* (New York, 2019).
Collin, Christian, 'Shakespeare and the Norwegian Drama', in Israel Gollancz, ed., *A Book of Homage to Shakespeare, 1916*, reissued with a new introduction by Gordon McMullan (1916; Oxford, 2016), 499–505.
Due-Nielsen, Carsten, 'The Beginning of a Beautiful Friendship: Denmark's Relations with Britain 1864–1914', in Bo Bjørke, Claus Bjørn and Jørgen Sevaldsen, eds, *Britain and Denmark: Political, Economic and Cultural Relations in the 19th and 20th Centuries* (Copenhagen, 2002), 171–197.
Hansen, Niels Bugge, 'Observations on Georg Brandes's Contribution to the Study of Shakespeare', in Gunnar Sorelius, ed., *Shakespeare and Scandinavia: A Collection of Nordic Studies* (Newark, 2002), 148–67.
Hansen, Niels Bugge, 'The Prince, the Poet and the Critic', in Bo Bjørke, Claus Bjørn and Jørgen Sevaldsen, eds, *Britain and Denmark: Political, Economic and Cultural Relations in the 19th and 20th Centuries* (Copenhagen, 2003), 391–406.
Hendley, Matthew C., 'Cultural Mobilization and British Responses to Cultural Transfer in Total War: The Shakespeare Tercentenary of 1916', *First World War Studies*, 3/1 (2012), 25–49.
Höfele, Andreas, 'Elsinore – Berlin: *Hamlet* in the Twenties', *Actes des congrès de la Société Française Shakespeare*, 33 (2015), 1–14.
Höfele, Andreas, *No Hamlets: German Shakespeare from Nietzsche to Carl Schmitt* (Oxford, 2016).
Jones, Henry Arthur, *Shakespeare and Germany* (London, 1916).
Joubin, Alexa Alice, 'Site-Specific Hamlets and Reconfigured Localities: Jiang'an, Singapore, Elsinore', in Graham Bradshaw, Tom Bishop and Tetsuo Kishi, eds, *The Shakespearean International Yearbook 7: Special Section, Updating Shakespeare* (Aldershot and Burlington, 2007), 22–48.
Kahn, Coppélia, 'Remembering Shakespeare Imperially: The 1916 Tercentenary', *Shakespeare Quarterly*, 52/4 (2001), 456–78.
Keinänen, Nely, 'Commemoration as Nation-Building: The Case of Finland, 1916', *Société Française Shakespeare*, 33 (2015), 1–14.
King, Edmund G. C., and Monika Smialkowska, eds, *Memorialising Shakespeare: Commemoration and Collective Identity, 1916–2016* (London, 2021).
McMullan, Gordon, 'Introduction to the 2016 Edition', in Israel Gollancz, ed., *A Book of Homage to Shakespeare, 1916*, reissued with a new introduction by Gordon McMullan' (Oxford, 2016), v–xxxiii.
McMullan, Gordon, and Philip Mead, 'Introduction: ANZAC and the Tercentenary in London, April 1916', in Gordon McMullan, Philip

Mead et al., *Antipodal Shakespeare: Remembering and Forgetting in Britain and New Zealand, 1916–2016* (London, 2018), 1–28.

Michaëlis, Sophus, 'Shakespearefesten paa Kronborg', *Teatret*, 15/18 (1916), 138–42.

Michaëlis, Sophus, 'Kronborg', in *Romersk Foraar og andre Digte* (1916; København, 1921).

Møller, Niels, 'Paa vej til Shakespeare (On the Way to Shakespeare)', in Israel Gollancz, ed., *A Book of Homage to Shakespeare, 1916*, 'reissued with a new introduction by Gordon McMullan' (1916; Oxford, 2016), 486–9.

Nielsen, Carl, *Carl Nielsens breve i udvalg og med kommentarer*, ed. Torben Meyer (København, 1954).

Nielsen, Carl, *Dagbøger og brevveksling med Anne Marie Carl-Nielsen*, ed. Torben Schousboe (København, 1983).

Refskou, Anne Sophie, 'Whose Castle is it Anyway?: Local/Global Negotiations of a Shakespearean Location', *Multicultural Shakespeare*, 15/30 (2017), 121–32.

Refskou, Anne Sophie, 'Unhomely Shakespeares: Interculturalism and Diplomacy in Elsinore', in Nicoleta Cinpoes, Florence March and Paul Prescott, eds, *Shakespeare on European Festival Stages* (London, 2021), 195–212.

6

Nynorsk and the Nordic spirit

Henrik Rytter's Shakespeare Translations, 1932–1933

Svenn-Arve Myklebost

In the early 1930s, Henrik Rytter (1877–1950) produced a twenty-three-play, ten-volume Shakespeare translation that at first glance seems quite peculiar.[1] It is written in *Nynorsk*, a form[2] of Norwegian based in dialects and Old Norse, but it is an idiosyncratic version of Nynorsk which feels both archaic and fresh, distant and close, strange and familiar, at the same time. The particular qualities of Rytter's Shakespeare are tied to the linguistic, spiritual, philosophical and political preoccupations that motivate his translation practice and above all his conception of *the Nordic*. In some respects his translations seem rustically retrogressive, but they are not fake antiques in the vein of Coleridge's 'Ancyent Marinere'. Instead, I argue in this chapter, they represent a 'Norwegian Shakespeare' that manages to be both 'authentic' and timely, reflecting something of the aesthetic identity of the plays as early modern texts while also using them to address central ideological issues of the 1930s.

Rytter's Shakespeare straddles a local/universal gap. As Lawrence Venuti discusses, translation is often viewed as 'an act of violence against a nation', whose 'essence' is 'usually given a biological grounding in an ethnicity or race and seen as manifested in a particular language and culture'.[3] But at the same time, '[n]ationalist movements have frequently enlisted translation in the development of national languages and cultures, especially national literatures'.[4] Such contradictions and complexities are rife in Rytter's project. He uses Shakespeare as a vehicle for assessing ideas about national identity, but his representation of Shakespeare is strangely at odds with itself: his introductions create the impression of a somewhat one-sided national-vitalist, Anglo-Nordic Shakespeare, whereas the translated play texts paint a more ambiguous and nuanced picture. This chapter explores this apparent inconsistency and seeks to explain it.

Rytter rendered several principal works of the Western canon into Norwegian, including Dante's *Divine Comedy* and Boccaccio's *Decameron*.[5] The main bulk of his translations, however, suggests a degree of Anglophilia. Among his numerous translations from English are *Beowulf*, works by Eliot and Dickens as well as twenty-three plays by Shakespeare.[6] He was a poet and playwright in his own right and published six original plays and seven collections of poems in his lifetime.[7] Aside from the *Decameron*, all his original works and translations are in Nynorsk, including his ambitious Shakespeare project. The historical, national, political and literary associations of Nynorsk are the foundations upon which Rytter's project is based. To explore Rytter's translations of Shakespeare, I must therefore first say something about the history of the target language and how it came to be connected with Shakespeare from its very inception.

Nynorsk

Even if it has tended towards regularization since the early twentieth century, Norwegian as spoken in Norway today still has considerable dialectal variability. Many words are not just pronounced differently in different fjords, bays and valleys but require completely different spellings to be rendered with orthographic fidelity. To name just one example, *korleis*, *åssen*, *korsen*, *koss*, *høss*, *kordan* and *hvordan* are all the same word: *how* in English. Not all words are so multifariously realized, but many have at least a handful of different forms. There are also syntactical and grammatical differences between the dialects.[8]

In the face of such plurality, it is not self-evident how spoken Norwegian should be written, something which became a question of major national importance in the nineteenth century. The Norwegian constitution had been signed in 1814 (when Sweden annexed Norway from Denmark) and, by the time independence arrived in 1905, two modes of written Norwegian had been established. In the capital of Christiania (from 1925 known as Oslo) the urban elite spoke a dialect of Norwegian reproducible in writing as an adapted version of Danish: the language of education, religion and privilege since the days of Danish rule in the unequal union of 1537–1814. This form of Norwegian was called *Rigsmaal* (approx. 'language of the realm') and after a series of reforms it is now used by up to ninety per cent of Norwegians under the name *Bokmål* (approx. 'book language').[9]

Nynorsk, for its part, emerged as *Landsmaal* (approx. 'language of the land') in the middle of the nineteenth century, and while Rigsmaal/Bokmål was an adapted version of an extant dialect partially based on Danish orthography and grammar, Landsmaal was an attempt to represent the entire variety of dialects used all over the country, with Old Norse as a guideline for word choice and grammar.[10] In the same way that Rigsmaal transformed into modern Bokmål, Landsmaal went through numerous reforms and has been known as Nynorsk since 1929. Although it is a minority language form in Norway, it is legally equal to Bokmål. It has at times been the language of choice for the labour movement, in opposition to the elite's Bokmål; at other times it has been appropriated by conservative nationalist forces. It has a strongly rural image, but many of the most important Nynorsk institutions (book publishers and newspapers) are found in cities, especially the Bokmål bastions of Bergen and Oslo.[11] Today, Nynorsk has a strong standing in the arts, in the theatre, among novelists and poets, and as a target language for translations.[12] At the same time, it is something of a linguistic underdog within Norway, something which plays a role in the history of its development as well as in Rytter's Shakespeare project.

Astonishingly, a single man was responsible for conceiving the idea of Landsmaal, travelling for years to document dialects from all over Norway, compiling the results, producing a dictionary and creating a grammar. Ivar Aasen (1813–1896) was a small-village autodidact who eventually moved to the capital and made a name for himself as a wielder and shaper of language. Seen in this way, there are parallels between him and Shakespeare, and the link is strengthened by the fact that Aasen too was a poet.[13] He started using his Landsmaal to write poetry from an early stage in its development, and he translated major works of world literature as a means to test and 'thicken' his creation.[14] One of his earliest attempts is the 'To be or not to be' monologue from *Hamlet*, produced in the early 1850s.[15] In this fragment, Aasen's Landsmaal is already a fully formed idiom, capable of doing justice to Shakespeare's rhythms and phraseology, and although some room for improvement exists regarding the metrics, this is not the fault of Landsmaal.

Aasen, then, not only created the language form that Rytter would be using more than half a century later (under the new name of Nynorsk), but he also provided a paradigm within which to act. Aasen and Rytter both grew up in the countryside, studied, worked and lived in the same communities (Ørsta/Volda in the west, Oslo and its surroundings in the east), wrote poetry and translated canonical works. Rytter even incorporated portions of Aasen's Shakespeare translations into his own.[16] Aasen emulated Shakespeare and Rytter emulated Aasen, and while these repetitions are largely accidental and unavoidable in a world where cities are hubs for theatre, publishing, education and culture, they also draw attention to the nature/rurality-culture/urbanity dynamic that exists in all three writers' works.

Rytter's Nynorsk is often deliberately archaic (or seemingly so) and rustic. That being said, his translations were produced at a time when Nynorsk was still somewhat new and malleable, and although the raw materials – the vocabulary as well as the dramatic source texts – were old, Rytter's linguistic recombinations were inventive, fresh and new. He tempered the venerable with the novel, the traditional with the modern, the retrospective with the progressive, resistance against Lutheran puritanism with a deeply felt spirituality, the national and local with the cosmopolitan, the individual with the universal. In a limited sense, there is a parallel between Rytter the Nynorsk translator and Shakespeare the 'tradapter' of French, Italian and Latin texts remade in the forge of Early Modern English.[17] Indeed, translation arguably had a similar function in early modern England as in early twentieth-century Norway. George Steiner summarizes the zeitgeist:

> At a time of explosive innovation, and amid a real threat of surfeit and disorder, translation absorbed, shaped, oriented the necessary raw material. It was, in a full sense of the term, the matière première of the imagination. Moreover, it established a logic of relation between past and present, and between different tongues and traditions which were splitting apart under stress of nationalism and religious conflict.[18]

Even though the 'time of explosive innovation' Steiner is speaking of is the Renaissance, his description applies, with some modifications, to 1930s Europe as well and especially to Rytter's situation as a Nynorsk poet and translator.

There is a parallel, Rytter believed, between his time and place and Shakespeare's and in his translations, he creates an image of Shakespeare that conforms to and validates his own political and spiritual ideas about language and nation, and the way these ideas inform his approach to translating the plays.

Rytter's world view: Nation, manliness, anti-Nazism and vitalism

Rytter's intellectual and poetic sensibilities run the gamut from turn-of-the-century Neo-Romanticism (a movement that resurged among Nynorsk poets in the interwar years) to modernism.[19] Seen from an English point of view, Rytter is kin to what Alexandra Harris calls the 'Romantic Moderns'[20] – intellectuals, painters and writers engaged in a search for Englishness in the decade before the Second World War, seeking answers in England's past and its countryside.[21] Around the same time, the Society for Pure English issued tracts where they suggested that dialect words be taken into educated speech and that efforts be made to save archaic words from extinction.[22] The society counted among its members the Shakespeare scholars Arthur Quiller-Couch and C. H. Herford. (The latter, who will turn up again later in this chapter, had a strong interest in Nordic literature and culture.)

Like his English counterparts, Rytter sought to identify a contemporary national 'spirit' and found it in tradition, in dialects and in old word forms, outside the cities; but as a Norwegian 'Romantic Modern' or 'Modern Romantic', Rytter's views cannot without complication be compared with those of English critics informed by modernism. Granted, he had in common with T. S. Eliot and F. R. Leavis an interest in agrarian matters, and also shared with the contemporary critic G. Wilson Knight an interest in 'spiritual' interpretations of the plays,[23] but while Eliot championed 'depersonalized' poetry and deplored the Romantic reading of Hamlet's inner turmoil, Rytter emulated the Norwegian nineteenth-century Romantic poet Henrik Wergeland and very much understood Hamlet's 'soul' Romantically, in the light of Shakespeare's personality.[24] There is no evidence that he studied the works of Eliot, Knight, Leavis or the Society for Pure English, but Rytter's Anglophilia bears out comparison with these Janus-faced artists and writers who looked to the past and the countryside to lay the course for the future.

This rural/spiritual turn had the potential to be deeply reactionary, as with Eliot's friend Viscount Lymington, who 'condoned Hitler's . . . fight for the pure soil of Germany'.[25] In Norway, Rytter's negative counterpart was the pro-German novelist and fellow Neo-Romantic-cum-modernist Knut Hamsun (1859–1952), author of *The Growth of the Soil* (1917). Both authors had an interest in nation, farming, nature and tradition, but while Hamsun would eventually be invited to a private audience with Adolf Hitler (in 1943), Rytter was strongly anti-Nazi. Hamsun was hostile towards English-language culture, and he found Shakespeare psychologically unsophisticated.[26] Rytter loved Shakespeare as much as Hamsun loathed him, and while Hamsun preferred to write in Rigsmaal, Rytter of course wrote in Nynorsk.

Hamsun and Rytter, then, stood on either side of a cultural war leading up to the Nazi invasion of Norway in 1940. This might easily have been different. Rytter, who had much in common with Hamsun and the Nazis, could potentially have gone down the same path as them. As a young man, embittered by financial difficulties and the lost status of his family name (Rytter means 'Rider' or 'Knight'), he expressed anti-capitalist and anti-semitic attitudes.[27] In the 1920s and 1930s, however, Rytter had begun moving to the left politically; he would never change his negative attitudes towards capitalism but would greatly adjust what he saw as its causes and solutions, adducing a Marxist explanation.[28] He was always a 'progressive' in spiritual matters (as opposed to being a piously socially conservative Lutheran), but the emergence of Nazism in Europe and Norway seems to have encouraged a more urgent and complete shift in him, towards a socialist or social-democratic world view.[29]

Rytter, then, became a strong critic of the Nazis as well as of Hamsun.[30] At stake in these debates was the idea of Nordic-ness, which the Nazis were eager to adopt. To the Nazis, the Nordic world – which ostensibly united Germans and Norwegians – was one of tough, purifying natural severity, birthing robust religious notions (such as a belief in warrior Gods and relishing battle) and hordes of Aryan fighters and conquerors: the Vikings. To Rytter, by contrast, there was no place for violence in the world of the Nordic. He revered the Old Norse farmer, sailor, fisherman, trader and explorer but did not hold the Viking warrior in high regard. As Rytter saw it, Nazism was a death cult, dabbling in things it could not comprehend.

Rytter was on the side of life, which is something he made clear in his writings of the time, for example in his pamphlet against Nazism, *Norden har ordet – eit stridsskrift* [The North Speaks – a Polemic].[31] Rytter's Shakespeare translations were produced in a period that overlapped with these ideological and philosophical quarrels with Hamsun and Nazi ideology, from the early 1920s (his *Othello* came out in 1923, about a decade before the other translations) until the early 1930s. The degree to which these topics can be traced in the translations is therefore interesting to determine. Luckily, the ten volumes of Rytter's *Skodespel* [Plays] are equipped with introductions written by the translator: one for the series as a whole and one for each play. The general introduction in the first volume contains a short sketch of Shakespeare's life and the early history of the plays in print and features the usual lamentations regarding the paucity of hard facts about Shakespeare. But, says Rytter, 'to know his works is to know the man himself'.[32] As a piece of biographic criticism, this foreword may have been outmoded even in the 1930s, but what Rytter says about Shakespeare is at any rate more interesting for what it reveals about Rytter's own world view.

At first glance, Rytter's project appears to be a clear case of what Venuti calls 'domestication' – an ideologically motivated

'Norwegianizing' of the Shakespeare canon, as opposed to a 'foreignizing' translation which does not seek to eradicate the fact that it is a translation. When domestication occurs, 'the aim of the translation is to bring back the cultural other as the same, the recognizable, even the familiar' to serve 'an appropriation of foreign cultures for domestic agendas'.[33] There are traces of such an agenda in Rytter's project, but a closer look indicates that things are not so clear-cut.

Throughout his introduction, Rytter calls Shakespeare a *'flogvit'*, which is a particular Nynorsk word for a fast thinker, a 'snapper up of unconsidered trifles' or a genius.[34] The word to some degree casts Shakespeare in the role of Nordic *skald*, something which had been quite common in earlier Landsmaal/Nynorsk treatments of Shakespeare.[35] Having said that, Rytter also uses the Latinate word 'genius' (Nynorsk: *geni*), for example, in the introduction to *Hamlet*, where he calls the play 'probably the only complete representation of genius in our possession'.[36] This is an early sign that while he is not trying to efface 'The Renaissance', he nonetheless creates a new William Shakespeare (Renaissance Humanist credentials included) to construct a contemporary Nordic framework of understanding for the translations of the plays. In essence, Rytter strongly implies that Shakespeare's England is Norway's 1930s.

The project also involves more apparently universalist attitudes. Rytter's subject is 'the spirit we meet in Shakespeare's works' and he claims this 'spirit' is familiar with all aspects of (human) nature,[37] as he details in the general introduction:

> Life flowed richly through it, as it flows through the works. It had experienced the highest elation and the deepest pain; defeat and victory, loss and love, depression and satisfaction – a surfeit thereof – impasses and insights into the futility of existence, curiosity and reverence for the mysteries of life, jokes and earnestness, love and friendship, but also bitter repulsion, indeed hatred, for mankind, pride and humility, fear – of madness –, desire – for ecstasy –, self-restraint – for the love of wisdom –, joy, merriment and melancholy in bitter mockery and corrosive longing, ... all this in excess, but also as if bathed in the very fount of life, with a luminous force within that nothing could extinguish or begin to taint. Everything is filled with the most discriminating and observant sensitivity towards nature, in

everything throbs the vivid pulse of life – everything is blessed and anointed with spiritual high vision [åndehøgsyn] and a longing for infinity [ævetråe].[38]

Rytter leaves ordinary prose to one side (along with regular punctuation) to more poetically evoke the energy, light, sensuality, life and almost religious omniscience he finds in the canon; clearly, he believes that everyday language cannot capture the special qualities of Shakespeare's supposed *Weltanschauung*. Notably, Rytter itemizes the characteristics of Shakespeare's spirit (which conflates the works and the person) in a list of pairs, many of them opposing dichotomies: love and hate, pride and humility, excess and self-restraint, melancholy and ecstasy. This indicates that Rytter sees Shakespeare as a spiritual ally, one who, like himself, views the universe as balanced or tempered. As argued, the foreword is an attempt to make Shakespeare into a spokesperson for Rytter's own world view, and this, in part, involves situating ideal nature as a balance between extremes. There are no ambivalences here, no simultaneous presence of dark *in* light or evil *in* good. Rytter's Shakespeare is very tidy: full of contrast but unpolluted by paradox.

The most crucial aspect is perhaps the emphasis on the perceived life-force running through Shakespeare's world and works. Ideas of 'spirit' and 'vital energy' form one piece in Rytter's Shakespeare puzzle.[39] Another related piece is Shakespeare's ties to the land. Rytter makes sure to emphasize the young Shakespeare's connection with rural Stratford and the integrity of farming and village life. He is especially interested in the Arden family's wealth and their long history of farming the land, because in his view there is nothing nobler. Rytter also perceives in Shakespeare's time a conflict between an adherence to the ideals of 'merry old England' and 'the dark puritanism that would soon turn the fate of England onto new pathways and put a mark on English society and popular temperament which is still traceable today'.[40] He places Shakespeare on the side of 'merry old England', which he ties both to the Renaissance and to England's medieval past, in opposition to the religious ideology that would come to dominate the civil war-torn seventeenth century. Again, Rytter's own preoccupations are visible in what he chooses to highlight in the biography. His Shakespeare represents nature, humanism, intellectual and spiritual liberty and tradition, and the opposing force of 'dark puritanism' calls to mind the austere and strict religion that was nearly ubiquitous in all aspects of Norwegian society until after the Second World War, as well as the totalitarian ideologies that were on the rise in Europe in the 1920s and 1930s, represented by Viscount Lymington's differently 'Merry' English countryside.[41]

In contrast to the Viscount or Hamsun, Rytter did not align nationalism with fascism, although it may appear logical that he should; when he addresses the surge of national feeling he perceives as running through England in Shakespeare's time, he describes it in unequivocally positive terms. Great deeds are piled on great deeds, the people are 'young and strong' and Shakespeare's role in this is to be one of many poet-dramatist geniuses as well as a chronicler of the greatness of English history.[42] That Shakespeare might have been ambivalent about nationhood, royalty or politics does not seem to occur to Rytter – and he is equally normative on the subject of sex. Rytter describes Shakespeare the sonneteer as overwhelmingly concentrated on the 'dark lady', glossing over the fact that more sonnets are devoted to an anonymous young nobleman and that these sonnets are easily as erotically charged as those directed at a woman. His Shakespeare is a manly, healthily heterosexual nationalist of rural stock with a cosmopolitan mindset, much like Rytter himself. He is even, based on no evidence whatsoever, 'tall' and 'stately'.[43]

Rytter's politics can be traced further in the forewords to the history plays. In *King John*, Falconbridge the Bastard is singled out as a personage of 'unique powers, . . . still reeking, as it were, of the soil whence he emerged' and his concluding speech is 'programmatic of all Shakespeare's history plays'.[44] Many current readers might see this speech as jingoistic ('This England never did, nor never shall / Lie at the proud foot of a conqueror' (5.7.112–13), and they might feel that Rytter's portrayal of it is uncomfortably reminiscent of German agrarian Romanticism (which the Nazis infamously formulated as '*Blut und Boden*' or 'blood and soil'), but Rytter evidently believed nationalism could be benign, and unlike the Nazis, he thought it could celebrate what is special to one nation without belittling other peoples and cultures. There is no *über Alles* in his ideology, although it is celebratory of national accomplishments and pride. Indeed, to be fair to Rytter, the Bastard never claims that England is superior, only that it is unassailable and only as long as it is true to itself. This latter point appears to be what matters to the translator and what he sees as Shakespeare's programme: to paint a picture of an ideal England, which in turn can act as a model for an ideal, anti-fascist Norway. The foreword to *Henry V* is the most explicit expression of how Rytter construed Shakespearean ideas about nation and history: 'If we look back at Shakespeare's history plays, it is clear that *Richard II*, the two parts of *Henry IV* and *Henry V* are in reality one single, continuous work where the main theme is the emergence of the *vital force of the English people* [*engelsk folkekraft*] through distinct displays of English character.'[45] As with the English people, so with Shakespeare himself: 'Shakespeare now stands, at the age of 35, at the pinnacle of his manhood, full of the force and joy of life.'[46] The dramatist becomes a microcosm to England's macrocosm and what they share, in Rytter's conception, is a particular kind of manly energy.[47]

Rytter's praise of *engelsk folkekraft*, then, evokes Rytter's ideal Norway more than Renaissance England. As Spaans explains, the 1920s and 1930s saw an emergence of a 'spiritual conception of Norwegian or Nordic ideals among Nynorsk language advocates' that he identifies as 'vitalism'.[48] Allegedly only certain uniquely Norwegian and Norse words could bring forth this special national-popular energy while also bringing out the 'sublime' qualities of Dante or Shakespeare in Norwegian.[49] The domesticated 'Nordic' identity of Rytter's Shakespeare is bolstered by his use of a Swedish model for his translations. According to Beyer, Rytter used Per Hallström's then recent translations as a guide, especially in his approach to metre.[50] This thirty-six-play, twelve-volume Shakespeare came out between 1922 and 1931, so the latest volumes would have been fresh off the press when Rytter started working on his own translations.[51] The introductions to Hallström's edition were written by the Swedish literary scholar Henrik Schück (1855–1948) as early as the 1890s, and Rytter appears to have borrowed freely from them, albeit with frequent and lengthy detours.[52]

Aside from this Swedish model, there is a constant intermingling of Nordic and Anglophone sources in Rytter's project. It has not been possible to ascertain which contemporary English-language editions Rytter used, but it is not hard to detect influences from such works in Rytter's commentary.[53] For example, notions that *King John* is not historically correct, that Falconbridge the Bastard harbours a special kind of power whose 'energy pervades and animates the whole drama' and that he brims with 'vitality' can all be found in the foreword to the play in C. H. Herford's 1904 edition for Macmillan.[54] Herford concludes his discussion of Falconbridge in the same way as Rytter by calling him a prototype and a mouthpiece for what was to come in English history, commending his closing speech and his general, English manliness.[55] Herford had an interest in Nordic culture: he edited a complete works of Henrik Ibsen in English (1906) and published a work on Norse myth in English poems (1919). Moreover, as mentioned, he was also a member of the Society for Pure English. This does not prove that Rytter definitely used Herford's edition. It does confirm, however, that preoccupations and ideas that may seem specifically Nordic and original to Rytter are in fact neither of those things, at least not completely.

Rytter may have borrowed ideas about vital energies and national character from Herford,[56] but it is not certain. Schück is not particularly interested in such matters either – so where did these ideas come from? Part of the answer can be gleaned from looking at Rytter's professional, personal, contemporary influences. In the process of translating Shakespeare, he relied on assistance from his close associate, the dictionary compiler Ola Raknes. Leif Høghaug explains that in 1932, 'attentive readers' would associate Raknes with 'the most substantial English-Norwegian dictionary yet made' and would recognize him as the force within Samlaget who had turned it into a modern, progressive publisher.[57] In addition to being a philologist, the prolific Raknes was a public intellectual, a scholar of religion, a socialist politician and a psychoanalyst associated with Wilhelm Reich. Rytter evidently took many suggestions for word choice from Raknes's dictionary, but there are grounds for assuming that they also conversed about the vitalist philosopher Henri Bergson,[58] Reich's liberal views and criticism of fascism as well as on religion and esotericism more generally.

Folkekraft would have been a central topic of conversation between Rytter and Raknes. The belief in a force or energy that courses through nature and humanity is one that is shared between the Qi of ancient Chinese folklore and religion, the Animal Magnetism of Mesmerism, Bergson's *élan vital*, Nietzsche, Schopenhauer, turn-of-the-century spiritualism, magic, theosophy and anthroposophy – and it is an important component of Reich's theories.[59] The light- and life-forces frequently evoked in Rytter's writings and applied to both nature and individuals such as Shakespeare are related to these concepts and very much in fashion in the 1920s and 1930s. It is instructive to read Rytter's pronouncements in this context, but his writings are lucidly decipherable without it. The energy and light of which he speaks are metaphors first and foremost, and the meaning is neither occult nor mystical (Rytter was no friend of the arcane) but robustly direct and clear: live free, create, procreate and be true to your nature and nation. Rytter appears to think that such energies are universal, but also that they are expressed in different ways in different nations. His attitudes to old and new, domestic and foreign, individual and universal, Romantic and modern, are not that easy to untangle.

As I begin to look more closely at Rytter's translations, some questions seem pertinent. How does Rytter's vitalist conception of Shakespeare's oeuvre manifest itself – or not – once I move past the introductions into the actual translations? Do the plays come across as 'Nordic', or do they retain substantial English Renaissance qualities? And are the plays in his translations what he claims that they are in his forewords?

The translations

Rytter had a few forebears in Norway and Scandinavia. As mentioned, Aasen had already translated fragments of Shakespeare, and a wealth of more comprehensive translations existed in Swedish and Danish – Hallström's edition has already been mentioned.[60] In Norwegian Rigsmaal, the first major effort at translating Shakespeare comprised twenty-one plays in eight volumes, made by a team of translators between 1923 and 1942, beginning before Rytter and finishing after.[61] In Norwegian Landsmaal/Nynorsk after Aasen, Rytter had fewer models on which to rely. Olav Madshus (1869–1927), with assistance from Arne Garborg (1851–1924), translated a complete *Macbeth* (1901) into Nynorsk. Madshus also completed *Kaupmannen i Venetia* (*The Merchant of Venice*) in 1905. Finally, the teacher and polymath Erik Eggen translated *Jonsokdraumen* (*A Midsummer Night's Dream*) in 1912 and *Kong Rikard den Tridje* (*Richard III*) in 1919. Beyond this, there are only a few sonnets translated by 'rs.' (1872) and Edvard G. Johannesen (1918).[62]

For some Norwegian readers, Rytter's renderings of Shakespeare's verse create a sense of what the Russian formalists called *ostranenje* – a 'making strange' of Shakespeare. His characters evoke the speech patterns of my grandparents; kings, queens and famous lovers are made to sound like a generation that has only recently passed away.[63] In between the incongruously familiar sections, however, are words and expressions that I only partially recognize, and which are often too obscure to be found in regular dictionaries. These phrases lend a different kind of strangeness to Shakespeare, an air of mystery that is barely dispelled when the sense is eventually discovered (usually by consulting an English version or a different Norwegian translation). Some of these forms recall the Norse sagas, but Rytter does not go as far in 'Vikingizing' Shakespeare as his predecessors Aasen and Madshus.[64] In their case, domestication was the undoubted goal – and it is a very profound case as well, since they in a sense attempted to appropriate Shakespeare as a writer of foundational Norse sagas. Almost despite himself, however, Rytter's translations avoid this – in part because the Nynorsk he employs is sometimes so obscure as to sound foreign – even to his own contemporaries.

Although the language might feel somewhat dusty and remote, Edvard Beyer thinks it is wrong to call Rytter's translations 'archaic'. In the English summary of his 'Problemer omkring oversettelser av Shakespeares dramatikk' (1953), he says that 'though some translators – Foersom and Rytter in particular – often apply obsolescent or archaic words and phrases, the aim is not consistent archaism but adequate rendering of the fullness, variety and freshness of the original'.[65] There is 'an abyss', Beyer goes on to say,

> between the exuberance, voracity, and latitude of Elisabethan [*sic*] English and the rigidity and sobriety of the modern Scandinavian languages. Henrik Rytter has here been in a unique position, because he has been able to utilize the rich and unexploited funds of Norwegian dialects, often obtaining an effect of forceful suggestion and expressive verbal music which in some cases approaches the effect of the original.[66]

Beyer – one of the great authorities on translation in post-war Norway – praises Rytter throughout his work on Norwegian translations of Shakespeare, singling out specific problems for discussion and demonstrating how Rytter has frequently been uniquely successful in solving them.[67] Beyer's appraisals are reflected in contemporary reception. The erudite review by Rolv Thesen in the socialist newspaper *Arbeiderbladet* (1 October 1932) actively compares Rytter to his ostensibly stiff and formal Norwegian and Danish forebears and the modern Swedish translation by Hallström, concluding that Rytter's version is superior.[68] Word choices and metrics are consistently praised by all commentators. As Høghaug and others have pointed out,[69] Rytter lifts significant portions from Aasen, but he improves the metre; where Aasen has an excess of unstressed line endings, Rytter stays much closer to the original scheme.

From a technical point of view, it is easy to agree that Rytter is one of the 'best' Norwegian translators of Shakespeare, in the sense that he more frequently manages to replicate Shakespeare's prosody than his predecessors and contemporaries. In the field of word choice, moreover, his extensive Nynorsk and dialectal vocabulary gives him a richer word stock than most of his competition, and according to Beyer (himself a Bokmål user) he frequently uses this larger vocabulary to hit upon just the 'right' word, such as *strøype* for 'choke' in *Macbeth*.[70] Rytter is also frequently commended for avoiding bowdlerization or euphemism: 'quivering thigh' is rendered literally as 'skjelvne lår' in Rytter's *Romeo and Juliet*.[71] When Rytter is criticized, it is because he is sometimes deemed too obscure for his own good,[72] that his punctuation is too heavy and too far removed from the Quartos and the Folio[73] or that his style fits the comedies less well than the tragedies or histories.[74] (These assessments, it should be noted, are made by specialists; the average reader today would unquestionably find Rytter difficult to read.)

The most useful insights into Rytter's Shakespeare might be derived from studying examples where the plays are most conspicuously of their time and place – where their identity as English Renaissance works comes most vividly to the fore, because it is at such moments they promise to clash most interestingly with the language and world view of Rytter's translations. One such work is *A Midsummer Night's Dream*, a play which according to Schück's foreword in Hallström combines and contrasts 'four different worlds': the heroic; the antique, ideal world; the fantastical; and the contemporary Elizabethan world of the mechanicals.[75] In the foreword to his translation, *Ein Midsumarnatt-Draum*, Rytter (in a typical manner) discusses only the play's Englishness, claiming that 'even though names of places, persons and events are mentioned from ancient classical ages, Shakespeare's own time, his England, is what emerges from the play'. While this is not entirely inaccurate, it nevertheless reveals preoccupations that run the risk of eclipsing the Renaissance elements of the oeuvre and which are strikingly at odds with Schück's analysis.[76] Rytter appears to see Norway as a monoculture, and he construes Shakespeare's England in the same way. In *A Midsummer Night's Dream*, however, names such as 'Hippolyta', 'Theseus' and 'Athens' are not mere window-dressing. Indeed, as has been frequently argued, the classical references and substructures of this and other plays significantly contribute to the creation of meaning and thematic thrust. The fact that Rytter apparently does not notice the importance of the clashes and synergies between English folklore and classical tradition speaks of his limitations as a reader or, more probably, the overshadowing force of his nationalist-vitalist interests. Not only do the classical references in the play generate meaning in and of themselves, they come to Shakespeare from a long tradition of intermingling the classical with the English that goes back to Chaucer and beyond, as Rytter surely knew.[77] 'Englishness' in Shakespeare's time incorporates and relies upon the classical, and this phenomenon extends to the warp and weft of the language itself, including its poetic and rhetorical devices.[78]

Although it is difficult to distinguish between what a translator foregoes deliberately and what is beyond their ability, it is worth investigating whether the text itself is influenced by Rytter's ideas. Perhaps surprisingly, despite his near dismissal of the Greek elements of *Dream*, Rytter keeps all the classical names, and, unlike with the mechanicals, he does not attempt to translate them. Reflecting Hallström's version, Theseus remains Theseus, but Bottom becomes *Botn* and Starveling becomes the nicely apt *Skrant* (skinny, ill, fruitless). Similarly, Titania is still Titania, but Cobweb is transliterated as *Kingelvev*. As such, some of the most obviously classical (and hence Renaissance-typical) elements are retained while most of the English material is rendered using Norwegian equivalents. English folk culture is equated with that of Norway (and thus domesticated, subsumed), while Athens is kept at arm's length (and thus foreignized, retained).

What then of the rhetoric? Brooks singles out Hermia's vow (1.1.169 ff.) as an exemplary use of anaphora in *The Dream*:

I swear to thee by Cupid's strongest bow,
By his best arrow with the golden head,
By the simplicity of Venus' doves,
By that which knitteth souls and prospers loves

Rytter retains the iambic pentameter and, as much as possible, the sense but not the anaphoric pattern:

Eg sver deg til ved Amors sterke boge
og ved hans beste pil med gylte odd,
ved Venus-duvom, deira uskuldssjel
kvart band frå sjel til sjel, kvar elskhug sæl

It is by no means impossible to reproduce the anaphora in Norwegian. André Bjerke (1958) and Øyvind Berg (2009) manage it in Bokmål, as does Halldis Moren Vesaas in Nynorsk (1980). Hallström also retains it in Swedish.[79] Does this mean that Rytter eschews such forms, eradicating Renaissance characteristics to make room for Nordic traits? Not really. For example, he very nearly retains the isocolon and parison of words at 3.2.155–6, as well as the sense: 'You both are rivals, and love Hermia; / And now both rivals to mock Helena' becomes the clunky but faithful, 'De tevlast båe, elskar Hermia; / no tevlast de te hæde Helena'. He also preserves the antimetabole in 3.2.91: 'Some true love turn'd, and not a false turn'd true' becomes, quite elegantly, 'sann elsk vart falsk, falsk elsk vart ikkje sann', which not only has the same pattern but also imitates almost perfectly the use of monosyllables.

As Beyer points out, Rytter's main goal is to preserve the metre, distributing the iambs, trochees and dactyls with stresses on pertinent words, as close to the source as he could make it.[80] The task of preserving classical rhetorical devices, stress patterns, rhymes and sense all at the same time is too much even for Rytter, and on the occasions where he is forced to make a choice, he prioritizes Germanic stresses above Latinate patterns of rhetoric, partly because he was interested in how meaning is carried across in performance. Despite the recurring claim that Rytter's translations work best as private reading matter and not on the theatre stage,[81] their aural qualities are obvious. His word choices are not just reflective of whichever dialect word contains the richest assonance in a metaphorical sense – it is also true quite literally, because Rytter's Shakespeare is designed with the aural dimension in mind. This is notable in his conscious handling of assonance and other aural effects, for example in *Macbeth*, where Rytter substitutes narrow, pinched vowel sounds for Shakespeare's rounded 'dudgeon gouts of blood' (i.e. frontal sounds for those articulated at the back of the mouth):

> frå blad og skjefte **tyt** og **dryp** det blod,
> som ikkje var der **fyrr**. – D'er ingenting;
> bloddåden berre hildrar dette fram
> for **syni** mi (2.1.46–9)

Ultimately, as far as classical rhetoric goes, there is no evidence that Rytter attempts to eradicate such patterns in the early plays, nor – conversely – is there any reason to believe that their presence is a conscious effort to preserve a specific Renaissance idiom *qua* Renaissance. The result of his efforts is a Shakespeare that achieves the merging of Jacobethan English and traditional/modern Norwegian that Rytter outlines in his forewords, but in its euphonious, strange multiplicity it does more than that, in the process possibly becoming too idiosyncratic for its own good.

Not for all time?

Looking at Rytter's introduction to *Hamlet* side by side with a modern example provides a fuller understanding of the transformations Nynorsk translations have gone through. For Edvard Hoem in his 2013 translation of the play,[82] the most striking characteristic of *Hamlet* is its changeability and its polysemy, especially 'the gulf between the truth about many things in a society and what those in power claim to be true'.[83] Hoem also highlights how different interpretations may coexist.[84] By contrast, Rytter, the 'Modern Romantic', appears uninterested in ambiguity or polysemy. He continues to focus on the human condition, nature, the light and force of life and the tribulations of the soul he believed Shakespeare must have gone through to create this 'wonderous' play. 'Since Shakespeare's time', he declares, 'men have increasingly heard Hamlet's voice in their own, seen their own struggles in his, understood that what gives him distinction gives distinction to them, studied and interpreted the profoundest depths'. Rytter's assertion is that this tendency is stronger in his time than ever before: 'One can say that mankind in our time hardly anywhere sees itself more clearly mirrored than in this more than 300-year old work of genius.'[85] Vitalism is present here too, and it mingles with a conviction that Hamlet represents – and acts as a model for – all of mankind. Of course, this is reductive, but it parses as a claim made in the fraught period before the Second World War and, as I have argued, what Rytter actually does with Shakespeare transcends what he says about him.

Where Hoem's contemporary Shakespeare is transparent and easy to read, Rytter's is original. As Venuti discusses in *The Translator's Invisibility*, transparency in writing is 'enforced by its economic value' and held aloft as an ideal by an endless range of critics and readers.[86] Rytter's translations, by contrast, offer something more complex (and sometimes difficult) that paradoxically makes Shakespeare feel both domestic and foreign, familiar and alien, ancient and contemporary – and for those that dare delve into his renderings of the plays, the rewards are considerable.

Indeed, there is something about Rytter's translations that make them feel fat where others feel lean, that makes them feel juicy where others are dry.[87] His Shakespeare gives the reader pause, placing unfamiliar words where they force us to think, not just 'what does this word mean?' but also 'what does this word mean *here*?'. Shakespeare lived in a time of rebuses, hieroglyphs, emblems and other verbal and visual riddles, and Rytter's translations capture some of the mystery of the era and strangeness of its cultural codes.[88] The most vivid expression of Rytter's vitalist, anti-puritan, anti-fascist Nordic-ness does not lie in the picture he paints in his forewords but in the linguistic diversity and invention that Beyer, Spaans and others have noted. Modern readers might find Rytter's Shakespeare daunting, but he, perhaps more than most Nordic translators, accentuates the Shakespeare canon's unending ability to generate, stimulate, merge, feed, blend with and provide a ground for something new, and his kaleidoscopic translations still have the ability to make us read Shakespeare as if for the first time.

Notes

1 Most commentators on Rytter claim that it is hard to read. See, for example, Sørbø, *Nynorsk litteraturhistorie*, 161. The first Rytter translation to be performed was *Othello* in 1926, described in a review by Erik Skavlan as 'incomprehensible' and 'remote from life' (*Dagbladet*, 13 October 1926, 4).

2 Nynorsk is neither a language nor a dialect but one of two ways to write Norwegian. It is hence a 'language form'. The vast majority of Nynorsk users write it but do not speak it as written.

3 Venuti, *Translation Changes Everything*, 116.

4 Venuti, *Translation Changes Everything*, 117.

5 A complete overview of Rytter's translations can be found in Ronny Spaans's article on Rytter in *Norsk oversetterleksikon*.

6 *Skodespel* [Plays]. Det Norske Samlaget, 1932–1933. The translations are organized thus:

    A. THE GREAT ENGLISH HISTORIES [*DEI STORE ENGELSKE SOGESPEL*]

Volume 1.	*King John*
	Richard II
Volume 2.	*Henry IV*
	Parts one and two
Volume 3.	*Henry V*
	Richard III

    B. THE GREAT COMEDIES [*DEI STORE LYSTSPEL*]

Volume 4.	*A Midsummer Night's Dream*
	Romeo and Juliet
	Much Ado About Nothing
Volume 5.	*Twelfth Night*
	As You Like It
Volume 6.	*The Merchant of Venice*
	Measure for Measure
	The Merry Wives of Windsor

    C. THE GREAT TRAGEDIES [*DEI STORE SYRGJESPEL*]

Volume 7.	*Julius Caesar*
	Antony and Cleopatra

Volume 8.   *Hamlet*
              Othello
Volume 9.   *Macbeth*
              King Lear

D. THE LATE WORKS [*SISTE ARBEID*]

Volume 10.   *Cymbeline*
               The Winter's Tale
               The Tempest

(Overview from Samlaget's promotional brochure, qtd. in Høghaug, 'Rytter i den shakespearske skuggeheimen', 135–6).

7 Heming Gujord supplies a short biography of Rytter: 'He was born in Trøndelag, grew up in Haramsøya and was schooled in Ørsta where his father was a teacher. He studied briefly in Trondheim and finished his education as a teacher in Volda in 1899. Subsequently, he worked at his father's "folk high school" in Ørsta and then ran his own folk high school in Gimnes until the family farm was repossessed, an event that would affect him deeply. After this he lived near Oslo where he made a living as a writer. Around 1940 he moved to Ustedal near Geilo, where he is buried next to his home at "Rytterhaugen".... Rytter was married twice, ... divorcing his first wife in 1930 [when he began translating Shakespeare] and marrying again in 1932 [upon completing the translations]' (Gujord, 'Frå daudingdans', 109; all translations into English are mine unless otherwise noted).

8 For an account in English, see Vikør, *The Nordic Languages*, 201–8.

9 See Vikør, *The Nordic Languages*, 51–4, 96.

10 In practice this meant that in the frequent cases where a choice had to be made between two word forms, the one most similar to Old Norse was selected.

11 Rytter's publishers, Det Norske Samlaget (Samlaget), are still the largest Nynorsk publisher. The role Nynorsk has played in the formation of Norwegian civil society since the late nineteenth century is too complex to fully account for here. For a more detailed investigation in English, see Bucken-Knapp, *Elites*; see also Vikør, *The Nordic Languages*. In short, Nynorsk users read Bokmål with ease, while Bokmål users tend to find Nynorsk difficult, rustic and unappealing.

12 A recent example of a successful translation published by Samlaget is Elena Ferrante's Napoli quartet, translated (2015–2017) by Kristin Sørsdal.
13 It was probably Aasen Rytter had in mind when he said that 'we have examples in our own country of how the gifted can reach far even with poor schooling' (Rytter, 'Introduction', 13).
14 'Ben Jonson . . . *Englishes* Martial in order to work over English, to *thicken* its texture and complicate its resonance'. Greene, *The Light in Troy*, 42. See also Venuti, *Translation Changes Everything*, 123.
15 Edvard Beyer provides an overview of Norwegian translations up to 1956. He notes that Aasen translated fragments from *Hamlet* and *Romeo and Juliet* before 1853 ('Problemer', 62).
16 Rytter copies Aasen 'almost verbatim' according to Høghaug ('Rytter', 139), but this is an exaggeration.
17 Spaans discusses this in '"Tiltak"', 98. Kristin Gjerpe notes a similar relationship between Latin and the Italian of Boccaccio and Dante in conjunction with Rytter's translations of these writers. See Gjerpe, 'Rytter', 73. It should be noted that Shakespeare frequently (and perhaps exclusively) based his work on English translations rather than continental originals.
18 Steiner, *Translation Studies*, 260–1.
19 Norwegian 'Neo-Romanticism' was a movement within literature and the arts that took place in the 1890s and 1910s as a counterreaction to realism. The 'Great Nynorsk Romantics' of the 1920s and 1930s postdated this movement and negotiated modernity in a way that earlier Neo-Romantics had not. See Sørbø, *Nynorsk litteraturhistorie*, 137–9. Spaans argues that Rytter could be called a modernist. See Spaans, '"Tiltak"', 96. Paal-Helge Haugen asserts, however, that Rytter's later poetry in free verse is significantly weaker than the regular poetry that makes up the main bulk of his production ('Poeten Henrik Rytter', 234). Even Rytter's obituarist Ragnvald Skrede politely implied that modernist styles were beyond Rytter's grasp (Høghaug, 'Rytter', 142–3).
20 See Harris, *Romantic Moderns*, esp. 206–26.
21 Harris, *Romantic Moderns*, 159–60.
22 Issued in 1920 by Logan Pearsall Smith. See Smith, *S.P.E. Tract No. III: A Few Practical Suggestions*, n.p.
23 'The soul-life of a Shakespearean play is an enduring power of divine worth', Knight, *The Wheel of Fire*, 13. For Eliot's and Leavis's interest in English village life, see Harris, *Romantic Moderns*, 180–4.

24 See Halpern, *Shakespeare and the Moderns*, 1–10.
25 Harris, *Romantic Moderns*, 184.
26 See Humpál, 'Knut Hamsun's Criticism'.
27 See, for example, Sørbø, *Nynorsk litteraturhistorie*, 162 or Gujord, 'Rytterstatue', 32–3.
28 See Gujord, 'Rytterstatue', *passim*, for an account of Rytter's journey towards the political left.
29 See Gujord, 'Rytterstatue', 32–3; after the Second World War Rytter eventually became both a vocal friend of the Jewish people and a sympathizer with the Norwegian Communist Party.
30 See Spaans, 'Ein stridsmann', 212.
31 Spaans discusses Rytter's quarrel with Nazism in more detail: Henrik Rytter ... wrote dramas ... [and] authored a powerful and captivating caution against Nazism in 1937, *Norden har ordet – eit stridsskrift*. A striking comparison of Nazism with the forces of Ragnarök and chaos prophesied in Voluspå [of Old Norse myth] ... it portends the catastrophes of the twentieth century. ... The conflict revolves around different interpretations of 'the Nordic spirit', which Rytter describes as a 'life-venerating spirit', i.e. a vitalist spirit. ... His spirit had a 'sacred reverence for humanity' while the maleficent spirit of Nazism was an aggressive Viking-spirit. ('"Tiltak"', 97)
32 Rytter, 'Introduction', 9.
33 Venuti, *The Translator's Invisibility*, 18.
34 It is a neologism first seen in the writings of the early Landsmaal pioneer Aasmund Olavson Vinje (1818–1870), made up of the Old Norse for 'to fly' and the noun 'vit', related to the English 'wit' or 'mind'. See 'Flogvit', *Det norske akademis ordbok*.
35 See, for example, Spaans, '"Tiltak"', 86.
36 Rytter, 'Introduction', 8.
37 'Med sanning kan ein segje at den ånd vi møter i Shakespeares diktverk var ikkje noko menneskjelegt framandt' ('Introduction', 9). This recalls Terence's 'I am human, and I think nothing human is alien to me'.
38 Rytter, 'Introduction', 9.
39 Here, Rytter mirrors D. H. Lawrence. See Zoll, 'Vitalism'.
40 Rytter, 'Introduction', 12.
41 Harris, *Romantic Moderns*, 184.
42 Rytter, 'Introduction', 20–1.

43 Rytter, 'Introduction', 28.
44 Rytter, introduction to *King John*, 37.
45 Rytter, introduction to *Henry V*, 7–8; emphasis added.
46 Rytter, introduction to *Henry V*, 7–8.
47 Again, Rytter's view stands in stark contrast with that of Eliot, who saw Elizabethan England as 'decaying'. See Marcus, 'T.S. Eliot and Shakespeare', 65.
48 Spaans, '"Tiltak"', 91.
49 Spaans, '"Tiltak"', 93.
50 Beyer, 'Problemer', 34.
51 According to Per Sivefors (personal communication), Hallström's translations are not much read today.
52 To name just one example: the first two sentences of Schück and Rytter's introductions to *A Midsummer Night's Dream* are identical, and much of the same information appears thereafter, in the same order, but as always, Rytter devotes space to his own interests, using the introduction to discuss national character.
53 Beyer notes that Rytter 'has taken some readings, directly or indirectly, from the bad Quarto' of *Romeo and Juliet* and observes that there are some 'imaginative' stage directions in *Othello*, 'but whether they are his own or lifted from some enterprising populariser is difficult to determine' (Beyer, 'Problemer', 13).
54 Herford, 'Introduction', 5–11.
55 Herford, 'Introduction', 11.
56 Or indeed D. H. Lawrence.
57 Høghaug, 'Rytter i den shakespeareske skuggeheimen', 116.
58 Raknes knew Bergson well and translated his *Le Rire* into Nynorsk in 1922.
59 Lee Irwin subsumes this phenomenon under the umbrella of 'panpsychism', which he defines as 'a combination of the Greek *pan*, "all or every," and *psuchê* (or psyche), "breath or soul," implying life-force, mental activity, and an animating spirit inherent in all of nature', in *The Cambridge Handbook of Western Esotericism and Mysticism*, 417.
60 For an English-language overview of Shakespeare translations into Norwegian up to 1916, see Ruud, 'An Essay'; for an overview and discussion in Norwegian of translations up to 1994, see Smidt, *Shakespeare*. For a Nordic overview, see Keinänen and Sivefors,

'Nordic Shakespeare until 1900: A Timeline' as well as their introduction to *Disseminating Shakespeare in the Nordic Countries*.

61 While Samlaget's Shakespeare was translated by one man – Rytter – the Somes Forlag/Aschehoug 'Rigsmaal' edition involved six translators: Rolf Hiort-Schøyen, Carl Burckhardt, A. Trampe Bødtker, G. Reiss Andersen, Gunnar Larsen and Aasmund Sveen.

62 Beyer, 'Problemer', 62.

63 Rytter generally wrote a form of Nynorsk based on 'Midlandsmål', a family of dialects with traits from eastern, central and western Norwegian as well as some Old Norse grammatical features. See Grepstad, 'Midlandsmål' (in Norwegian). A more detailed account of his particular form of Nynorsk can be found in Johannes Gjerdåker, 'Mannen som elska ord', especially 42–4.

64 See Spaans's remarks on how Aasen's rendering of 'O that I were a glove upon that hand' (*R&J* 2.3.24) uses *vott* ('mitten') instead of *hanske* ('glove') to involuntarily comic effect and on how Madshus's saga-inflected, National Romantic vocabulary suits his *Macbeth* to a tee while making a nonsense of *The Merchant of Venice* ('"Tiltak"', 85–6).

65 Beyer, 'Problemer', 59.

66 Beyer, 'Problemer', 59.

67 Rytter's phrasings are variously described as 'quite precise' (23), 'masterful' (35), 'very exact' (40) and 'closer [than other translators]' (46); his deviations from the original sense are praised when they retain the metre (49); and he deems Rytter's 'To be or not to be' monologue the very best Norwegian rendering (41).

68 See Thesen, 'Shakespeare på nynorsk'. Since this is a socialist newspaper, a third of his review is devoted to justifying reading Shakespeare in the first place, concluding it is acceptable since Lenin advocates acquainting oneself with the literature of the bourgeoise. See n. 1 for an opposing view.

69 See n. 22.

70 Beyer, 'Problemer', 22.

71 Spaans, '"Tiltak"', 98.

72 Spaans, '"Tiltak"', 98.

73 Beyer, 'Problemer', 9.

74 Spaans, '"Tiltak"', 90.

75 Schück, 'Introduction', 180–1.

76 Rytter, 'Introduction', 7.
77 Theseus and Ypolita feature in 'The Knight's Tale' in Chaucer's *Canterbury Tales*.
78 Brooks, 'Introduction', xxlv–xlix.
79 Hallström and many of the Norwegian translators achieve the effect by commencing the anaphora one line later than Shakespeare. Rytter also postpones the opening in the same manner as Hallström but then abandons the *Ved* ('By') line opening almost immediately.
80 Beyer, 'Problemer', 45.
81 See n. 1.
82 His translations comprise *King Lear* (1981), *Romeo and Juliet* (1985), *The Merchant of Venice* (1990), *Troilus and Cressida* (1993), *Othello* (1996), *The Taming of the Shrew* (1997), *Richard III* (1998), *Macbeth* (1999), *As You Like It* (2000), *Henry IV, Parts I and II* (2008–2009) and *Hamlet* (2013).
83 Hoem, 'Introduction', 5.
84 Hoem, 'Introduction', 7–8.
85 Rytter,' Introduction' to *Hamlet*, 9.
86 Venuti, *The Translator's Invisibility*, 6.
87 Rytter exerted a silent influence on other translators and poets, in particular those working in Nynorsk. The most direct descendant of Rytter is Sigmund Skard (1903–1995). Upon Rytter's death in 1950 a complete translation of Dante was found among his papers. This was never published, but Skard, who was a professor of American literature at the University of Oslo and central within Samlaget, used it as the point of departure for his own Nynorsk edition of Dante's *Divine Comedy* (1965). As for Norwegian translators of Shakespeare's plays, some of the most significant have tended to be Nynorsk users. The Norwegian Theatre (Det Norske Teateret) – a Nynorsk-only theatre with considerable cultural capital – began to require new translations for stage use in the 1960s, prompting Hartvig Kiran (1911–1978) to translate *Macbeth* (1962) and *Hamlet* (1967). The above-mentioned Halldis Moren Vesaas (1907–1995) supplied a *Romeo and Juliet* in 1964 and, as has been mentioned, *A Midsummer Night's Dream* in 1980. She also translated *The Tempest* in 1971, though this was not published until 1998 (Spaans, '"Tiltak"', 102). These translators often follow Rytter, but there is a tendency for their efforts to become nimbler, lighter and – for better *and* worse – more straightforward. Also worth mentioning is Ragnvald Skrede (1904–1982), who translated *Othello* in 1974. His greatest

Shakespearean effort was a complete Nynorsk edition of the sonnets, *Sonettar*, which came out in 1972. Skrede had studied Rytter's translations and poetry closely and wrote his obituary in the national newspaper *Verdens Gang* (19 September 1950; see Høghaug, '"Far vel"', 142).

88 For more about esoteric imagery in Shakespeare, see Myklebost, 'Early Modern'.

Works cited

Berg, Øyvind, trans., *En midtsommernattsdrøm* (Oslo, 2009).
Beyer, Edvard, 'Problemer omkring oversettelser av Shakespeares dramatikk', in *Universitetet i Bergen, Årbok 1956* (Bergen, 1956).
Bjerke, Andrè, *En midtsommernattsdrøm* (1958; Oslo, 2013).
Bucken-Knapp, Gregg, *Elites, Language, and the Politics of Identity: The Norwegian Case in Comparative Perspective* (New York, 2003).
'Flogvit', in Carina Nilstun, ed., *Det norske akademis ordbok*, Naob.no, accessed 20 September 2021.
Gjerdåker, Johannes, 'Mannen som elska ord: Henrik Rytter i den Norske språkutviklinga', in Hovdenakk and Høghaug, eds, *Skrift og Strid*, 41–52.
Gjerpe, Kristin, 'Rytter som omsetjar av Boccaccio: Frå folkemål til folkemål', in Hovdenakk and Høghaug, eds, *Skrift og Strid*, 73–86.
Greene, Thomas M., *The Light in Troy: Imitation and Discovery in Renaissance Poetry* (New Haven and London, 1982).
Grepstad, Jon, 'Sigmund Skard', in *Allkunne.no* (2012), https://www.allkunne.no/framside/biografiar/s/sigmund-skard//102/6260/, accessed 17 September 2021.
Grepstad, Jon, 'Midlandsmål', in *Allkunne.no* (2019), https://www.allkunne.no/framside/sprak/omgrep/midlandsmal/67/87698/, accessed 17 September 2021.
Gujord, Heming, 'Frå daudingdans til fridomskamp – Henrik Rytter', in Jørgen Sejersted and Eirik Vassenden, eds, *Norsk litterær årbok 2005* (Oslo, 2005), 108–34.
Gujord, Heming, 'Rytterstatue for ein ordkrigar', in Hovdenakk and Høghaug, eds, *Skrift og Strid*, 11–36.
Hallström, Per, trans., *Shakespeares Dramatiska Arbeten: Lustspel* (Stockholm, 1923).
Halpern, Richard, *Shakespeare among the Moderns* (Ithaca, 1997).
Harris, Alexandra, *Romantic Moderns: English Writers, Artists & the Imagination from Virginia Woolf to John Piper* (London, 2010).

Haugen, Paal-Helge, 'Poeten Henrik Rytter: Ei ti-pakning', in Hovdenakk and Høghaug, eds, *Skrift og Strid*, 225–44.

Herford, C. H., 'Introduction', in *The Works of Shakespeare*, viii, *Julius Caesar*, ed. C. H. Herford (New York and London, 1908).

Herford, C. H., 'Introduction', in *The Works of Shakespeare*, iv, *King John* (New York and London, 1912).

Hoem, Edvard, trans., *Hamlet* (Oslo, 2013).

Høghaug, Leif, '"Far vel, far vel! – Hamlet, å, minnast meg!": Rytter i den shakespearske skuggeheimen', in Hovdenakk and Høghaug, eds, *Skrift og Strid*, 131–50.

Hovdenakk, Sindre, and Leif Høghaug, eds, *Skrift og strid: Essay om Henrik Rytter* (Oslo, 2011).

Humpál, Martin, 'Knut Hamsun's Criticism of Shakespeare', in Keinänen and Sivefors, eds, *Disseminating Shakespeare*, 269–90.

Irwin, Lee, 'Panpsychism', in Glenn Alexander Magee, ed., *The Cambridge Handbook of Western Mysticism and Esotericism* (Cambridge, 2016), 417–28.

Keinänen, Nely, and Per Sivefors, 'Introduction', in Keinänen and Sivefors, eds, *Disseminating Shakespeare*, 1–30.

Keinänen, Nely, and Per Sivefors, eds, *Disseminating Shakespeare in the Nordic Countries: Shifting Centres and Peripheries in the Nineteenth Century* (London, 2022).

Keinänen, Nely, and Per Sivefors, 'Nordic Shakespeare until 1900: A Timeline', in Keinänen and Sivefors, eds, *Disseminating Shakespeare*, 297–316.

Knight, G. Wilson, *The Wheel of Fire* (1930; London, 2001).

Marcus, Phillip L., 'T. S. Eliot and Shakespeare', *Criticism*, 9/1, 63–79. http://www.jstor.org/stable/23094254, accessed 10 January 2022.

Myklebost, Svenn-Arve, 'Early Modern Visual-Verbal Esoteric Imagery and the Theatre: *Julius Caesar* 1.3', *Nordic Journal of English Studies*, 17/1 (2018), 3–25.

Ruud, Martin B., 'An Essay Toward a History of Shakespeare in Norway', *Scandinavian Studies and Notes*, 4/2 (1917), 89–202, www.jstor.org/stable/40915005, accessed 26 August 2021.

Rytter, Henrik, 'Ein midsumarnatts-draum', in Rytter, trans., *Skodespel*, iv, 11.

Rytter, Henrik, 'Innføring', in Rytter, trans., *Skodespel*, i, 7–33.

Rytter, Henrik, 'Kong Henrik den femte', in Rytter, trans., *Skodespel*, iii, 7–8.

Rytter, Henrik, 'Kong Jon', in Rytter, trans., *Skodespel*, i, 37.

Rytter, Henrik, 'Kong Richard den andre', in Rytter, trans., *Skodespel*, i, 135.

Rytter, Henrik, trans., *William Shakespeare Skodespel*, 10 vols (Oslo, 1932–1933).

Schück, Henrik, 'Innledning', in *Shakespeares Dramatiska Arbeten* (Stockholm, 1922).
Shakespeare, William, *A Midsummer Night's Dream*, ed. Harold F. Brooks (1979; London, 2003).
Shakespeare, William, *Julius Caesar*, ed. David Daniell (London, 2006).
Shakespeare, William, *King John*, eds John Tobin and Jesse M. Lander (London, 2018).
Skavlan, Erik, 'Det Norske Teateret', *Dagbladet*, 13 October 1926.
Smidt, Kristian, *Shakespeare i norsk oversettelse: En situasjonsrapport* (Oslo, 1994).
Smith, Logan Pearsall, *S.P.E. Tract No. III: A Few Practical Suggestions* (1920). Project Gutenberg, 2004, https://www.gutenberg.org/ebooks/12390, accessed 11 January 2022.
Sørbø, Jan Inge, *Nynorsk litteraturhistorie* (Oslo, 2018).
Spaans, Ronny, 'Henrik Rytter', in Eva Refsdal and Kristina Solum, eds, *Norsk oversetterleksikon*, https://www.oversetterleksikon.no/2017/05/18/henrik-rytter-1877-1950/, accessed 9 April 2021.
Spaans, Ronny, '"Tiltak det var merg og makt i"': Om vitalisme i nynorske Shakespeare-tolkingar', in Jørgen Sejerstedt and Eirik Vassenden, eds, *Norsk litterær årbok 2006* (Oslo, 2006), 81–109.
Spaans, Ronny, 'Ein stridsmann tek ordet: Henrik Rytter og nordisk folkeånd', in Hovdenakk and Høghaug, eds, *Skrift og Strid*, 205–24.
Steiner, George, *After Babel* (Oxford, 1975).
Thesen, Rolv, 'Shakespeare på nynorsk', *Arbeiderbladet*, 1 October 1932.
Venuti, Lawrence, *The Translator's Invisibility: A History of Translation* (London and New York, 1995).
Venuti, Lawrence, *Translation Changes Everything: Theory and Practice* (London and New York, 2013).
Vesaas, Halldis Moren, trans., *Ein midtsommarnattsdraum* (Oslo, 1980).
Vikør, Lars S., *The Nordic Languages: Their Status and Interrelations* (Oslo, 1995).
Zoll, Allan R., 'Vitalism and the Metaphysics of Love: D. H. Lawrence and Schopenhauer', *The D. H. Lawrence Review*, 11/1 (1978), 1–20, http://www.jstor.org/stable/44233593, accessed 11 January 2022.

7

'A great interpreter of modern life'

Eyvind Johnson and the changing perception of Shakespeare

Per Sivefors

> *To be, or not to be ---. William S-e is a great, lovely liar*
> *--- It's not to be -- it's: to live or not to live --. Maybe he*
> *intended it that way?*[1]

When Eyvind Johnson (1900–1976) included these lines in a letter to his friend and soon-to-be colleague Rudolf Värnlund, he may also have articulated a line of thought that would preoccupy him for decades to come. Presumably, Johnson distinguishes between a passive notion of life – simply existing – and an active, vital one, but his 'maybe' also indicates that he does not have a neat resolution to the dilemma. His lines moreover hint at the role his reading of Shakespeare would have in his literary articulations of the problem. Indeed, among the significant generation of Swedish authors of working-class background who began publishing in the 1920s and 1930s, no one referenced Shakespeare more extensively than Johnson. Spending much of the 1920s abroad, mostly in Berlin and Paris, he made his début in 1924 and published a series of novels and short stories that eventually made him a recognized yet controversial literary voice. Clearly, Johnson's wide reading shaped and influenced his work throughout his career: *Return to Ithaca* (1946) is an extended pastiche of the *Odyssey*; *The Days of His Grace* (1960) draws on Paulus Diaconus's *Historia Langobardum*; and his earlier works from the 1920s and 1930s display influences from contemporary modernists like Joyce and Proust. His extensive use of allusion and meta-techniques has even led one critic to label his work 'postmodern'.[2] In terms of politics, while his ideals in the 1920s and 1930s veered towards anarchism, in the 1940s, adopting a more mainstream liberal position, he would go on to write a series of political allegories on the struggle against fascism.

In other words, Johnson's outlook was shifting, and as we will see so was his use of Shakespeare in his work until the 1940s. Accordingly, this chapter argues that far from being a static point of reference, Shakespeare in general and *Hamlet* in particular become closely aligned with Johnson's changing political and aesthetic outlook from the 1920s into the 1940s. While Hamlet is embodied in the early novels as a more or less homogenous set of variations on the theme of passivity and ambivalence in Europe after the First World War, later, in the 1930s, Johnson articulates more deliberate attempts at overcoming that ambivalence. Subsequently, Shakespeare is reconfigured as part of a canon to be conquered in the author's own past; yet, during the political turmoil of the 1930s, Johnson questions Shakespeare as an irrelevant cultural expression. In yet another apparent turn, Shakespeare's works seem to be made to symbolize the ongoing and hopeful struggle against fascism during the Second World War. To shed light on these changing conceptions of Shakespeare, the present chapter will be structured around a series of chronologically organized readings of most of Johnson's novels from the mid-1920s to the early 1940s, with an emphasis on the complex re-negotiations of Shakespeare in the 1930s and onward, when there is a greater prevalence of direct allusions to Hamlet, but also to, for example, *The Winter's Tale*. As the letter cited earlier indicates, even when *Hamlet* and Shakespeare are not explicitly mentioned, they were a presence in Johnson's creative mind from the very beginning of his career. There is no shortage of allusions to Shakespeare in Johnson's letters from the 1920s. For example, he jokingly signs another of his letters to Värnlund 'Hamlet VII' and variously addresses his friend as 'Coriolanus II Rudolfus' and 'Coriolanus I+II'.[3] Clearly, the Hamlet figure was both a point of identification and a source of references, and while Johnson's use of Shakespeare has been noted by critics, it has received little focused attention and criticism has not acknowledged the shifts in Johnson's construction of Shakespeare.[4] Nils Schwartz, in a dissertation from 1979, argues that many of Johnson's early characters can be divided into 'passive' and 'active' Hamlet figures. The passive Hamlet is characterized by ambivalence, hesitation and indecision, by 'reflexive non-action', whereas the active Hamlet is, in addition to thinking and considering, capable of 'reflexive action'.[5] While such a view is over-schematic, especially if applied to Johnson's subsequent work from the 1930s and 1940s, it hints at the importance of psychoanalysis as a context for Johnson's early work. While the present chapter is not specifically concerned with Johnson's debt to Freud, it bears remarking that Johnson certainly knew Freud's theories[6] although he never makes any clear allusions to Freud's writings on Shakespeare.[7] In fact, Johnson's own ambivalence towards biographical readings, which is often reflected in his own prefaces and afterwords to his works,[8] does not square well with Freud's take on Hamlet in *The Interpretation of Dreams*; if there are any relevant Freudian affinities in his works, it is more the late Freud of *Civilization and Its Discontents*.[9] Indeed, the theme of civilization and its associated problems is a crucial facet of Johnson's Shakespeare, although in sharp contrast to Freud's pessimistic notion of neurosis as the inevitable result of living together in society, Johnson makes very clear and politically motivated attempts at overcoming negativity and indetermination. In this regard, his work can be said to participate in a more general discussion on the adverse effects of culture in the 1920s and 1930s.[10]

Also in terms of intellectual context, Johnson's early work has been considered modernist in significant ways,[11] but in its treatment of Shakespeare it both has similarities and dissimilarities to the notions of Shakespeare articulated in, for example, Anglo-American high modernism. Richard Halpern has suggested that modernism saw – and praised – Renaissance theatre as a form of expression aligned with 'primitive' cultures like ancient Greece and contemporary Japan and Bali. At the same time, modernists emphasized 'the *transitional* character of [the Renaissance] – its passage from a primitive state to the condition of modernity'.[12] It is notable that Johnson's incarnations of Hamlet both confirm and do not confirm these views. For Johnson, the Hamlet figure unquestionably reflects the indeterminacy and lack of direction of his own time; Hamlet in other words serves as an emblem of the difficult period of transition after the First World War. On the other hand, there is little sense of distancing or exoticizing in Johnson's adoption of Shakespeare. In a letter from June 1929 to Värnlund, Johnson declares that 'As for myself, I know of no literary figure that's more modern than Hamlet. Dress him up in [the ready-made suit] Collins ettan, a low collar, a motley tie and shoes with crêpe soles and have him speak this year's Swedish'.[13] Hamlet does not offer an exotic or 'primitive' counterpart to modern man; he *is* modern man. What is more, the implication is that Hamlet is not necessarily a figurehead of high culture to be rescued from commercialization; in that sense, Johnson's version of Shakespeare is clearly different from that of, say, T. S. Eliot, who was, as Cary DiPietro argues, concerned with distancing Shakespeare and the Renaissance from Victorian mass culture.[14]

However, to Johnson in the 1920s, Hamlet was not simply the modern human; he could also be configured in more conventional terms as a universal figure of *all* humans. This idea is reflected elsewhere in Johnson's writing. In another letter, also from 1929, he describes his work on his novel *Avsked till Hamlet* [Farewell to Hamlet] (1930): 'To me, Shakespeare's Hamlet isn't a unique type, a Danish prince who was taken aback by visions – I understand him simply as humankind. Everyone is likely to have a piece of Hamlet in them, and if you're going to assess the spiritual content of a person, I'll be hanged if the Hamlet [sic] isn't the best.'[15] Johnson in some ways shares modernist affinities with primitivism, although Shakespeare has a rather complex role in this relation. To Johnson Hamlet is, immediately and already, *there* in 1920s Europe and his own life.[16] It is illuminating to contrast this treatment of

Shakespeare to Knut Hamsun's dismissal of the Bard in the late nineteenth century. Indeed, Johnson knew Hamsun's work and, in some ways, his early novels could be said to be related to Hamsun's *Growth of the Soil* (1917) in their reservations about modernity.[17] But while Hamsun dismissed Shakespeare as irrelevant to the hectic pulse of contemporary life, *Hamlet* has a crucial bearing on Johnson's understanding of civilization and culture as he knew them in the 1920s and early 1930s.[18] In that sense, his Shakespeare is diametrically opposed to Hamsun's. Johnson's novels from the 1920s all suggest that the Hamlet figure reflects the problematic aspects of post-war existence, and, as we will see, his subsequent work in the 1930s made hints as to how that passivity and ambivalence might be overcome.

Johnson's novels from the 1920s may not make explicit reference to *Hamlet* or Shakespeare but repeatedly depict Hamlet-like figures whose ability to overcome passivity is problematic at best. This series of Hamlet characters seems to represent a homogenous set of variations on the theme of post-war rootlessness. Johnson's first novel, *Timans och rättfärdigheten* [Timans and Righteousness], from 1925 features a character named Stig, whose similarities to Hamlet were even pointed out by one reviewer at the time.[19] Stig is the son of a wealthy industrialist – a 'prince' – who contemplates suicide and is considered by his parents to be mentally ill. But as Schwartz points out, the family relations are reversed compared to Shakespeare's play: it is the mother who has died and 'reappears' in Stig's character and facial features, and the father has married his wife's sister.[20] After the father has handed over the leadership of the factory to his greedy stepson, there is a strike among the workers that results in a violent altercation with the police. The novel depicts Stig's passivity as impossible to overcome, and he remains incapable of stepping outside his role as a cynical observer even when his father succumbs to dementia and his sister dies giving birth. What is interesting here about the Hamlet character is the context of class struggle: by implication at least, Hamlet is represented as antithetical to the revolutionary force of the working class – a theme that, as we will see, resurfaces in some of Johnson's other work from the later 1920s and early 1930s.

There is certainly a family resemblance between the 'passive' Hamlet figures in several of Johnson's books from the 1920s, although the class perspective is not always as pronounced: for example, in the virtually plotless *Stad i ljus* [City in Light] (1928) the young man Torsten walks around Paris and observes city life with vague dreams of becoming an author; he is a flaneur who walks around the city awaiting a *lettre recommandée* that will put him out of his financial difficulties. In another of Johnson's novels, *Minnas* [Remembering], from 1928, the middle-aged librarian Clerk seems incapable of channelling his intellectual knowledge into commitment or action. Civilization has not taught him to resolve his discontents into an active intervention into the world.[21] It should be emphasized, however, that not all of Johnson's Hamlet figures remain passive and reflecting. Particularly, while the schoolteacher Andersson in *Stad i mörker* [City in Darkness] (1927) is locked up in the winter darkness of a small town in northern Sweden and certainly is 'something of a Hamlet', after a sexual encounter with a widowed cleaning woman at his school, he actively decides to stay with her and build a permanent life together.[22] In this plot, the novel also hints at the possibility of reconciliation between the classes – a note of almost programmatic hopefulness after all.

After this series of more or less related characters who in turn seem related to Hamlet, Johnson's next novel *Kommentar till ett stjärnfall* [Notes on a Shooting Star] (1929) brings up Shakespeare as an explicit point of reference. It is also here that we can notice a more overtly politicized attempt at overcoming the impasse that has prevailed among most of the previous Hamlet characters. The novel, set in 1920s Stockholm, depicts two half-brothers, Magnus Lyck and Andreas Sonath, one of whom is a political radical whose revolutionary fervour is compromised by personal problems, the other one a less-than-talented musician and parasite. Johnson himself said of the two that 'one of them is a Hamlet communist, the other son a sort of Hamlet dandy'.[23] Despite their dissimilarities, neither brother is fully capable of shedding his 'Hamletism', and Magnus's dismissal of the Danish prince clearly smacks of protesting too much: 'To be or not to be, that's not the question. . . . I'm one of those who have an outlook on life, I'm the one who puts himself above individualist fancy and I don't potter around with my soul, with my heart, no I don't . . . I'm no coward, I, no Hamlet' (34). It may be, as Gavin Orton suggests, that Magnus, for all his anti-Hamlet sentiment, is a 'passive Hamlet' figure.[24] However, by the end of the novel Magnus seems to have found his own way forward – precisely by continuing to be a reflecting Hamlet:

> We question our way. We solve old riddles with new questions. We question heaven to pieces to find truth. We dig in the earth with our questions: deeper, deeper. And we're fortunate to be able to question, to make grand gestures and throw up our question marks as firebrands against the vault above us. All progress perhaps lies in a new, more intelligent, more creative manner of questioning. (312)

Compared to Hamlet's description of the heavens as a 'foul and pestilent congregation of vapours', this is a skyward challenge that suggests a belief in progress and political change.[25] Indeed, Magnus's questioning turns into an expression of solidarity with the working classes. The episode takes place on 1 May, and for Magnus the workers' marches he witnesses in Stockholm spark a paradoxical sense of (almost) belonging with them:

> And I've seen them walk past by, how they've believed. Not that I believe, no. No, that would be a lie. Not that I believe the way they believe. But in my own way, and my way of believing can't be theirs. Yet: I wanted to say, and always say: Believe, go on believing, and the world will be better for you. (313)

This politicization of Hamlet seems to have suggested a way out of the philosophical impasse that characterized the earlier novels. While the ambivalent Hamlet figure is a clearly recurring pattern in Johnson's allusions to Shakespeare throughout the 1920s, by comparison, his work from the 1930s represents a more consistent way of moving beyond Hamlet. It is plain that the already-mentioned *Avsked till Hamlet*, with its valedictory title and its publication in the first year of the decade, was conceived of as a turning point. 'I'm re-working the legend of Hamlet, a present-day Hamlet, and it's likely to be my last thing in that mould', he wrote to Värnlund in a previously cited letter.[26] The novel can be said to hint at the notion of civilization and its discontents, which, as suggested previously, was a current topic in intellectual debates at the time (Freud's already-mentioned work of that title was published the same year as Johnson's novel). Also in 1930, Johnson had expressed his admiration for the young Rousseau, who of course insisted that civilization had been detrimental to humankind.[27] It is obvious that such ideas were intimately entwined in Johnson's creative mind with the Hamlet figure, not just because of the title of the novel but because of its themes and political allegiances. The novel, like several of his subsequent works, is a partly autobiographical story of a young man named Mårten Torpare, who has been adopted as a child by a well-to-do couple, leaves home for failed university studies and travels around Europe, eventually moving back to Sweden and actively engaging in a quest for a meaningful life in the area where he grew up. Moving forward here spells going back: in other words, overcoming the 'passive' Hamlet by connecting with one's roots.[28]

What is striking, then, is that the novel emphatically suggests ways of defeating Hamlet, again in the context of class struggle. At one point, the often ironically depicted Mårten travels to Copenhagen to visit his sister, who is an aspiring actress. He begins discussing *Hamlet* with his sister and her Danish fiancé, an ex-military man, and, being prompted on his current situation, confidently asserts the present-day relevance of Shakespeare's prince: 'I'm an interpreter of Hamlet, Mårten said. A great interpreter of modern life.' After this declaration, Mårten ruminates on just how right he is: 'I, he thought. An interpreter of Hamlet. How come I never thought of that before? There's something rotten in the world. Certain young authors had a predilection for the word rotten, including comrade Shakespeare. Hamlet, prince of Denmark. Now I'm here. A good word, rotten.' However, the Danish lieutenant is unperturbed by the play's negative depiction of Denmark: 'We don't worry at all about that line from Hamlet, he said. But people think so. Maybe Shakespeare didn't even know where Denmark was.' Again, though, Mårten asserts the immediacy of Shakespeare's presence: 'He was here, Mårten expertly said. Perhaps he walked on this very spot' (92). Clearly, this passage expands on Johnson's idea that Hamlet is here and now, and while the narrator pokes fun at Mårten's tendency towards intellectual abstraction – he 'schillerized and goethecized with authority' (93) – Johnson also has Mårten articulate more straightforward political messages, especially towards the end of the novel. Culture, Mårten says there, is 'ennobled nature, the disciplining of instincts, the will to justice, the knowledge of justice. The most important cultural moment right now is the working-class movement because it has the will without which everything is dead. It may not foster the greatest, the finest spirits; but it keeps their work alive' (188–9). It is the collective struggle of the working class that is the driving force behind the new human, even if Mårten, with his education and personality, is never fully a part of it. This may be a limited victory but a victory nonetheless.

Homecoming, finding one's roots and negotiating the confinement of culture and civilization are similarly at the focus of *Regn i gryningen* [Rain at Dawn] from 1933, perhaps Johnson's most programmatic novel with respect to the theme of 'discontents'. The protagonist Henrik Fax, a farmer's son who has received an education and married into a comfortable middle-class life, is increasingly frustrated with the shallowness of his existence. At one point, he goes to the theatre with his wife and sees a tragic play that the wife admires but Henrik dismisses as hollow and pretentious: 'It's of course something you've read again?', his wife asks, and Henrik retorts, as if echoing Hamlet's 'words, words, words': 'Read, he says, read, read ...' (*Regn i gryningen*, 56). Even though Shakespeare is not mentioned at this point, it is clear that his works represent a cultural heritage that Henrik seeks to reject. Indeed, Henrik leaves his wife and his work as an office clerk and returns to the now deserted rural cottage where he grew up.[29] At one point, he is engaged in discussion with the local landowner Ceder, and Henrik's antagonistic stance towards bourgeois education, specifically Shakespeare, is made clear. Ceder asks him whether he knows *The Winter's Tale*, and Henrik believes that earlier on, he would have pretended he had read the play but forgotten it, whereas now he is only too pleased with his own cockiness: 'No, I don't, I said. I've probably never read the Winter's Tale. And I imagine it's a pretty boring play' (123). But Ceder quotes the concluding lines – in English – from the play, which makes something of an impression on Henrik:

> *lead us from hence, where we may leisurely*
> *each one demand, and answer to his part*
> *performed in this wide gap of time, since first*
> *we were dissevered: hastily lead away.* (*Regn i gryningen*, 124;
>   italics in the original).

Unsurprisingly, Ceder interprets the 'lead us from hence' as an admonition to transcend the stalemate of current life. For Ceder, however, the solution is not the introduction of a Nietzschean superman or the bliss of a Christian afterlife; it is, simply and bluntly, the eradication of the human race. 'Mankind, in its present shape, is perhaps just a transitional form, he said. A failed experiment. What do people consist of? As for myself, I have to say: lots of bones and flesh and fifty percent insomnia. You couldn't call that particularly successful' (124). Johnson's tendency towards ironic distancing – a common technique throughout his oeuvre – does not allow for easy identification with any of the characters in the text, but the novel is perhaps the most explicit articulation of the problems of finding happiness and a fulfilled life in Europe between the wars. To be sure, Henrik Fax is not a simple mouthpiece for the author; in fact, in a metafictional turn, an author referred to as 'E. J.' gets to read a lengthy autobiographical account Henrik has been writing and mostly dismisses Henrik as a hypocrite. Significantly, however, E. J. rehearses the familiar critique against civilization as a straitjacket. As he comments to Henrik, 'Let's believe in the struggle for a better human. By "better" I don't mean good under any circumstances, but one that is less narrow-minded, a more open human. When culture is an obstacle for the fresh, happy, life-affirming in people, they should give culture a kick' (237). In the end, therefore, and underneath the layers of irony and narrative complexity, Shakespeare's role in civilizing humankind comes with certain problems: his work serves as a target of reservations about contemporary culture yet also helps to articulate those very reservations.

In one sense, Johnson's extended questioning of the merits of capitalist civilization can be read biographically as reflecting his search for new artistic motifs; indeed, it is around this time that he begins to focus more systematically on his own proletarian background and writes a series of four autobiographical novels that would constitute his real breakthrough as an author. In these *Bildungsromane* set in early twentieth-century northern Sweden and depicting a proletarian teenage boy, Olof, from age fourteen to eighteen, Hamlet becomes not so much a figure of passive ambivalence as part of a Western cultural heritage to be actively embraced by the protagonist. Gradually, the novels reflect the autodidact Olof's conquest of language and education not only thematically but in their language and style. The third novel, *Se dig inte om* [Don't Look Back], from 1936 has Shakespeare casually enter the picture as a point of reference for Olof's emotional reactions.

A fleeting sexual encounter with a girl leaves him in doubt about his own guilt: 'it occurred to him that he perhaps left this Maja in – as Shakespeare put it – a sea of troubles' (222). Appropriately, in the fourth novel, *Slutspel i ungdomen* [Endgame in Youth] (1937), Olof's increasingly wide reading becomes the basis for a more elaborate set of intertextual references. One of them is Shakespeare and in a lengthy chapter depicting a fever dream Olof has, *Hamlet* is even paraphrased in blank verse over several pages (*Slutspel i ungdomen*, 212–17). Along with Goethe, Dickens and others, Shakespeare represents a canon that Olof has literally incorporated into his mind. This process clearly reflects Johnson's own ambitions to educate himself, as reflected by his accounts of his wide reading in letters and articles. It also, arguably, posits Shakespeare as part of a process by which Olof, unlike most of Johnson's earlier characters, becomes a mature, responsible person.[30] At the end of the last novel, Olof embarks on a long southbound journey and is also realizing that words – unlike Hamlet's despondent 'words, words, words' – are precisely what give his life a sense of meaning and direction:

> Strange, he thought, that you've never seen a windmill even if you know exactly what it's like. And basically you know what people were like five hundred years ago, even if you haven't met anyone from that time.
>
> In fact, you already knew a lot, although you obviously had to find the words for it. Precisely this: finding the words for what you actually knew. There were no manuals that you could use. You have to begin by making inventions. Invent words. (*Slutspel i ungdomen*, 385)

At the same time, the insistence on Shakespeare and other literature as crucial to the identity and *Bildung* of the young man begs the question of what importance that heritage has to the time in which the novels were written. Indeed, as Jimmy Vulovic notes, the Olof novels represented a new direction in Johnson's work: instead of the mostly contemporary setting of the previous novels, the perspective was now backward-looking to the early twentieth century.[31]

Yet the political unrest of the 1930s and the imminent Second World War made the call for commitment in the present more urgent than ever. This concern is visible in Johnson's next novel,

Nattövning [Night Manoeuvre], from 1938, a symbolic depiction of anti-fascist struggle in which one of the protagonists, Tomas Gyllem, finally decides to join the republican forces in Spain. Here, *Hamlet* has become irrelevant to the political problems that are looming across Europe. The novel begins with a funeral procession in Stockholm to a 'great actor' (6), presumably Gösta Ekman, who died in early 1938 and was famous for his interpretation of Hamlet. However, the Hamlet figure has now lost its contemporary bearing, as the politically committed onlooker Tomas ruminates:

> In our time, Hamlet is something that only an actor can seriously be, and he must still be Hamlet on a stage. Perhaps the time will come when he is resurrected, not as a saviour, that's not his kind, but as the spirit of the problem of life among people – and then an author writes a tragedy about him and calms the audience down for a few centuries: thank god he's just a theatrical figure. (7)

This is far removed from Johnson's earlier idea that Hamlet is universally 'modern'. In fact, the tendency to question the contemporary relevance of the figure is not limited to Shakespeare but amounts to a general rethinking of the role of literature and culture in times of political crisis. Even Johnson's own previous work seems to be included in this questioning, judging from the recurring character Mårten Torpare's reflection that 'there may have been too much walking in the woods in Nordic literature for quite some time now' (38), which could be construed as an allusion to Johnson's own earlier *Regn i gryningen*.[32] If that earlier novel had questioned the role of literature to foster a new human being, the questioning now has a more specific bearing on European politics. There is a paradox here, though: such dismissal or bracketing of a lot (but not all) literature and culture raises the question of what is to be defended against fascism in the first place. Johnson was demonstrably aware of this issue as it was articulated by one reviewer of his novel, the Finnish-Swedish poet Rabbe Enckell.[33] The novel, however, does not resolve it: in the end, Hamlet seems left as a conflicted symbol of something that is somehow both worth and not worth defending. In that sense, perhaps this ambivalence is reflective of what Elliott Brandsma has recently termed the 'decentering of master narratives' in Johnson's work in the 1930s:

Hamlet cannot serve as a universal key to understanding the contemporary world.[34]

However, in his subsequent novels, as if yet again rethinking Shakespeare's significance to the present, Johnson would invest previous allusions with a new and more emphatically positive meaning. For most of the Second World War, in which Sweden was formally neutral, Johnson was busy editing the clandestine periodical *Håndslag* for the Norwegian resistance movement and writing a series of massive novels known as the Krilon trilogy (1941–1943).[35] In these densely allegorical accounts of politics and warfare, a group of middle-aged men in Stockholm are attacked by personifications of Nazi powers and Stalinism, who conspire to take over their businesses and workplaces. The leader of the group, Johannes Krilon, who has sometimes been considered another variation on the theme of the 'active Hamlet',[36] represents the allied powers (in fact, he even shares some physical attributes with Winston Churchill[37]); he is temporarily disgraced and his office is burnt down. In a final battle, however, the dark forces are defeated but only at the price of losing one of the members of the group, Emil Hovall. This character is a quiet but staunch defender of democracy and humanism who is sometimes given to dream visions in which he articulates the need for a better, peaceful and tolerant world. In the last vision he has, just before the final battle between Krilon and the symbolic embodiments of fascism, he meets a bearded man named Johannes Johannesson, whose name is obviously similar to that of Krilon, from whom Hovall has been estranged for some time. Hovall declares to the bearded man that he wants to be removed from his daily struggle and find a better place to live. He articulates his wish using a familiar quote.

> Above all, I'm looking for harmony, and lately I have often felt that life has disturbed me. I want to wander far away. My English isn't that good, but I read it and can express myself reasonably well in it. In the last couple of days, I have been thinking of Shakespeare's Winter's Tale, some words from it have been ringing in my ear. (*Krilon*, 935)

'*Lead us from hence*', Hovall hesitantly begins, but Johannesson

> gave him a friendly look, patted his beard and recited in a low voice:

*Lead us from hence, where we may leisurely
each one demand, and answer to his part
performed in this wide gap of time, since first
we were dissevered: hastily lead away.* (936; italics in the
original)

These four lines, again quoted in English, in one sense sum up the entire trilogy, with its wish for people to be 'led hence' from the war and yet again become responsible human beings who 'answer to their part' after having been 'dissevered'. This is a far cry from Ceder's pessimistic outlook in *Regn i gryningen* as prompted by the very same lines: a declaration of the belief in humankind to persist rather than being destroyed or radically changed. The battle now concerns nothing less than 'human value' (936), and Shakespeare is accordingly enlisted in the struggle for a better world. From the perspective of the novels, the 'wide gap of time' is not to be taken literally, since the members of the discussion group are only apart for a few months; yet the extent of their separation, with the consequences for their friendship (and, of course, at the allegorical level, for the unity of Europe and the world), has been huge. The adverb 'leisurely' now comes to stand in for the time and reflection needed to heal the wounds. Remarkably, then, during the decade from 1933 to 1943 Shakespeare's lines have taken on a completely new resonance. True, the idea of individual responsibility, indeed accountability, can be said to form a continuity with Johnson's earlier citation of the lines. Yet this time, the responsibility is at once wider and more specific: it concerns the fate of the entire world and the question of how to make everyone, in this particular political moment, 'answer to his part'. Of course, the ending of Shakespeare's play, with its symbolic resurrection of Hermione, can be said to find its reflection in the call for peace and unity with which Johnson's novel concludes. It also, in a more oblique way, hints at how the author saw his own artistic effort under the circumstances. Johnson considered his work on the Krilon trilogy to be his war service, and the lines from *The Winter's Tale* hint at the power of art to be an agent in the struggle for a better world: as the statue of Hermione is capable of moving Leontes, so, presumably, would Johnson's own work be capable of moving its audience.[38] In other words, the implication is that Johnson's allegiances have shifted towards a more programmatically hopeful vision in which Shakespeare serves a positive role and that the paradox from *Nattövning* has been resolved, at least to an extent. After such a resolution, it is significant perhaps that the Hamlet figure would not continue to be a strong presence in Johnson's work from the 1940s and onward, even if some of his anti-heroes like the seventeenth-century clergyman Urbain Grainier in *Dreams of Roses and Fire* (1949) or Johannes in *The Days of His Grace* (1960), set in the reign of Charlemagne, have a certain resemblance to Hamlet as the reflecting onlooker of Johnson's previous novels. As previously noted, from his previous support for anarchism, Johnson's political outlook during and after the Second World War would turn towards a more centrist liberal ideology, although the question of literature's role in politics and the world continued to preoccupy him until his death in 1976. His penultimate novel, *Favel ensam* [Favel Alone], is largely set in Britain; in its extended critique of political utopias (including More's *Utopia*) and its insistence on the right of the artist to *not* be politically or programmatically committed, it was not well received in 1968.[39] Shakespeare makes some appearances in the novel, this time in a way that suggests a critique of literary allusion as a form of escapism: 'Quote Shakespeare or dig up something he has quoted: one of the eternal companions: that word rubbish. Quote Shakespeare and others in order not *to have to bother yourself*. Be Mistress Quickly in the Merry Wives for five or ten seconds so you don't have to say the word rubbish about life, about death' (*Favel ensam*, 230–1). If such a late statement yet again testifies to the shifting nature of Johnson's responses to Shakespeare, it also demonstrates that Shakespeare continued to be a sounding board and a point of reference throughout his career. Indeed, Johnson's very last novel, *Några steg mot tystnaden* [Some Steps Towards Silence] (1973), features a frame-maker, Peidar Urais, whose close relative, the hotel manager Giachim, is unwilling to repair the old palace which he owns and where Peidar's workshop is housed. The embittered Peidar, who has also been abandoned by his wife years ago, reflects, 'Whether 'tis nobler in the mind to suffer – or to take some kind of arms in a sea of troubles, *nymph?*'. Peidar further elaborates on his kinsman, 'He knows a bit of art, he secretly reads books, I believe, he comes up with quotes – for suitable better guests – but mumbles Hamlet to himself or to impress me, who also knows how to mumble quotes' (208). As if coming full circle, Hamlet, like in

Johnson's series of novels half a century earlier, serves as a point of reference for passive, abandoned and defeated men.

In short, Johnson's Shakespeare was as amorphous as Johnson's own political allegiances and the rapidly transforming European political map. What began in his work as a fairly static series of Hamlet figures, emblems of 'modern life' who are mostly incapable of finding direction in their lives, continues as a more programmatic attempt at overcoming passivity by tentative displays of solidarity with the working classes. Later elements of Shakespeare in the novels take different directions: Shakespeare becomes part of a Western cultural heritage that confers a sense of identity and meaning on the author's younger alter ego; at the same time this heritage is depicted as problematic and insufficient in the present of the 1930s. In the end, though, Shakespeare is recycled and absorbed into a political and moral vision for the world after the devastation of the Second World War. Johnson's consistent yet shifting attention to Shakespeare may be atypical of authors from his generation and background, but it testifies to how malleable Shakespeare was when shaping an extended series of literary responses to twentieth-century politics and culture.

Notes

1 Eyvind Johnson, letter to Rudolf Värnlund, 5–6 November 1923, cited in Munkhammar and Bergh, *Bara genom breven till dig*, 380. English translations are my own; in the case of titles of Johnson's works, I use English whenever a translation is available and Swedish for untranslated works, with my translation of the title within square brackets. Citations to Johnson's works will be given parenthetically in the text.

2 Jansson, *Självironi*.

3 Munkhammar and Bergh, eds, *Bara genom breven*, 462, 456, 461.

4 Johnson's use of Shakespeare tends to be noted in passing – see, for example, Lindberger, *Norrbottningen*; Orton, *Eyvind Johnson*; Stenström, *Romantikern Eyvind Johnson*; Tormud, *Till en berättelse* – but mostly in connection with the early novels from the 1920s. The most extensive treatment can be found in Schwartz, *Hamlet i klasskampen*, which also, however, only focuses on Johnson's work to 1930.

5 Schwartz, *Hamlet i klasskampen*, 120.
6 In the preface to a later edition of his novel *Minnas*, first published in 1928, Johnson recalls, 'It is highly likely that an early reading of Sigmund Freud and Marcel Proust has influenced the shaping of the book; that, and other literature. And life' (Johnson, *Minnas*, 5). Apparently, Johnson was introduced to Freud's work in 1923 (Stenström, *Romantikern Eyvind Johnson*, 213).
7 Schwartz argues that Johnson's first novel *Timans och rättfärdigheten* is indebted to Freud's and Ernest Jones's reading of *Hamlet* but ignores the biographical element in that reading (Schwartz, *Hamlet i klasskampen*, 123).
8 See, for example, Johnson, *Slutspel i ungdomen*, 389; *Sju liv*, 487. On the other hand, Johnson did repeatedly claim that all writing is autobiographical in some way or other (Lindberger, *Människan*, 424).
9 Obviously, this latter work cannot have been a direct influence on Johnson's books from the 1920s since it was first published in 1930, but he certainly was familiar enough with it by 1933 to allude to its Swedish title, *Vi vantrivas i kulturen*, in his novel *Regn i gryningen* (234).
10 As an example of the debate in Sweden, one might suggest the psychoanalyst Pehr Henrik Törngren's essay 'Dikten kontra livet' ('Literature Versus Life') in the short-lived but influential periodical on culture, *Spektrum*, in December 1932. Törngren drastically likens a dependence on literature to alcoholism since it removes the reader or writer from reality; literature becomes a projection area for ambivalence about life but does not ultimately resolve it. If this view of literature as escapism can easily be dismissed as simplistic, it still articulates one position in the wide-ranging debate on the culture that took place in the 1930s, with its social reforms and ambitions to build a new and better society. While Johnson's views of culture and literature were much more complex, he was presumably familiar with Törngren's essay since he had a short story in the very same issue of *Spektrum* in which it appeared.
11 For recent discussions of Johnson, modernism and modernity, see Brandsma, 'Recovering a "Lost Europe"'; Salmose, 'Swedish Social Modernism'; Thomsen, 'New Nordic Environments'.
12 Halpern, *Shakespeare among the Moderns*, 26.
13 Munkhammar and Bergh, eds, *Bara genom breven*, 1170. Although Johnson does not seem to have known about them, it bears remarking that the first modern-dress performances of *Hamlet* had taken place

just a couple of years earlier, in 1925 (in London, Berlin and Prague). See Thompson, 'Introduction', 109.

14 DiPietro, *Shakespeare and Modernism*, 25–42; also, the Introduction to the present volume.

15 Quoted in Stenström, *Romantikern Eyvind Johnson*, 303 (n. 46).

16 It can be noted that beyond his broader contemporary significance, Shakespeare could serve as confirmation of a homosocial bond between the two young authors, to the point of forcing them to declare the non-sexual nature of their relationship. As Värnlund puts it in a letter to Johnson from February 1929, back in the day 'even the worst crook risked death rather than letting down those he had promised friendship. And that *mostly* without the existence of any perverse relationship -! It's this philosophy of friendship that you find in Schakspeare's [sic] plays and that makes them so magnificent, despite all their Punch and Judy spirit' (Munkhammar and Bergh, eds, *Bara genom breven*, 1102).

17 Johnson had evidently read Hamsun's novel as early as 1920; see Lindberger, *Norrbottningen*, 66.

18 Humpál, 'Knut Hamsun's Criticism of Shakespeare'.

19 Lindberger, *Norrbottningen*, 137.

20 For these and other parallels to *Hamlet* in this novel, see Schwartz, *Hamlet i klasskampen*, 123.

21 For the notion of Clerk as a 'passive Hamlet', see Schwartz, *Hamlet i klasskampen*, 132.

22 For the (undeveloped) suggestion that Andersson is a Hamlet figure, see Lindberger, *Norrbottningen*, 155.

23 Munkhammar and Bergh, eds, *Bara genom breven*, 1132. The actual term Johnson uses for the second son is 'jazzgosse', which literally translates 'jazz boy'; it was introduced in a popular song in 1922 to satirize young, male and slightly effeminate followers of fashion.

24 Orton, *Eyvind Johnson*, 31.

25 *Ham*, 2.2.268–9.

26 Quoted in Stenström, *Romantikern*, 303 (n. 46).

27 In a letter to Finnish-Swedish poet Elmer Diktonius, quoted in Lindberger, *Norrbottningen*, 271; available in its entirety in Lindberger, ed., *'Och så vill jag prata med dig'*, 20–3.

28 Cf. Orton, *Eyvind Johnson*, 40.

29 The gender patterning is evident: the woman represents a confinement within culture from which – of course – the man must break free.

'Discontents' in Johnson's novels are almost invariably gendered as male. For discussion, see Witt-Brattström, *Ur könets mörker*, esp. 241.

30 For the claim that this maturation also represents a distancing from the Hamlet figure, see Tormod, *Till en berättelse*, 356.

31 Vulovic, *Ensamhet och gemenskap*, 200.

32 Orton, *Eyvind Johnson*, 38.

33 Review in *Hufvudstadsbladet*, 18 November 1938, cited in Lindberger, *Människan*, 34.

34 Brandsma, 'Recovering a "Lost Europe"', which mainly focuses on Johnson's short story collection *Natten är här* [The Night Has Come] (1934).

35 Sweden's neutrality was, for parts of the war, dubious and included a fair amount of collusion with Nazi Germany, including allowing troop transports through the country.

36 Schwartz, *Hamlet i klasskampen*, 143.

37 For these parallels, see Orton, *Eyvind Johnson*, 79–80.

38 For Johnson's process of writing the trilogy, see Lindberger, *Människan*, 64–135.

39 For Johnson and utopian thinking, see especially Stenström, *Romantikern*, 71–196.

Work Cited

A. Works by Eyvind Johnson:

Timans och rättfärdigheten (Stockholm, 1925).
Stad i mörker (Stockholm, 1927).
Stad i ljus (Stockholm, 1928).
Kommentar till ett stjärnfall (Stockholm, 1929).
Avsked till Hamlet (Stockholm, 1930).
Regn i gryningen (Stockholm, 1933).
Se dig inte om (Stockholm, 1936).
Slutspel i ungdomen (Stockholm, 1937).
Nattövning (Stockholm, 1938).
Sju liv (Stockholm, 1944; collected edition of short stories).
Krilon (Stockholm, 1948; collected edition of the three novels *Grupp Krilon*, *Krilons resa* and *Krilon själv*, published in 1941–1943).

Minnas (Stockholm, 1950 [1928]).
Favel ensam (Stockholm, 1968).
Några steg mot tystnaden (Stockholm, 1973).

B. Other sources:

Brandsma, Elliot J., 'The De-Centering of Master Narratives in Eyvind Johnson's *Natten är här*', *Humanities* 10/1 (2021), n. p.
DiPietro, Cary, *Shakespeare and Modernism* (Cambridge, 2006).
Halpern, Richard, *Shakespeare Among the Moderns* (Ithaca, 1997).
Humpál, Martin, 'Knut Hamsun's Criticism of Shakespeare', in Nely Keinänen and Per Sivefors, eds, *Disseminating Shakespeare in the Nordic Countries: Shifting Centres and Peripheries in the Nineteenth Century* (London, 2022), 269–89.
Jansson, Bo G., *Självironi, självbespegling och självreflexion: Den metafiktiva tendensen i Eyvind Johnsons diktning* (Stockholm, 1990).
Lindberger, Örjan, *Norrbottningen som blev europé: Eyvind Johnsons liv och författarskap till och med Romanen om Olof* (Stockholm, 1986).
Lindberger, Örjan, *Människan i tiden: Eyvind Johnsons liv och författarskap, 1938–1976* (Stockholm, 1990).
Lindberger, Örjan, ed., *'Och så vill jag prata med dig': Brevväxlingen mellan Eyvind Johnson och Elmer Diktonius* (Stockholm, 1997).
Munkhammar, Birgit, and Magnus Bergh, eds, *Bara genom breven till dig, vän! Eyvind Johnsons och Rudolf Värnlunds brevväxling* (Stockholm, 2018).
Orton, Gavin, *Eyvind Johnson: En monografi* (Stockholm, 1974).
Salmose, Niklas, 'Swedish Social Modernism: The Inward and Outward Turn in Eyvind Johnson's *Stad i ljus*', in Helen Rydstrand and John Attridge, eds, *Modernist Work: Labor, Aesthetics, and the Work of Art* (London, 2019), 163–78.
Schwartz, Nils, *Hamlet i klasskampen: En ideologikritisk studie i Eyvind Johnsons 20-talsromaner* (Lund, 1979).
Shakespeare, William, *Hamlet*, eds Ann Thompson and Neil Taylor, The Arden Shakespeare (London, 2006).
Stenström, Thure, *Romantikern Eyvind Johnson: Tre studier* (Lund, 1978).
Thompson, Ann, 'Introduction', in William Shakespeare, *Hamlet*, eds Ann Thompson and Neil Taylor (London, 2006), 1–137.
Thomsen, B. Thorup, 'New Nordic Environments in Eyvind Johnson's Factual and Fictional Prose, 1928–1932', *European Journal of Scandinavian Studies* 48/1 (2018), 19–41.
Tormod, Mats, *Till en berättelse om tröst: Eyvind Johnson omläst* (Stockholm, 2012).

Törngren, Pehr Henrik, 'Dikten kontra livet', *Spektrum* 8 (December 1932), 26–34.

Vulovic, Jimmy, *Ensamhet och gemenskap i förvandling: Vägar genom Eyvind Johnsons och Rudolf Värnlunds mellankrigsromaner* (Stockholm, 2009).

Witt-Brattström, Ebba, *Ur könets mörker etc.* (Stockholm, 2003).

Afterword

Michael Dobson

Reading this fine collection of essays about Shakespeare's multiple roles in Nordic theatrical and literary culture during the great age of conflict between emerging European nation states and crumbling European empires, one question occurs again and again: Would Shakespeare have meant as much in this part of the world, or at least would he have meant in the same ways, had his most famous play not depicted a legendary prince of Denmark whose dynasty is eventually supplanted by that of his Norwegian rival Fortinbras? Not the least of this volume's achievements is to provide substantial further resources for Anglophone scholars interested in the modern afterlives of *Hamlet*, a play whose Northern inflections usefully served not only those Scandinavians, Icelanders and Finns who wanted their different languages recognized as worthy of a classic of world literature but those who sought to localize Shakespeare's tragedy for their own more immediate purposes. When I spent a month at the Nasjonalbiblioteket in Oslo in 2019, mainly examining the archives of the nearby Nationaltheatret, I was intrigued to learn that the chief painting adorning the ceiling of a playhouse built for Ibsen and Bjørnson is generally known by a title which alludes not to a Norwegian classic but to an English one. Directly above the stalls, Eivind Nielsen's image of a nymph dismaying a satyr by showing him his own image in a looking glass, though its artist called it 'The Mirror of Truth' (1899), is more often referred to as 'The Mirror Up to Nature', as though its chief purpose is to remind actors and audiences alike of Hamlet's advice to the players. By either title, its neo-rococo style – a pink, fluffy pastiche of Fragonard or Boucher – seems incongruous for what must originally have been intended as a visual manifesto for the redemptive rigours of late nineteenth-century theatrical realism, but the currency of the latter name both assumes and demonstrates that any Norwegian National Theatre, Ibsen aside, is to be regarded as a natural venue for revivals of *Hamlet*. The most striking image in the theatre's archives, to me at least, which might serve as an epilogue to this entire volume, depicts the final tableau from one of those revivals, Hans Jacob Nilsen's 1946 production, in which the bodies of Hamlet (seated in a chair), Claudius, Gertrude and Laertes are upstaged by three figures who stand on a raised platform directly behind and above the defeated Danes. Their backs to the audience, the entire surviving court kneel and bow their heads in supplication and fealty towards these interlopers, the outermost two of whom bear large banners. One of the banners shows the three lions of the English royal standard: this, clearly, is an English ambassador. The other, borne by a soldier, shows the single lion of the Norwegian royal crest, making it clear (as if it weren't obvious) that the messianic figure in shining armour beside him, at the very centre of the stage picture, is Fortinbras. A character who has often been cut entirely elsewhere here arrives to provide what looks like the play's climax.[1] Giving the English and Norwegian flags symmetrical and equal prominence, Nilsen's production uses this locally patriotic moment to highlight post-war Norway's desire to be seen, Quisling apart, as victorious Britain's faithful ally. And how pleasantly convenient that the fictionalized version of Scandinavian history provided by English literature's most famous tragedy should also be the only history in which Norway defeats and takes over Denmark for once, rather than vice versa.

But as this volume repeatedly shows, even at less charged historical moments than this one it was hard to perform Shakespeare in any of the emerging Nordic nation states without also showing allegiance – aesthetic, political or both – to one or other of the empires and imperial monarchies whose hegemonies were liable to extend into the domain of theatre as well as that of government. As in Nilsen's *Hamlet*, playing Shakespeare at all might be presented as a gesture of alliance with Britain, but all around the Baltic and to the north other, previous versions of what and how Shakespeare might mean on stage haunted what local companies might do. France, the main influence for years on Danish drama in particular, had neoclassicized and then Romanticized Shakespeare well before the period explored by this collection; Germany had in part founded its modern theatrical and literary tradition on the translation and appropriation of Shakespeare, and for those persuaded by Ferdinand Freiligrath's 1844 poem *Hamlet*, with its famous opening lament that 'Deutschland ist Hamlet!', the newly unified territory's late nineteenth-century military adventures, including the invasion of Schleswig-Holstein, could be understood as attempts specifically to prove that Deutschland was no longer Hamlet. Russia, too, had its own tradition of reviving Shakespeare and despite its official non-existence so did Poland. *Hamlet* was thus a key text for imperialists, nation-builders and would-be nation-builders for the Nordic countries' influential neighbours too throughout the period covered by this volume – witness Stanislaw Wyspiański's *Hamlet Study* (1905), which imagined the ghost of Poland's royal independence stalking the battlements of Wawel Castle in Kraków.

It might be a salutary exercise, then, to turn from the histories described in this volume back to the text of *Hamlet*, to consider how far the most northerly of Shakespeare's plays really underwrites the various interests which this volume's contributors have so adeptly shown to have been at work in the Nordic Shakespeares of the modernist period. Promisingly, the words 'nation' or 'nations' occur four times in *Hamlet*, but they do so only twice in connection with Denmark: on the other two occasions they refer instead to France. The offstage Norman cavalryman Lamord is reported to have ranked Laertes's skill at fencing above that of all 'th'escrimers of their nation' (4.7.98),[2] and Laertes in his turn regards Lamord as 'the very brooch indeed / And gem, of all the nation' (4.7.91–92). This is perhaps an appropriate metaphor in the light of Polonius's earlier advice to his son that he should wear 'rich, not gaudy' clothes while he is in Paris so as not to offend against the fashion-consciousness of the French aristocracy (1.3.70–3). Claudius, who has seen 'and served against, the French' (4.7.82), shares this admiration for Gallic chivalry and culture, but he and his queen seem much less impressed with their own countrymen. Surprised by Laertes's short-lived rebellion, Claudius calls for the foreign mercenaries he has hired as his personal bodyguard in preference to using Danish troops: 'Where is my Switzers? Let them guard the door' (4.5.97). Gertrude, hearing that the 'rabble' are acclaiming Laertes as king, dismisses the local population as so many incompetent and innately disloyal hunting hounds: 'How cheerfully on the false trail they cry. / O, this is counter, you false Danish dogs!' (4.5.109–10). Prince

Hamlet likewise, whatever else he may be, is hardly a conventional epitome of patriotism: one of the first things we learn about him is that he has requested permission to leave Denmark and return to university at Wittenberg in Germany (1.2.112–19). While his father defeated the Norwegians, vanquishing old Fortinbras in single combat in the process, and on one memorable occasion even smote the sledded Polacks on the ice (1.1.62), young Hamlet, when confronted by the spectacle of Fortinbras's army advancing on Poland in 4.4, is moved only to admiration and self-reproach. By contrast his sole observation on the subject of the Danes in general is a comment on his compatriots' reputation for alcoholism:

> This heavy-headed revel east and west
> Makes us traduced and taxed of other nations:
> They clepe us drunkards and with swinish phrase
> Soil our addition[.] (1.4.17–20)[3]

The overall narrative of *Hamlet, Prince of Denmark*, then, depicts the extinction of a royal family who cannot be said to die as willing martyrs in their country's cause. Perhaps the only nation which comes out worse in the play than Denmark is England, a vassal state represented in the cast list solely by the ambassadors who arrive on their fruitless errand to the dead Claudius during the last seconds of the fifth act, and described by the Gravedigger as home to general insanity:

> HAMLET: Ay, marry. Why was he sent into England?
> FIRST CLOWN: Why, because 'a was mad. 'A shall recover his wits there. Or if 'a do not, 'tis no great matter there.
> HAMLET: Why?
> FIRST CLOWN: 'Twill not be seen in him there. There the men are as mad as he. (5.1.141–46)

The fourth use of the word 'nation' or 'nations' in *Hamlet*, though, is slightly different: arguably, paradoxical as it may sound, it might even gesture towards something potentially cosmopolitan. As Claire McEachern points out, in the Tudor period, though 'nation more often means race, or kind – the kith and kin of a common nativity, or birth, *natio*,[. . .] in the course of the sixteenth century it comes to denote that principle of political self-determination belonging to a people linked (if in nothing else) by a common government'.[4] But Rosencrantz appears to use the word in a different sense than either of these when, describing to Hamlet the quarrel between newly fashionable private companies of boy actors and the adult common players whose audiences they are stealing, he reports that 'there has been much to-do on both sides, and the nation holds it no sin to tarre them to controversy' (2.2.353–5).[5] The 'nation' which is happy to have the proponents of the boy players and those of the adult companies egged on to further mutual recrimination and satire is surely not exactly 'all those who are ethnically Danish' or 'all subjects of the Danish crown', especially given that these lines originally alluded to the War of the Theatres, a set of showbusiness rivalries which was taking place not in Copenhagen but in London. Instead it means something more like 'the theatregoing public at large', so membership of a 'nation' is here fleetingly construed not in terms of birth or of power but in terms of participation in public theatrical culture. In a play in which the examples of drama we witness are one play about Troy and another, based on Italian sources, about a murder done in Vienna, that culture is not an insular or xenophobic one at all.

The conspicuous presence of this foreign playwright in the theatre repertories of Northern Europe from the 1880s through the 1940s, then, however strenuously some of the playhouses involved should have been imagined and designed as instruments of exclusive cultural nationalisms, is perhaps a tribute to Shakespeare's own productive vagueness about national identity: however vigorously he may have been co-opted posthumously as a figurehead for nationalism and imperialism, both within his erstwhile homeland and beyond, they are not phenomena which even his history plays exactly hymn. It is sad to reflect that this book, which thinks of the nationalisms which arose, converged and conflicted to produce the First and Second World Wars as historical phenomena from a long-past epoch, should have gone to press in, of all years, 2022 – a year in which the multilingual international Shakespeare festivals which once looked set to supplant national theatres as the dominant venues for European theatrical Shakespeare have yet to recover either from the Covid pandemic or from the preceding decade's resurgence of nationalist populism (the Giulya festival in Hungary, for instance, has been denied funding for any productions not performed in Hungarian), and in which the invasion of Ukraine has put the Nordic region once more into a state of high alert about the Russian Empire immediately to the east. The conflicts which shadow the translations and productions discussed between these covers, alas, had not, after all, been settled once and for all. When the governments of Sweden and Finland chose to join Nato in response, one wonders whether they did so with a quotation from *Hamlet* ringing in their ears: President Zelensky's invocation of 'To be, or not to be' as a description of the stark choice facing his own nation. I hope that by the time this volume has appeared the inhabitants of Northern and Eastern Europe will once more be members of the same cosmopolitan theatregoing 'nation' and that the only wars in which we will be engaged will be strictly theatrical ones.

Notes

1 On this, see Dobson, 'Cutting'.
2 This passage occurs only in the second quarto: in, for example, the Oxford edition it is given as additional passage L.
3 In the Oxford edition, it occurs as additional passage B, 1–4.
4 McEachern, *Poetics*, 1.
5 The Arden edition reprints these lines from the Folio in Appendix 2, passage 2 (16–18).

Works cited

Dobson, Michael, 'Cutting, Interruption, and the End of *Hamlet*', *New Theatre Quarterly*, 32/3 (2016), 269–75.
McEachern, Clare, *The Poetics of English Nationhood, 1590–1612* (Cambridge, 1996).
Shakespeare, William, *Hamlet*, ed. Ann Thompson and Neil Taylor, The Arden Shakespeare (London, 2006).

Appendix

A timeline of significant Shakespeare-related events in the Nordic countries, 1880–1940

The editors are grateful to Anne Sophie Refskou for some important information concerning the Danish context and, as ever, to Kent Hägglund for sharing his extensive knowledge on Shakespeare in Sweden.

1880 – Norwegian church publication declares Shakespeare 'safe reading for Lutheran Christians', *WT* performed at the New Theatre, Bergen; *Mac* at the Nya Teatern (later Svenska Teatern), Stockholm.

1881 – In Finland, first Finnish-language production of a Shakespeare play, *RJ*, at the Finnish Theatre in Helsinki, starring Ida Aalberg as Juliet, performance hailed as a 'cultural victory' for Finnish culture; in Norway, *Oth* at the New Theatre, Bergen, Hartvig Lassen translates *MV* into modern Norwegian for use in schools, indebted to Hagberg's Swedish, Schlegel's German and possibly also Lembcke's Danish version, Lassen cuts passages deemed inappropriate for students; in Sweden, first performances of *AC* and *JC* at the Royal Theatre, Stockholm, and *Ham* starring Edward Swartz.

1882 – In Finland, *MV* at the Finnish Theatre in a translation by Paavo Cajander published the same year, review compares Finnish translation to Hagberg's Swedish, Swedish-language *Cym* at the Swedish Theatre in Helsinki; in Iceland, the first Icelandic *Oth* is published by Matthías Jochumsson, attacked for inaccuracy, causing translator to issue an apology and defend his translation, saying it is indebted to Nicolaus Delius, Hagberg and Edvard Lembcke; in Norway, Lassen translates *JC* into modern Norwegian for use in schools; *RJ* at the Royal Theatre, Stockholm.

1883 – In Finland, *TS* performed in Vyborg by the Finnish Theatre company; in Norway, Lassen translates *Mac* for schools, also cut for reasons of propriety, for example, parts of the porter scene; in Sweden, premiere of Anne Charlotte Leffler's *En räddande engel* [A Saving Angel] contains allusions to Juliet. Swedish literary historian Henrik Schück publishes *William Shakspere: Hans lif och värksamhet* [William Shakespeare: His Life and Work].

1884 – In Finland, first Finnish-language performance of *Ham*, in a translation by Paavo Cajander by the Finnish Theatre company, *TN* at the Swedish Theatre in Helsinki; in Stockholm, two premieres: *AYL*, at the Svenska Teatern and *MM* at the Royal Dramatic Theatre, the latter not well received; *H4* at the Royal Dramatic Theatre, Stockholm, starring the Norwegian actor Johannes Brun as Falstaff; *Ham* at the Royal Theatre with the famous actor and director August Lindberg in the title role; Swedish writer Anne Charlotte Leffler travels to London, writes about her experiences, for example, on seeing Ellen Terry play Beatrice (published in 1885).

1885–6 – Guest appearances by Italian actor Ernesto Rossi at the Danish Folketheatret and the Royal Theatre, Stockholm.

1885 – First complete Danish translation of *Son* by Adolph Hansen and appearance of an annotated English school edition of *Mac*, eds Mr A. Stewart MacGregor and Mrs S. Kinney, for use in Danish schools; Eiríkur Magnússon's Icelandic translation of *Tem* published to mixed reviews, with some asking who wants to read Shakespeare anyway.

1886 – The Finnish actress Ida Aalberg invited to perform Ophelia in Finnish in Stockholm and Copenhagen; first Finnish-language performance of *KL* in Finland, translated by Paavo Cajander; in Norway, *Ham* at the New Theatre, Bergen; *Mac* played by Ernesto Rossi at the Royal Theatre opposite Elise Hwasser alternating with Olga Björkegren.

1887–8 – Valdemar Østerberg publishes new Danish translations of *Ham*, *RJ* and *KL*.

1887 – In Finland, first Finnish-language performance of *Mac* at the Finnish Theatre, translated by Paavo Cajander, also performances of *Ham* and *MV*; *RJ* published for the first time in Icelandic, translated by Matthías Jochumsson; in Norway, *JC* at the Christiania Theatre.

1888 – Norwegian periodical publishes a character study of Ophelia by Just Bing, calling her the 'finest woman' in Shakespeare; the famous German Meiningen Ensemble plays Shakespeare at the Svenska Teatern, Stockholm (the previously named Nya Teatern).

1889 – In Finland, first Finnish-language *JC* and *Oth*, with Ida Aalberg as Desdemona, Aalberg goes to Berlin to train as an actor; in Norway, Knut Hamsun criticizes Shakespeare as outdated, anti-Shakespeare statements continue in the early 1890s.

1890 – *Oth* at Copenhagen's Dagmartheatret; Finnish actress Ida Aalberg plays Juliet (in German) at the Ostend theatre in Berlin, with Josef Kainz as Romeo; *Viola*, Sille Beyer's Danish adaptation of *TN*, performed in Norway at the Christiania Theatre; *TS* and *Ham* at the Finnish Theatre.

1891 – *TN* performed in Danish using Lembcke's translation, at the Casino theatre; in Finland, first Finnish-language *MND*, with lavish costumes and set decorations, music by Mendelssohn, *MW* at the Swedish Theatre in Helsinki.

1892 – In Norway, *TN* at the New Theatre, Bergen, using Lembcke's Danish translation; *MV* at the Finnish Theatre.

1893 – *WT* at the Royal Theatre, Copenhagen, this time using Lembcke's Danish translation.

1894 – *Mac* at the Royal Theatre, Copenhagen, in Lembcke's translation; Swedish actress Charlotte Raa-Winterhjelm invited to Finnish Theatre to play Lady Macbeth in Finnish, but two decades after early triumphant performances in Finnish, audience react negatively to her accented Finnish, also *TS* at the FT; the Finnish actress Ida Aalberg performs in Stockholm, Gothenburg, Christiania, Copenhagen, guest performance at Helsingborg of *Oth* by Danish troupe under Pavel Friis; Norwegian periodicals publish on the authorship question, outlining Baconian theories.

1895 – Theodor Caspari, a Norwegian poet, publishes an essay comparing Ibsen and Shakespeare, to the detriment of Ibsen; guest appearance of *Ham* at the New Theatre, Bergen, by Swedish troupe led by August Lindberg, who has previously toured with the production in Finland.

1895–1896 – In Denmark, Georg Brandes publishes his biography of Shakespeare, read all over the world, the book attacked by Theodor Bierfreund (1855–1906), who publishes his own Shakespeare bio two years later.

1896 – In Finland, first Finnish-language *AC*, with Ida Aalberg as Cleopatra, and *WT*; Finnish translator Cajander celebrated for his contributions to Finnish literature.

1897 – In Finland, first Finnish-language *R3*, also *TS* and *KL* at the FT, translations by Cajander; in Norway, *RJ* at the New Theatre, Bergen; *Ham* at the Royal Dramatic Theatre, Stockholm.

1898 – Theodor Bierfreund publishes a book on Shakespeare, in part as a response to Brandes; in Finland, Nikolay Bobrikov is appointed Governor General, leading to further censorship and restrictions on the Finnish language, *MV* revived by the Finnish Theatre for the third time; *CE* at the Royal Dramatic Theatre, Stockholm.

1899 – *MW* performed at the Casinotheatret, Copenhagen, *MND* at the Royal Theatre, Copenhagen, this time using Lembcke's translation; in Finland, *WT* at the Finnish Theatre; in Norway, *TN* at the Nationaltheatret, Christiania.

1900–1901 – Valdemar Østerberg publishes Danish translations of eight plays, several more to follow.

1900 – *R3* at the Royal Theatre, Copenhagen; in Norway, *TS* at the Nationaltheatret; first Swedish *Tem* as a one-man show by August Lindberg, premiere in Gothenburg and tours in the provinces.

1901 – In Denmark, Niels Møller publishes translations of *H4*, *MV* and *Ham*; premiere of Finnish *TN* at the Finnish Theatre, Helsinki, using title *Viola*, also *Ham*, *Mac* in Viipuri (the theatre company based in Viipuri, also known as Vyborg in English, travelled all over Finland, so their Shakespeare productions here and below might have been seen elsewhere too); translation of *Mac* into Norwegian Nynorsk, by Olav Madshus assisted by Arne Garborg; fiasco for first Swedish *LLL* at the Dramatic Theatre, Stockholm, play not performed again until 1971.

1902 – Guest performance in Copenhagen of French production of *Ham* starring Sarah Bernhardt in the title role; *TS*, *KL* and first *Tem* in Finnish at the Finnish Theatre, Helsinki, farewell performance at the Arkadia Theatre in Helsinki includes fourth act of *MV* starring Benjamin Leino as Shylock, *MV* at Suomen Maaseututeatteri; in Sweden, *MA* at the Dramatic Theatre.

1903 – In Norway, *MND* at the Nationaltheatret; in Finland, *MV* in Viipuri.

1904 – *Oth* at the Royal Theatre, Copenhagen; *JC*, *MND* and *RJ* at Finnish National Theatre, *Ham*, starring Kosti Elo, and *TS* in Viipuri; in southern Sweden, the only extant copy of the first quarto of *TA* surfaces, sold in 1905 to Folger.

1905 – Translation of *MV* into Nynorsk by Olav Madshus; in Finland, *RJ* at Tampere Theatre, *AC* at Suomen Maaseututeatteri, translation of Mary Macleod's *Shakespeare Story-Book* into Finnish by A. and K. Forsman, translation of the Norwegian Christen Collins's 'Shakespeare's Hamlet' in a Finnish literary magazine, short article in several Finnish newspapers on how much money Shakespeare brings to Stratford-upon-Avon.

1906 – In Norway, *MV* at the Nationaltheatret; in Finland, *Ham* (starring Aarne Orjatsalo), *TN* and *RJ* at Tampere Theatre, *Ant* (with Ida Aalberg visiting as Cleopatra), *Oth* and *MW* in Viipuri. Aalberg's Cleopatra was so successful that patrons threw roses onstage; *KL* at the Royal Dramatic Theatre, Stockholm, directed by and starring August Lindberg.

1907 – In Denmark, lawyer August Goll publishes study *Forbrydertyper hos Shakespeare*, later translated into English under the title *Criminal Types in Shakespeare*; in Finland, *TS* and *MV* at Tampere Theatre, *MA* in Viipuri, *H4* at FNT; in Norway, *Ham* at the Nationaltheatret.

1908 – In Denmark, Valdemar Østerberg's translation of *Mac*; in Finland, *MW* at Tampere Workers' Theatre; in Norway, *Oth* at the Nationaltheatret.

1908–9 – August Strindberg writes a series of articles and open letters on theatre, several of which focus on Shakespeare, *Mac* at the Dramatic Theatre, Stockholm; in Finland *Ham* and *TN* in Viipuri, *MW* at Tampere Workers' Theatre.

1910 – *Ham* at the Dagmartheatret, Copenhagen; in Finland, *Oth* at the Tampere Theatre with Aarne Orjatsalo in the title role, *RJ* in Viipuri; in Norway, *H4* at the Nationaltheatret.

1911 – *JC* at the Royal Theatre, Copenhagen, Danish actress Ellen Aggerholm plays Puck in a production of *MND* at His Majesty's Theatre, London, Danish director August Blom makes a silent film based on *Ham*; in Finland, *AC* and *MND* at FNT, *Tem* in Viipuri, Aarne Orjatsalo tours around Finland playing a large repertoire of plays including *TN*.

1912 – In Finland, *AYLI* and *Cor* at the FNT, *KL* in Viipuri, *R3* in Swedish at Svenska Teatern in Helsinki; in Norway, *AYL* at the Nationaltheatret in a free translation by Herman Wildenwey, translation of *MND* into Nynorsk by Erik Eggen, translation of *Ham* into Riksmaal by C. H. Blom.

1913 – *H4* and *Livet i skoven* [Life in the Woods], the latter a nineteenth-century adaptation by Sille Beyer of *AYL*, at the Dagmartheatret, Copenhagen; in Finland, *Ham* at FNT, *KL* in Viipuri, with Kaarle Halme directing and playing the title character; Elli Tompuri becomes the first female Hamlet in the Nordic countries, tours around Finland.

1914 – In Finland, *Oth* and *MW* at FNT, *TS* at Tampere Theatre with Simo Kaario celebrating his tenth anniversary as an actor by playing Petruchio.

1915 – In Denmark, Valdemar Østerberg publishes a school edition of *MV*; in Finland, *MA* at FNT, *MV* in Viipuri, *TN* at Tampere Theatre, Elli Tompuri tours with *RJ*; guest performances of Max Reinhardt's *MND* and *TN* at the Royal Opera, Stockholm.

1916 – The Shakespeare *Mindefest* is celebrated in Elsinore; Sir Israel Gollancz's anthology *A Book of Homage to Shakespeare* features several contributions by Nordic scholars; Swedish literary historian Henrik Schück publishes *Shakspere och hans tid* [Shakespeare and His Time], his second book on the topic, critic August Brunius publishes study *Shakespeare och scenen* [Shakespeare and the Stage].

1917 – The Royal Opera, Stockholm, features Max Reinhardt's production of *Oth*, *Ham* at the Nya Teatern, Gothenburg; in

Finland, *MV* at FNT, *Ham* at the Tampere Workers' Theatre with Aarne Orjatsalo in the title role, *KL* at the Tampere Theatre with Wilho Ilmari in the title role.

1918 – Selection of sonnets translated into Norwegian by Edvard G. Johannesen; *R3* at the Dramatic Theatre, Stockholm, starring Lars Hanson; in Finland, *RJ* at FNT, *MND* at the Tampere Workers' Theatre (Finland), directed by Aarne Orjatsalo who also plays Bottom.

1919 – In Denmark, *MND* at Aarhus; in Finland, *TN* in Viipuri, *RJ* at Tampere Theatre; in Norway, translation of *R3* into Nynorsk by Erik Eggen.

1920 – In Copenhagen, Max Reinhardt's *MV*, also performed in Stockholm; in Sweden, Lorensbergteatern in Gothenburg is the first theatre outside the capital to get public funding, new director Per Lindberg (son of August L) stages *AYL* and *Ham*, with incidental music by Wilhelm Stenhammar; in Finland, *Oth* in Turku.

1921 – Danish Asta Nielsen stars as a female Hamlet in German film production directed by Svend Gade and Heinz Schall, *Ham* at the Betty Nansen Teater, *Oth* at the Scala Teater, *H4* at the Royal Theatre, Copenhagen, *MND* at Odense, Valdemar Østerberg publishes translation of *Ham*, Johannes Poulsen tours Danish provinces as Petruccio in *TS*; in Finland, *MND* at FNT, *AYL* and *MV* at Tampere Theatre; in Norway, Ingolf Schanche stars in *Ham* at the Nationaltheatret, Oslo, also performs role in Stockholm; in Sweden, the Helsingborg city theatre opens with performance of *TN*, first Swedish performance of full text of *Tem* at the Dramatic Theatre, Stockholm, *KL* and *Oth* at the Lorensbergteatern, Gothenburg.

1922–31 – Per Hallström's complete translation of the plays, the first in Swedish since C. A. Hagberg's, which is reissued (1925–8) in a version revised by Nils Molin.

1922–1930s – Indriði Einarsson translates twelve plays in the canon into Icelandic, two performed although apart from small excerpts, all remain unpublished by his death in 1939.

1922 – In Denmark, August Goll publishes *Romeo og Juliet og andre Shakespearestudier* [Romeo and Juliet and Other Studies in Shakespeare]; in Copenhagen and Stockholm, the Moscow Art Theatre performs *Ham*, *RJ* at the Lorensbergteatern, Gothenburg, music by Stenhammar, in Finland, *Cym* at FNT, *WT* in Viipuri.

1923 – Danish actor Johannes Poulsen stars as Shylock in *MV* at the Royal Theatre, Copenhagen, with guest performance at the Dramatic Theatre, Stockholm, *Ham* at Odense, open-air performance of *TN* at the Dyrehaven, Copenhagen; in Finland, *WT* at FNT, *Ham* and *RJ* in Viipuri.

1923–42 – Twenty-one plays translated into Norwegian Rigsmaal by a team of six translators.

1924 – Valdemar Østerberg publishes study *Prince Hamlet's Age* in English; in Sweden, August Brunius publishes *Shakespeare: liv, drama, teater*, intended for the general reader and partly adapting his earlier *Shakespeare och scenen* (see under 1916); in Finland, *TS* at Vaasa Worker's Theatre, *AYL* in Turku; in Malmö, Sweden, guest performance of *MV* by the Danish Royal Theatre.

1925 – In Denmark, *MND* at Aarhus, *WT* at Odense, first Swedish radio performance of Shakespeare, featuring scenes from *Ham* by Gustaf Molander, to be followed by another thirty-six radio versions of various plays until 1940; in Finland, *TN* at FNT, *RJ* at both FNT and in Turku.

1926 – In Denmark, open-air performances of *TS* at Kronborg castle in a reconstruction of the Swan Theatre and of *MND* at the Dyrehaven, Copenhagen, premiere, also in Copenhagen, of Jean Sibelius's incidental music for *Tem*; in Finland, performances of *Ham* at three different workers' theatres; first performances of *TN* and *WT* in Iceland by the Leikfélag Reykjavíkur [The Actors' Guild of Reykjavík], using translations by Indriði Einarsson; *AC* at the Konserthusteatern, Stockholm, directed by Per Lindberg, starring Harriet Bosse, featuring music by Kurt Atterberg and costumes by Isaac Grünewald.

1927 – *TS* at the Royal Theatre, Copenhagen; *Tem* at the Finnish National Theatre, productions of *Ham*, *MA*, *MND*, *MV*, *MW* at regional theatres; modernist production of *MND* at the Dramatic Theatre, Stockholm, directed by Olof Molander, design by Isaac Grünewald.

1928 – In Denmark, first radio performances of Shakespeare, of *MV* and *Ham*, to be followed by thirteen more to 1940, *AYL* at the

Royal Theatre, Copenhagen; in Finland, *TN* at FNT; in Sweden, new translation of selection from the Lambs's *Tales from Shakespeare*.

1929 – *MV* at the Betty Nansenteatret, Copenhagen; in Finland, productions of *Ham* in Pori, Tampere and Viipuri, *TS* in Turku, *RJ* in Tampere; *KL* at the Dramatic Theatre, Stockholm.

1930 – *Ham* in Aarhus, Denmark, open-air performance of *TN* at Copenhagen; *MND* at FNT; Swedish author Eyvind Johnson publishes novel *Avsked till Hamlet* [Farewell to Hamlet], Swedish premiere of *H8* at the Oscarsteatern, Stockholm, directed by the British Thomas Warner.

1931 – In Denmark, Poul Henningsen's revue *Pæn og høflig* [Nice and Polite], which reverses the gender roles of *TS* and presents a 'modern' young woman who 'tames' her conservative fiancé, another adaptation of *TS*, by Henry Hellssen, at the Dagmartheatret, German guest performance of *AYL* at the Dagmartheatret, *MA* at the Royal Theatre; in Finland, scenes from *Oth* and *Ham* on radio, Tampere Theatre celebrates its thirtieth anniversary with a performance of *Oth*, *MV* in Lahti and Viipuri, *H4* at FNT; in Sweden, Nils Molin's academic dissertation *Shakespeare och Sverige intill 1800-talets mitt* [Shakespeare and Sweden Until the Mid-Nineteenth Century].

1932–3 – In Norway, Henrik Rytter's translation of twenty-three plays into Nynorsk, in ten volumes.

1932 – In Finland, *The World of Radio* magazine advertises English-language full-length productions of various plays, including *Ham* and *TS*, *Ham* in Pori, *MV* in Hämeenlinna and Tampere.

1933 – *TN* at the Royal Theatre, Copenhagen, *RJ* at Odense, German guest performance of *MV* at the Dagmartheatret; in Finland, productions of *Ham* and *MV*; German guest performance of *MV* at the Dramatic Theatre, Stockholm.

1934 – Kaj Munk's controversial modern-dress adaptation of *Ham* premieres at the Betty Nansen Teater, Copenhagen, *MV* in Aarhus, guest performance in Copenhagen of *Ham* by the Swedish Vasateatern, *MM* at the Dagmarteatret; in Finland, *Cor* at the FNT, influenced by controversial Comédie Français production in Paris (1933/4), *Ham* at Tampere Theatre, with Wilho Ilmari in title role; in Sweden, Gothenburg's new city theatre is inaugurated by *Tem*.

1935 – WT at the Royal Theatre, Copenhagen; contentious adaptation of *Hamlet* by Kaj Munk, at the Betty Nansen Theatre in Copenhagen; *Ham* in Kuopio and Tampere, Finland; *H4* at the Dramatic Theatre, Stockholm, directed by Alf Sjöberg, *Ham* at the Gothenburg City Theatre, directed by artist and set designer Knut Ström, *TN* at the Komediteatern, Stockholm.

1936 – Guest performance of *Mac* by the English Players at the Casinoteatret, Copenhagen, *RJ* at the Folketeatret, Copenhagen, *Oth* at Odense; in Finland, *TS* at the Tampere Theatre, with Wilho Ilmari as Petruchio, Elli Tompuri performs Shakespeare monologues on Finnish radio; in Sweden, *MV* at the Gothenburg City Theatre, *RJ* at the Dramatic Theatre, Stockholm, with guest performances in Gothenburg and Copenhagen.

1937 – *Ham* at the Royal Theatre, Copenhagen, using translation by Johannes V. Jensen, in Elsinore, first international guest production of *Ham*, starring Vivien Leigh and Laurence Olivier; in Finland, *KL* at the FNT, productions of *Ham*, *TN*, *Oth* and *MV* at various regional and workers' theatres; in Norway, *KL* at the Nationaltheatret, directed by Johanne Dybwad; Swedish composer Lars-Erik Larsson is commissioned to write music for a radio broadcast of *WT*.

1938 – Open-air performance by the Royal Theatre of *MND* in Brønderslev, Denmark, in Elsinore, visiting production of *Ham* by Gustav Gründgens and Staatliches Schauspielshaus, Berlin; in Finnish *TN* and *Oth* on radio, the latter in both Finnish and Swedish, *TS* in Viipuri, directed by Glory Leppänen; *AYL* at the Dramatic Theatre, Stockholm, directed by Alf Sjöberg, using a rococo-inspired setting.

1939 – Open-air performance of *TN* in Copenhagen, in Elsinore, visiting production of *Ham* starring John Gielgud, Valdemar Østerberg publishes Danish translation of *R3*; *TN* at the Gothenburg City Theatre; *TS* on Finnish radio, actors from Viipuri Theatre, directed by Glory Leppänen.

1940 – In Denmark, open-air performance of *CE* in Copenhagen, *MND* at the Royal Theatre; in Finland, *MA* at the FNT; in Sweden, amateur performances of *Mac* and *MV* directed by 21-year-old Ingmar Bergman, *MA* at the Dramatic Theatre, Stockholm, directed by Alf Sjöberg.

INDEX

Aabel, Hauk 166
Aakjær, Jeppe 181, 186
Aalberg, Ida 7, 16, 21, 69–71, 74–90, 91 n.11, 92 n.30, 93 n.48, 94 n.75, 94 n.77, 94 n.81, 94 n.83, 107, 110, 112–16, 123–4, 137 n.44
Aasen, Ivar 202, 212–13, 219 n.13, 219 n.16, 222 n.64
Addison, Joseph 46
Ahlberg, Axel 77–8, 82, 84, 112, 114, 116, 119, 124, 128–9, 132, 135 n.28, 136 n.39, 136–7 n.40
Aho, Juhani 87–8, 138 n.59, 192 n.7
Aldis-Wright, W. 59
Aldridge, Ira 106, 134 n.18
Alexander II of Russia 78, 100, 116, 153
Alexander III of Russia 111, 116
Alexandrine, Queen of Denmark 179
Amundsen, Roald 168 n.14
Archer, William 188
Aspegren, Aurora 84, 92 n.40
Atterberg, Kurt 28 n.53
Avellan, Kaarola 111, 114–15

Bab, Julius 16
Bacon, Francis 151
Berg, Øivind 215

Bergbom, Emelie 72, 75–7, 90, 91 n.17, 125–6, 131, 134 n.9, 138 n.55
Bergbom, Kaarlo 3, 18, 21, 72, 74, 76, 78, 89, 91 n.14, 91 n.17, 99–141
Bergen 6, 12, 200
Berger, Alfred von 155
Bergson, Henri 210, 222 n.58
Bernhardt, Sarah 18, 26 n.50, 29 n.79, 70
Beyer, Sille 152
Bhabha, Homi 38
Bierfreund, Theodor 151
Birch-Pfeiffer, C. 135 n.26
Bismarck, Otto von 154
Bjerke, André 215
Bjørnson, Bjørn 157–8, 173 n.100
Bjørnson, Bjørnstjerne 22, 135 n.26, 143, 145, 147–50, 155, 158, 160, 173 n.112, 182, 251
Björnsson, Guðmundur 60, 66 n.54
Blatchford, Robert 151
Bleibtreu, Karl 151
Blom, August 16
Bobrikov, N. L. 117
Boccaccio, Giovanni 200, 219 n.17
Bolin, Wilhelm 16, 94 n.66, 135 n.27

Böök, Bruno   77, 84, 92 n.40,
  93 n.48, 111, 135 n.28
Borg, Inez   114
Börjesson, Johan   122, 134 n.7
Boucher, François   251
Brachvogel, A. E.   135 n.26
Brandes, Georg   2, 13, 22, 23 n.1,
  151, 180, 187–90, 194 n.32,
  194–5 n.34, 195 n.37
Brandsma, Elliott   240
Brontë, Charlotte   91 n.11,
  135 n.26
Brun, Johannes   159, 162
Brynjúlfsson, Gísli   41
Bull, Henrik   6
Bull, Ole   6, 147
Burckhardt, Carl   222 n.61
Burns, Robert   44
Byron, George Gordon   40–1,
  43–4, 152

Cajander, Paavo   3, 5, 11, 21,
  73–4, 76, 80, 100, 110, 112,
  120, 126, 128, 131, 133,
  138 n.57
Calderón de la Barca, Pedro   11,
  30 n.87
Canth, Minna   70, 73, 89, 113,
  138 n.54
Carlyle, Thomas   155
Charlemagne   230, 243
Chaucer, Geoffrey   214
Christian X of Denmark   179,
  185
Churchill, Winston   241
Clark, G. W.   59
Coleridge, Samuel Taylor   199
Collin, Christian   182–3, 192 n.9
Cukor, George   15
Cygnaeus, Fredrik   104

Dahlqvist, Georg   105
Dante Alighieri   152, 154, 200,
  208, 219 n.17

Darwin, Charles   155
Delius, Nikolaus   43
Diaconus, Paulus   230
Dickens, Charles   200, 239
Didriksen, Aagot   166
Diktonius, Elmer   246 n.27
DiPietro, Cary   10, 232
Drachmann, Holger   154
Duse, Eleonora   70
Dybwad, Johanne   89, 155, 158,
  160–2, 166, 174 n.133, 180,
  182

Eggen, Erik   211
Egilsson, Sveinbjörn   36
Einarsson, Baldvin   37
Einarsson, Indriði   4, 8, 61
E. K. (signature)   129
Ekman, Gösta   240
Elfving, Betty   76–7
Eliot, T. S.   10, 13, 22,
  200, 204, 220 n.23,
  221 n.47, 232
Elizabeth I of England   153, 156
Elo, Kosti   11, 14, 28 n.59
Enckell, Rabbe   240
Engel, C. L.   133 n.1
Erkko, J. H.   138 n.59
Estlander, C. G.   94 n.66
Ewald, Johannes   172 n.77

Fairbanks, Douglas   15
Falkman, Severin   93 n.40, 110
Finne, Jalmari   10, 119, 126–8
Finne, Olga   120
Foersom, Peter   152, 212
Forsman, Jaakko   134 n.9
Fragonard, Jean-Honoré   251
Frasa, Alina   135 n.24
Frederik II of Denmark   180
Freiligrath, Ferdinand   253
Freud, Sigmund   231, 235,
  245 n.6, 245 n.7
Furnivall, Frederick James   151

INDEX

Gade, Niels, W.   188
Galilei, Galileo   154
Garborg, Arne   152, 154, 211
George V of Britain   185
Gerok, Karl   44
Gestur. *See* Björnsson, Guðmundur
Godenhjelm, B. F.   8, 73, 76, 84
Goethe, Johann Wolfgang   44, 77, 91 n.17, 113, 150, 152, 154, 186, 239
Gogol, Nikolai   91 n.17
Gollancz, Sir Israel   182, 189, 192 n.8, 193 n.15
Grace, Gilbert   155
Gregori, Ferdinand   16, 29 n.69
Grieg, Nordahl   19
Grímsson, Sigurður   63
Gröndal, Benedikt   58
Gröneqvist, Oskar. *See* Wilho, Oskari
Gründgens, Gustaf   17
Grundtvig, N. F. S.   44
Guðmundsson, Sigurður   41–2, 47–9, 61
Gustaf II Adolf of Sweden   117

Hagberg, Carl August   5, 16, 20, 43, 102, 135 n.29
Hálfdanarson, Helgi   64
Hallgrímsson, Jónas   38–40
Hallström, Per   5, 208, 211, 213–14, 224 n.79
Halme, Kaarle   10–11, 116, 119
Hamsun, Knut   154, 170–1 n.70, 204, 233, 246 n.17
Hauch, Carsten   44
Hauptmann, Gerhart   184
Heide Steen, Signe   166
Heine, Heinrich   39, 44
Henry VIII of England   153
Herford, C. H.   193 n.15, 203, 210
Hiort-Schøyen, Rolf   222 n.61

Hirn, Yrjö   192 n.7
Hitler, Adolf   204
Hoem, Edvard   215–16
Högdahl, Lilli   129
Høghaug, Leif   210
Holberg, Ludvig   152, 154
Hölderlin, Friedrich   44
Holmberg, Kalle   133
Homer   154
Hugo, Victor   19, 108

Ibsen, Henrik   6, 22, 70, 73, 77, 79, 89, 91 n.17, 143, 145, 150, 154–5, 165, 167–8, 182, 210, 251–2
Ilmari, Wilho   11–12, 14–16, 131, 133

Jochumsson, Matthías   4–5, 20, 41–5, 47–9, 51–3, 57, 60–2, 64
Johannesen, Edvard, G.   211
Johnson, Eyvind   19, 22, 229–50
Jones, Ernest   245 n.7
Jones, Henry Arthur   184
Joyce, James   194 n.32
Jylhä, Yrho   3

Kajanus, Robert   120
Kallio, Hemmo   139 n.75
Kallio, Ismael   84, 91 n.14
Kiran, Hartvig   224 n.87
Kivi, Aleksis   7, 73, 94 n.76, 105, 107, 138 n.59
Kivinen, Anton   84
Knudsen, David   166
Koskinen, Yrjö   134 n.9
Kott, Jan   133
Kramsu, Kaarlo   111

Lagervall, J. F.   134 n.23
Larsen, Gunnar   222 n.61
Larsson, Lars-Erik   28 n.53
Lawrence, D. H.   222 n.56

Leavis, F. R. 204, 220 n.23
Leffler, Anne Charlotte 95 n.93
Leigh, Vivien 195 n.39
Leino, Benjamin 7, 84, 93 n.40, 111–12, 114, 116, 119, 124
Leino, Eino 129–30, 138 n.59, 192 n.7, 192 n.9
Leino, Olga 129
Lembcke, Edvard 4, 43, 152, 158, 164
Lenning, Hjalmar 129
Leppänen, Glory 16, 19, 30 n.83, 133
Lessing, Gotthold Ephraim 77
Lindberg, August 10
Lindberg, Per 10, 13, 28 n.55
Linde, Herman 153
Lindfors, Adolf 11, 111, 114, 120, 124–6, 129, 139 n.75
Longfellow, Henry Wadsworth 44
Lönnrot, Elias 6
Løvaas, Johan 159, 166
Luther, Martin 155
Lymington, Viscount (Gerard Wallop) 208

Madshus, Olav 211–12
Magnússon, Eiríkur 4, 43, 46, 57–60
Manzoni, Alessandro 152
Marryat, Frederick 152
Martin, Hilda 18
Mary Stuart 153
Mendelssohn, Felix 120, 131
Mendez, Catulle 153, 170 n.63
Michaëlis, Sophus 185–6, 189, 191, 193–4 n.22, 194 n.24
Milton, John 36, 46
Moissi, Alexander 27 n.50
Molander, Harald 135 n.27
Molière 48, 91 n.17, 109, 150, 152, 154

Molin, Nils 5
Møller, Niels 5, 183–4
More, Thomas 243
Moren Vesaas, Halldis 215, 224 n.87
Morris, William 57
Moser, Gustav von 76, 78
Moszkowski, Moritz 125
Mozart, Wolfgang Amadeus 150

Nansen, Fridtjof 146, 155, 167–8
Napoleon Bonaparte 168
Närhi, Otto 129–30
Nicholas II of Russia 117
Nielsen, Asta 15, 19
Nielsen, Carl 180, 187, 191 n.1, 194 n.27, 194 n.31
Nielsen, Eivind 251
Nielsen, Johannes 185
Nietzsche, Friedrich 154, 165, 210
Nikulásson, Ingivaldur 12
Nilsen, Hans Jacob 252
Numers, Gustaf von 125, 138 n.54
Nyblin, Daniel 85

Oddvar, August 166
Oehlenschläger, Adam 154, 183, 187, 189, 193 n.12, 194 n.24
Olavson Vinje, Aasmund 221 n.34
Olivier, Laurence 14–15, 195 n.39
Ollila, Yrjö 7
Olsen, Karl 152
Orjatsalo, Aarne 11, 14–15
Østerberg, Valdemar 4–5

Paavola, Jouku 133
Pálsson, Lárus 15

Perander, J. J. F.   82
Pétursson, Hannes   42, 55
Pickford, Mary   15
Pope, Alexander   36
Proust, Marcel   245 n.6
Pulkkinen, Rosa   18
Puro, Teuvo   11

Quiller-Couch, Arthur   203
Quisling, Vidkun   252

Raa, Charlotte   71–2, 84, 90,
   91 n.12, 94 n.75, 107–9,
   134 n.22, 135 n.24
Raa, Frithiof   135 n.24
Racine, Jean   154
Rajala, Panu   14
Raknes, Ola   210, 222 n.58
Rängman, Maiju   138 n.62
Raphael   154
Rasco, Oscar   16
Rautio, Aleksis   129, 139 n.75
Rautio, Katri   78, 114, 125
Reich, Wilhelm   210
Reinhardt, Max   15–16
Reiss Andersen, G.   222 n.61
Rode, Helge   180, 187, 189,
   194–5 n.34
Rossi, Ernesto   16, 113
Rousseau, Jean-Jacques   236
'rs.' (signature)   211
Runeberg, Johan Ludvig   44
Rutland (Roger Manners, 5th Earl
   of)   151
Ruud, Martin   23 n.9
Rytter, Henrik   4, 19, 22,
   199–227

Sachsen-Meiningen, Duke of   117
Sala, Niilo   112, 114, 118–20,
   122, 136 n.40
Salo, Oskari   129
Saxo Grammaticus   183

Schanche, Ingolf   16, 166
Schibsted-Hansson,
   Agnethe   166
Schiller, Friedrich   39, 44, 77,
   91 n.17, 105, 109, 117, 122,
   131, 154
Schlegel, August Wilhelm   102
Schlegel, Karl Wilhelm   102
Schopenhauer, Arthur   210
Schück, Henrik   5, 23 n.11, 208,
   210, 213, 222 n.52
Schwartz, Nils   231, 233
Seebach, Marie   77
Shakespeare, William
   All's Well that Ends Well   19
   Antony and Cleopatra   104,
      109, 119, 123–5, 218 n.6
   As You Like It   12–13, 15, 44,
      62, 143, 158–62, 164–7,
      218 n.6, 224 n.82
   Coriolanus   104, 120, 231,
      138 n.53
   Cymbeline   41, 44, 62,
      219 n.6
   Hamlet   4, 7–9, 11–19, 22–3,
      25 n.30, 26 n.37, 27 n.43,
      27 n.48, 27 n.52, 29 n.73,
      29 n.76, 29 n.79, 43–5, 57,
      65 n.17, 70, 72–3, 75, 85,
      89, 92 n.37, 108–9, 112–14,
      143, 156–7, 163, 165, 180,
      183, 186, 189–91, 191 n.3,
      195 n.39, 202, 206, 216–17,
      219, 220 n.15, 224 n.82,
      224 n.87, 230–6, 238–41,
      243–4, 245 n.7, 245 n.13,
      246 n.20–2, 247 n.30,
      251–6
   Henry IV 62, 104, 143, 158,
      160, 162–3, 209, 218 n.6,
      224 n.82
   Henry V 104, 209, 218 n.6
   Henry VI 62

Julius Caesar 60–3, 66 n.54, 104, 109, 113, 116–19, 218 n.6
King John 104, 208–9
King Lear 12, 42, 44–5, 48, 53–5, 57, 61, 109, 113–15, 219, 224 n.82
Love's Labour's Lost 44
Macbeth 4, 29 n.76, 43–6, 48–53, 55, 57, 61, 71–2, 108–9, 113–15, 134 n.22, 152, 211, 213, 216, 219, 223 n.64, 224 n.82, 224 n.87
Measure for Measure 218 n.6
Merchant of Venice 5, 7, 13–14, 18, 20, 27 n.49, 62–3, 75, 109–11, 115, 117, 136 n.29, 143, 152, 157, 164, 211, 218 n.6, 223 n.64, 224 n.82
Merry Wives of Windsor 11, 218 n.6, 243
Midsummer Night's Dream 11, 13, 15, 26 n.37, 62, 109, 120–2, 131, 143, 157, 163–4, 167, 172 n.84, 193 n.12, 211, 213–14, 218 n.6, 222 n.52, 224 n.87
Much Ado about Nothing 20, 30 n.83, 30 n.86, 62, 218 n.6
Othello 4, 10–11, 15, 27 n.49, 43–4, 57–8, 105–6, 109, 113–16, 134 n.18, 143, 155, 158, 165, 172 n.87, 186, 205, 218 n.1, 219 n.6, 222 n.53, 224 n.82, 224 n.87
Richard II 209, 218 n.6
Richard III 62, 104, 109, 119, 125, 133, 211, 218 n.6, 224 n.82

Romeo and Juliet 4, 8, 11–15, 21, 27 n.49, 29 n.73, 43–4, 55, 57, 63, 69–97, 108–10, 112, 114, 132, 135 n.28, 158, 213, 218 n.6, 220 n.15, 222 n.53, 224 n.82, 224 n.87
Sonnets 73, 208, 211, 225 n.87
Taming of the Shrew 12–13, 15, 17–19, 27 n.49, 29 n.70, 30 n.83, 48, 109, 111–12, 115, 143, 145, 157, 163–5, 173 n.97, 224 n.82
The Tempest 4, 10–11, 28 n.53, 43–4, 46, 56, 58–9, 109, 120, 128–31, 219 n.6, 224 n.87
Troilus and Cressida 224 n.82
Twelfth Night 8, 11–12, 14, 62–3, 109, 126–8, 143, 145, 157, 162–4, 218 n.6
Two Gentlemen of Verona 19
Winter's Tale 10, 12–13, 23, 62–3, 109, 117, 120, 122–3, 128, 169 n.1, 219 n.6, 231, 237, 241–2
Shaw, George Bernard 10
Shelley, Percy Bysshe 44
Sheridan, Richard Brinsley 109
Sibelius, Jean 28 n.53, 128, 130
Sjöberg, Alf 20, 30 n.86
Skard, Sigmund 224 n.87
Skrede, Ragnvald 219 n.19, 224 n.87
Sløk, Johannes 4
Slöör, Kaarlo, A. (Kaarlo A. Santala) 71, 108
Snellman, Ruth 130, 140 n.86
Socrates 154
Sophocles 154
Stefánsson, Jón 193 n.13
Steiner, George 203

Stenhammar, Wilhelm 28 n.53
Strindberg, August 8–10,
 25 n.31, 30 n.87, 122
Sturluson, Snorri 36
Sudermann, Hermann 70, 89
Sudraka 154
Sullivan, Arthur 130
Sveen, Aasmund 222 n.61

Tauber, Wilhelm 130
Terence 221 n.37
Tervo, Juhana 84
Thomsen, Grímur 40, 60
Thorarensen, Bjarni 37
Þorbergsson, Magnús Þór 61–2
Þorláksson, Jón 36, 43
Thorsteinsson, Steingrímur 41–9, 52–5, 60, 65 n.17
Thorvaldsen, Bertel 154
Tieck, Ludwig 39, 102
Tolnæs, Gunnar 166
Tolstoy, Leo 154
Tompuri, Elli 7, 15, 18–19, 28 n.59, 89, 129
Topelius, Zacharias 117, 125, 138 n.59
Törngren, Pehr Henrik 245 n.10
Törnquist-Tarjanne, Onni 6
Trampe Bødtker, A. 222 n.61

Ulrici, Hermann 103

Valéry, Paul 190, 195 n.38
Vanor, M. 153
Värnlund, Rudolf 229–30, 232, 246 n.16
Verdi, Giuseppe 110, 150
Vining, Edvard, P. 19

Waage, Indriði 16
Wahl, Anders de 180
Warburg, Karl 192 n.7
Weber, Carl Maria von 150
Wecksell, J. J. 108
Wellington (Arthur Wellesley, 1st Duke of) 167–8
Wergeland, Henrik 154, 182–3, 204
Wessely, Josephine 77
Westermarck, A. 108
Wiberg, Stub 166
Wikström, Alma 84, 94 n.75
Wildenwey, Herman 159–60, 162, 173 n.112
Wilhelm II of Prussia 189
Wilho, Oskari (Gröneqvist) 75, 108, 110, 136 n.29
Wilson Knight, G. 204
Wyspiański, Stanislaw 253

www.ingramcontent.com/pod-product-compliance
Lightning Source LLC
Chambersburg PA
CBHW071810300426
44116CB00009B/1268